Key Concepts in International Relations

Series Editor: Paul Wilkinson

2
Sovereign Statehood

Key Concepts in International Relations

*Series Editor:*Paul Wilkinson

Sovereign Statehood

The Basis of International Society

Alan James
University of Keele

London
ALLEN & UNWIN
Boston   Sydney

Allen & Unwin (Publishers) Ltd,
40 Museum Street, London WC1A 1LU, UK

Allen & Unwin (Publishers) Ltd,
Park Lane, Hemel Hempstead, Herts HP2 4TE, UK

Allen & Unwin, Inc.,
8 Winchester Place, Winchester, Mass. 01890, USA

Allen & Unwin (Australia) Ltd,
8 Napier Street, North Sydney, NSW 2060, Australia

First published in 1986

British Library Cataloguing in Publication Data

James, Alan, *1933–*
    Sovereign statehood: the basis of international society. – (Key
concepts in international relations: 2)
1. Sovereignty
I. Title   II. Series
320.1'57   JC327
ISBN 0-04-320190-3
ISBN 0-04-320191-1 Pbk

Library of Congress Cataloging in Publication Data
James, Alan, 1933–
    Sovereign statehood
(Key concepts in international relations: 2)
Bibliography: p.
Includes index.
1. Sovereignty. I. Title. II Series.
JX4041.J35 1986 341.26 85-26707
ISBN 0-04-320190-3 (alk. paper)
ISBN 0-04-320191-1 (pbk. : alk. paper)

Set in 10 on 11 point Times by Fotographics (Bedford) Ltd
and printed in Great Britain by
Billings and Sons Ltd, London, Worcester

To
Val
and
Morien   *Nesta*   *Gwyn*
Gareth   *David*   *Ceri*

Contents

General Editor's Introduction

The word 'concept' is derived from a Latin root meaning literally gathering or bundling together. In any organized body of knowledge the major concepts developed and deployed by scholars are the vital instruments for organizing information and ideas; they are as indispensable for the tasks of gathering classification and typology as they are in the more ambitious work of model and theory-building. And in any study of human history and society these key concepts inevitably constitute weapons and battlefields in the conflict of normative theories, ideologies and moral judgements. Every major concept of international relations has a very different connotation depending on the philosophical beliefs, ideology, or attitude of the beholder. Take the terms 'imperialism' and 'revolution': although liberal and Marxist writers frequently use these words the precise meanings and significance they attach to them will vary enormously, and even if a single author is perfectly consistent in usage in a single book, he may alter his usage, either consciously or unwittingly, over time. None of us is immune against this process of continual redefinition and reevaluation. This is one of the reasons why it is so important for us all, whether laymen or specialists, to become more aware, vigilant and critical of the problems and pitfalls of conceptualization both for ourselves and others. The review and clarification should not be left to a small coterie of professional philosophers and linguistic analysts. It should be a regular part of our own mental preparation for study, reflection, writing, and the practical burdens of communicating and participating in a democratic society. Careful and informed use of the full range of major concepts developed in any field of knowledge, with due attention to clarity and consistency and the interrelatedness of concepts is also obviously a vital heuristic tool, a prerequisite for good scientific research. More than this, the refinement, modification and reevaluation involved in operationalizing well-tried concepts often lead to the introduction of new concepts, fresh building-blocks in the development of knowledge, discovery and fuller understanding, whether of the physical universe, human history and society, or the nature and development of the individual human spirit, personality, and imagination.

If one examines the standard range of introductory texts on international relations used by universities in America and Western

Europe, one is struck by three features of their conceptual apparatus, aspects which are now so widespread that they can be said to typify the stock-in-trade of the discipline. First, there is the astonishingly wide consensus on the basic checklist of key organizing concepts in the subject, almost invariably reflected in the contents outline: international system, nation–state, sovereignty, power, balance of power, diplomacy, military strategy, nuclear deterrence, alliances, foreign policy-making, international law, international organization, trade, aid, and development. These are the almost ubiquitous repertoires. Other themes such as human rights, conflict resolution, ideology, and propaganda find inclusion in a minority of contents pages: almost invariably in the modern texts they will be mentioned only briefly at some point in the introductory survey course.

A second recurrent feature is the lack of attention to the origin and development of the concepts themselves. This characterizes nearly all the well-known texts. It is almost as if the text-book writers wish to leave the student in innocence of the major historical developments of their subject. How many of the introductory texts, for example, even bother to mention such seminal contributions as those of Grotius in international law, Clausewitz in military strategy, or Mitrany in the field of international organization? Only rarely is attention given to problems of definition, to conflicting theories and approaches, and to the problems of conceptual obsolescence and innovation.

The third major weakness, in the editor's view, is the failure to adequately relate the key concepts of international relations to the real world thinking and activities of statesmen, officials, political parties, media, public, and other key participants in the international system. Yet the language of international relations we use as academic teachers, researchers, and students, is not the esoteric product of a research laboratory or seminar room: our major concepts are the very stuff of international diplomacy, foreign policy, and intercourse. True, on occasion, as in the case of the key concepts of nuclear deterrence and functionalist and neo-functionalist theories of integration, academicians and scientists serving or advising governments have also played a key role in developing new concepts. Yet the plain fact is that many of our newer concepts – in, for example, military strategy, economic development and inter-national organization – have been originated, modified, developed and debated mainly among politicians, diplomatists, civil servants, service chiefs, guerrilla leaders, and even journalists. And because we need to be closely in touch with the nuances and subtleties of the constant evolution of ideas and assumptions of the main participants in the international system, narrowly-based surveys of conceptual usage and development in the scholarly literature would also be inadequate and distorting.

It is to remedy these grave deficiencies that this new series of individual monographs, each devoted to a thorough review of a major international relations concept, has been devised. The editor and publishers hope that the series will educate and illuminate at both the undergraduate and post-graduate teaching levels in all universities and colleges that offer courses in international relations. It is also hoped that the volumes will provide valuable background, sources, and stimulus to teachers and researchers, many of whom have long complained about the absence of such guides. Finally, the series should also be of value to officials, politicians, industrial executives and others whose professional work involves some degree of participation in, and understanding of, international developments, trends, policy-making and problems. The series should also be of interest and value to students and specialists in cognate disciplines, such as history, economics, political science, and sociology.

It may help to recapitulate the brief given to each contributor in the series. It is intended that each volume will deal thoroughly with the following aspects: The origins and evolution of the concept, including significant variations and changes in usage, and in relation to changes in the international system and in the political systems of major powers; an attempt at an authoritative definition of the concept in order that it may be employed as a more effective tool in the analysis and theory of international relations; the identification of any important sub-concepts and typologies; a critical review of the ways in which the concept is utilized in major theories, models and approaches in the contemporary study of international relations; the relationship between the concept and the contemporary practice of international relations; the relationship between the concept and policy-making in international relations; the future of the concept in international relations.

It should hardly be necessary to add that the publishers and the series academic editor should have chosen the individual authors commissioned to review each concept, with considerable care, taking into account not only their previous record of scholarly work in the field, but also their experience as teachers and expositors. We hope and believe that the completed series will provide a boon to international relations teaching and research world-wide. We welcome suggestions, responses and even practical proposals for additional contributions to the series. Please correspond in the first instance with Gordon Smith of Allen & Unwin at the address printed on the reverse of the title page.

*   *   *

Few would dispute that *Sovereign Statehood* should be included in a series on Key Concepts in International Relations. The sovereign state is still the fundamental unit of organization in the international system, despite frequent predictions of its demise and complaints about its inherent inadequacy and weakness. There are now 170 of them, and numerous national liberation movements around the world still aspire and struggle for the status of sovereign statehood.

It is a great privilege to be able to include within our Key Concepts Series a new and rigorous analysis of sovereign statehood in the modern international system. Professor Alan James, a gifted and experienced teacher in international relations and author of a classic study of UN peacekeeping, has deliberately eschewed yet another dry discussion of jurisprudential theories of sovereignty. The inestimable advantage of his approach is its frank acceptance that sovereignty is a protean term referring to a number of core attributes of a modern state. Using illustrations from recent and contemporary international relations, he shows the practical value of viewing the acquisition of the key attributes of statehood, relating to both internal and external sovereignty, as a continuum and as a practical process within the international system. By shifting his gaze from the metaphysical notions of Absolute Sovereignty he is able to illuminate the degree to which sovereign statehood *in practice* is invariably limited or qualified by the realities of international power politics and economic interdependence. The author's refreshingly down-to-earth approach and his profound knowledge of modern cases enables him to present a more realistic and nuanced assessment of the role and implications of sovereign statehood, revealing the ways in which it is already being modified and even transcended in certain respects by the development of new international norms and institutions. Just as Bodin's famous dictum 'Majestas est summa in cives ac subditos legibusque soluta potestas' (Sovereignty is supreme power over citizens and subjugated peoples and is bound by no other law) became overtaken by the realities of constitutional and legal limits to internal sovereignty in the modern democratic state, so the notion that sovereignty is somehow vested in national society is dangerous and misleading. It is dangerous because it can be used by a ruthless and powerful regime to justify totalitarian power over the individual. It is misleading because, in reality, as Alan James demonstrates, most states in the international system are to some degree dependent on others for their survival and their ability to maintain a minimal level of internal sovereignty. And in order to become a member of the international society of states every new state must acquire the minimum degree of formal recognition by other states necessary to confer external sovereignty. As his study makes clear, there is in practice a considerable variation in the degree of international acceptance secured by the various states, and in the pace at which they acquire additional recognition.

It is illuminating to apply Professor James's insights to three of the major problems he raises concerning sovereignty in the modern states system. First there are the acute difficulties that arise when a state claiming external recognition is in fact only erratically or partially able to command internal sovereignty within its internationally agreed frontiers. If we take the extreme case of Lebanon in the late 1970s and early 1980s, it is clear that this state enjoys the conventional forms of external recognition. It has a seat at the UN. It has diplomatic representatives abroad and receives diplomats from abroad in Beirut. It conducts international trade and is formally party to many international agreements. Yet internally its territory is occupied by the armies of Syria and Israel and effective control of Lebanon is divided among the various factions within their militias which predominate in specific areas. President Amin Gemayel's writ does not extend beyond the doors of his Presidential palace. Thus the Lebanese government's decisions are neither enforceable indirectly, by means of the sanctions of the law, or directly by coercive power, because the authorities lack the means to enforce their decisions. The Lebanese state cannot be said to exercise internal sovereignty *in practice* because its procedures for decision are not omnicompetent, and far from possessing a monopoly of coercive power, the government faces a patchwork of armed factions and occupying forces. The key problems for the international society in such circumstances are (i) how do you prevent such a country from being annexed or divided by predatory neighbouring states?, and (ii) how do you help to restore a stable and legitimate government which enjoys the general support of the population and has the ability to enforce its laws?

A second major problem is that of outrageous abuse of the sovereign right of domestic jurisdiction (enshrined under Article 2(7) of the UN Charter) by a regime which unquestionably possesses a monopoly of coercive power, but which is using that power to commit genocide or other massive crimes against the human rights of sectors of its own population. Should domestic sovereignty allow such outrages as those which have occurred in recent years in Kampuchea, Uganda, Tibet and the Central African Republic? Could the international community develop some mechanism of international humanitarian intervention for the enforcement of human rights, on similar lines to the UN's mechanism for the enforcement of peace? Even if it could, how could one prevent the machinery being paralysed by disagreements between the super-powers?

A third and far more dangerous problem for the international system arises from conflicts between rival sovereign states in cases where one or both of the parties to the dispute are not prepared to resolve the matter by peaceful negotiation or mediation and where at least one party is ready to defy international law by an act of aggression against the other state. Recent events in the Gulf War, and in the Falklands and Lebanon in 1982, show that the problem of sovereign states threatening international peace is still as acute as ever. Such conflicts inevitably carry the risk of major power involvement with all its concomitant dangers in a world with nuclear weapons.

In the light of these severe drawbacks and dangers of the system of sovereign states, it would be tempting to theorize in optimistic terms about international institutions that could one day supersede or transcend the nation state. Professor James is too much of a realist to engage in such speculations. He recognizes that sovereign states are likely to remain the basic units in the international system for a long time ahead. But under his steady gaze many of the myths and illusions about the nature and theory of sovereign statehood are stripped away.

Paul Wilkinson
Professor of International Relations
University of Aberdeen

Acknowledgements

My interest in the concept of sovereignty as it applies to the state in its international aspect was stimulated by the late Professor C. A. W. Manning, and he also shaped my understanding of it. I owe him a considerable intellectual debt. It is therefore very appropriate that the typing of the manuscript should have been assisted by a grant from the CAWM-ites Fund. For this I thank two of the fund's trustees, Professor G. L. Goodwin and Dr B. E. Porter. I am also grateful to the late Professor F. S. Northedge for encouraging me to write this book, and to Professor P. Wilkinson for including it in his series on Key Concepts in International Relations.

The writing of the book has almost entirely been done during two periods of leave from the University of Keele. The first was financed by the Social Science Research Council in the form of a personal research grant, and the second by the university under its leave of absence arrangements. I am grateful to the SSRC and the university for these favours, and also to my colleagues in the International Relations Department at Keele for so willingly 'closing ranks' during the second leave of absence.

The manuscript has been typed by Betty Appleby, Kath McKeown and Patricia Knight. I thank them all very warmly for their cheerful co-operation and skilful deciphering of my handwriting. I must, however, add a special word of thanks to Betty Appleby, not just because she has done most of the typing but also for the keen interest she has always shown in the project.

Chapter 2 has appeared in an earlier version in the January 1984 issue of the *Review of International Studies*. I thank the editor, Professor R. E. Jones, and the publishers, Butterworth, for their ready assent to my request to use the article.

Finally, I am greatly indebted to Val James for her support and encouragement. I am also deeply appreciative of all the help I have had from Lorna Lloyd.

1

Quagmire

Sovereignty is so emotive a term that it very naturally finds an important place in international rhetoric. Any proposed diminution of a state's political freedom or legal jurisdiction is likely to evoke a response which will be expressed, in part at least, as a defence of its sovereignty. Claims and counter-claims in a negotiating process will, if at all possible, be supported by references to the state's sovereignty or to some idea of sovereignty which amply justifies its claim. Criticism of another state's behaviour will very probably refer to its cavalier approach to the sovereignty of its adversary, and, if the facts conceivably permit it, the charge of 'trampling' on the other's sovereignty will almost certainly be advanced. By contrast, no state is slow to remind its auditors how great is its own respect for the sovereignty of its fellows, of the punctilious care it invariably exercises in any matter which touches on an attribute so sensitive and hallowed as this.

Within the state, too, when issues of foreign policy are discussed they may well be defended and attacked by reference to the criterion of sovereignty. Again, of course, no one is likely to pour buckets of cold water over the term – at least no one who is a serious participant in the political game. Instead, those on the defensive will expound on how they have interpreted or applied the term in a wise or far-seeing way, while those on the other side will have the luxury of a direct and unambiguous assault on those who dare to play fast and loose with the state's (or perhaps even better, the nation's) sovereignty. Governmental proponents of Britain's entry to the European Economic Community, for example, saw fit to emphasize how Britain must now learn to exercise her sovereignty 'in a new and larger dimension'[1] – to take one very typical remark. Those on the same side of the argument but on the opposite side of the political spectrum could appeal to the Labour Party's internationalist tradition, railing against a 'blinkered obstinacy' which would preserve 'parochial powers', and 'isolationist efforts to hug the rags of our sovereignty closer around us'; instead Britain should share in 'the greater sovereignty of a united Europe'.[2]

Across the Channel, those on the far left who were opposed to

French membership in the Community (and to much else) could pull out all the ideological stops: 'France's sovereignty is being torn from her morsel by morsel . . . The fate of our peasantry is decided today in Brussels, that of our money in Washington; that of our nation will be decided tomorrow, if the people does not take care, in Luxembourg, or rather in Bonn, by the general staff of the forces of reaction and the multinational trusts of Atlantic Europe.'[3] And, staying in the same country but changing the issue, one can cite an attempt to hoist General de Gaulle – so often criticised for his 'mystical' and 'anachronistic' devotion to sovereignty – with his own petard. The matter concerned the president's Algerian policy, and particularly the signs that he was moving away from the idea of *Algérie française*. An opponent of this development declared: 'It is not within the power of any authority to decide upon the relinquishment of a part of the territory where France exercises her sovereignty.'[4]

Turning back to the international scene, one ominously tendentious use of the term 'sovereignty' can be taken from the mouth of Adolf Hitler, who, in 1938 at the time of Germany's annexation of Austria, asked: 'What can words like "independence" or "sovereignty" mean for a state of only six million?'[5] Only twenty years later, at the first UN Conference on the Law of the Sea, a number of smaller and weaker states were seen to be defining sovereignty in a manner which gave maximum support to their negotiating positions; the term was 'appropriated by the dissatisfied as a means of maintaining tactical freedom'.[6] And in the Middle East crisis of 1967, when the question of a declaration by the maritime powers in favour of freedom of navigation through the Gulf of Aqaba was being discussed, President Nasser of Egypt declared that 'We shall consider any declaration by them as a transgression of our sovereignty. It would be considered a preliminary to an act of war'.[7] (Before the next decade was out his country had set its hand to a peace treaty with Israel which, *inter alia*, declared that the Gulf of Aqaba was an international waterway, through which all traffic was entitled to pass.)

All this is part of the stuff of politics. Here some imprecision of language is to be expected, some stretching of terms, a rather hasty grabbing for any semantic ammunition which can be plausibly pressed into service. It would not be unreasonable to suppose, however, that there might be some substance behind the terminology, that, in this case, it was in some way meaningful to speak of states as sovereign entities. The identification and elaboration of this meaning, as also the making of judgements about its significance, is the task of academic students of international relations, and the subject has not been ignored. But there is nothing approaching unanimity in the conclusions reached. Some, indeed, assert that sovereignty is clearly on the way out. One of the best known writers in the field, for example, said twenty years ago that the 'sovereign nation-state is in the process of becoming obsolete'.[8] Others go further and declare, in the words of a prominent international lawyer, that sovereignty is 'factually inaccurate'.[9] Yet others make essentially the same point in a more powerful way. A British professor of politics (and a specialist in international relations) said of the introduction of sovereignty into the discussion of an international matter: 'let not the issue be fuddled by shibboleths and phantasms'.[10] A distinguished modern historian observed that the use of the phrase 'sovereign equality' was an instance of how 'we encumber our thinking with gibberish phrases'.[11] And a professor of law at a leading American university (Yale) urged people to 'forget all that blather about . . . sovereignty . . . all that abstract garbage'[12] – although admittedly, despite the use of his professional address, he was here perhaps acting more in a political than an academic capacity.

Alongside this line of comment lies the fact that it is not only states and politicians who employ the term 'sovereignty' in a variety of ways. Academics also are to be found using it in a number of quite different senses. As one eminent international lawyer observed at the start of the century, 'there exists perhaps no conception the meaning of which is more controversial than that of sovereignty. It is an indisputable fact that this conception, from the moment when it was introduced into political science until the present day, has never had a meaning which was universally agreed upon.'[13] The position has not improved since then, and his lament has been echoed. The result, in the view of one analyst, is that scholars have been 'puzzled' by the notion of sovereignty 'ever since they noticed the emergence of what we now call states'.[14] Another has put it more strongly, saying that it is 'doubtful whether any single word has caused so much intellectual confusion'.[15] Nor, of course, has this confusion been confined to the ranks of the senior scholars, for its has also, very naturally, spread to their students. Thus there is in existence on this subject a substantial intellectual quagmire, rather than that clarity and light which is supposed to pervade the academic world.

Most if not all of this problem stems from the fact that the theorizing about sovereignty which has taken place over the centuries has focused almost entirely on the internal nature of the state. What sovereignty refers to at this level is the presence, within a governed political community, of supreme legal authority – so that such a community can be said to possess sovereignty, or to be sovereign, if it does not look beyond its own borders for the ultimate source of its own legitimacy. This concept was first developed in the

Roman Empire of the early Christian era. Then it was lost to political discourse, as the European political communities of the medieval period all considered themselves to be part of a wider entity – Christendom – which had a secular overlord in the shape of the Emperor and a religious head in the Pope. It was not until the break-up of this scheme that the modern state system emerged, and with it the revived doctrine of sovereignty.[16]

Christendom was showing signs of political disintegration as early as the thirteenth and fourteenth centuries. But so powerful was the idea that the known world formed, in essence, a single unit that the independent political communities which were, *de facto*, beginning to emerge did not see themselves as entirely separate, in law, from Christendom's central institutions. By the sixteenth century, however, the substantial changes which had taken place could no longer be invariably denied. In England Henry VIII formally broke with the Papacy in 1533. And in France the philosopher Jean Bodin both crystallized and developed much of the new thinking which was beginning to appear by declaring, in 1577, that effective rule required absolute power – or sovereignty. In the following century the English political philosopher Thomas Hobbes wrote his famous work *Leviathan* (1651), likewise arguing that supreme law-making power within a political society must lie with the ruler – or sovereign.

Both Bodin and Hobbes were much influenced in their writing by the experience of domestic disorder. Bodin had seen France in confusion and chaos on account of civil and religious wars, and Hobbes had lived through the English Civil War. It is not surprising, therefore, that their formulations of the idea of sovereignty supported the case for strong rule from above. In other words, they seemed to be saying that sovereignty involved political absolutism. Even Hobbes, however, admitted that a government would lose its legitimacy if it failed to protect its subjects. And Bodin certainly claimed that the sovereign should respect both divine law and the customary laws of the political community. From this last basis it could be argued that sovereignty lay not with the ruler but with the ruled. In this way ultimate authority could be claimed for the people, with the government simply acting as their agent. This was the argument of another famous English philosopher of the seventeenth century, John Locke. Writing later than Hobbes, and in more tranquil times, he asserted that personal rights and individual property were at the basis of the state, and inviolable. Thus if the government failed to protect them the people had the right of rebellion, and could set up a new government which would better attend to the requirements of the ultimate sovereign. Here was the claim for what came to be called popular sovereignty. It was taken even further in the middle of the eighteenth century by the French philosopher Jean-Jacques Rousseau, who, in his *Social Contract*, depicted the state as nothing more than the political organization of all the people.

A slightly different way of looking at the matter was to see sovereignty as inhering in the state as such. Debate could then proceed as to whether sovereignty was actually exercised, on behalf of the state, by the monarch, the government, some part of the government (such as the legislature), the people, a section of the people, or a combination of these elements. Clearly there would be plenty of scope for argument on these matters – and in fact it has often led to considerable uncertainty about the more detailed meaning of the term 'sovereignty'. But what would remain above argument would be the claim that the state itself was sovereign, in the sense of possessing ultimate authority. This is the position which has actually evolved, so that the political world has come to be depicted as made up of sovereign states. However, while this gets over some of the problems which can arise so far as inward-looking state sovereignty is concerned, it has frequently created problems regarding the state in its international aspect. For the most fundamental characteristic of the international scene is the absence of an overarching authority. Accordingly, it seems nonsensical to talk of states being sovereign in the sense of possessing ultimate authority and legal supremacy when this is exactly what none of them has, or claims, in relation to any of the others. This is the conundrum which has given rise to the confusion which was outlined above.

One possible way of solving it is to envisage state sovereignty, at the international level, as connoting not supremacy but independence. Internally the state is supreme, and the external corollary of this internal condition is that all states are independent of each other. For, if one state has ultimate control over its own internal affairs, no one else can exercise that control. Which, in turn, means that in principle the state can do what it likes not just within its borders but also in its external relations. In other words, it acts independently on the international stage. This is fine so far as it goes, but the trouble is that it does not go far. For it simply leads to all sorts of difficult questions about what, exactly, independence means, and whether states can, in their international capacities, properly be spoken of as independent.

The response of some has been to suggest that the word 'sovereignty' should be banished. Having surveyed six meanings attributed to it in the domestic context alone, a British political scientist concluded that it was a mistake to think that the matter could be dealt with by treating sovereignty as 'a genus of which the species can be distinguished by suitable adjectives'. Accordingly, he was of the opinion that there was 'a strong case for giving up so protean a word'.[17] And in a book on international relations the leading French political scientist came to the same conclusion, saying that 'because of the ambiguities it sustains' he would 'offer no objection to abandoning'[18] the word. A prominent Australian student of international relations did not go as far as this in his comment on the matter, merely observing that attempts to define sovereignty were usually 'arid'.[19] His implication seemed to be that the matter could be left on one side, as it did not have much bearing on what was actually happening between states. A British scholar, on the other hand, while agreeing that the definitional exercise had little point, did not think that sovereignty was of little relevance to the international scene. Instead, by analogy with the familiar observation about the elephant, he suggested: 'Although conceptually difficult, sovereignty is usually easy to recognize in practice.'[20]

This last suggestion is hardly satisfactory. It is, after all, the academic's job to clarify the meaning of words, and so to assist understanding. And in this particular case the matter is of more importance than some. For the object to which the word 'sovereignty' refers is notional in character. This does not mean that it lacks significance. The fact that no one has ever seen a sovereign state (except in the eye of the mind) does not lessen the huge impact which decisions taken by the state can have on the lives of millions of its people, and, maybe, on those of other states. But the absence of a physical referent has the consequence that one cannot tell those interested to go and have a look at the object in question and make up their own minds about its essential nature. In these circumstances inquirers need guidance of a specific kind. It is up to the academic to provide it, provided always that there is point in retaining the word.

The suggestion that there is not is based on two main grounds. One has to do with the word's ambiguity. However, if in these circumstances 'sovereignty' was simply replaced by another word the source of the ambiguity would simply have been transferred. The new word would have the same wide-ranging application as the old, and would be used to the same ambiguous effect. One way round this problem, of course, would be to substitute many words for the one which, singly, causes offence. The difficulties involved in such lexicographical reform, however, are legion: who is to organize it and how is agreement to be reached on the variety of usages and terms which would be involved? And, in any event, who are academics to tell states how they should describe themselves?

The other main objection to the word 'sovereignty' arises from the belief that the concept involved – the meaning, that is, which is given to the word – does not accurately reflect the reality it is supposed to be depicting. If that is the case, then here is something which academics should indeed be pointing out. It is still not up to them to lay down the law on the matter, for states may have good rhetorical grounds for maintaining their tried terminology. But academics could properly draw attention to the gap between the ostensible and the real reason for the use of the word. This is in fact what many of them have been doing, as the examples given above testify. But care should be taken before assuming that this is a good basis on which to criticize, in a blanket way, the use of the word 'sovereignty'. For 'what all too many writers seem not to notice is that by this same term, sovereignty, there are commonly connoted more concepts than one'.[21] While, therefore, someone may be directing his ire in an entirely appropriate direction, it is entirely inappropriate for him to assume that the usage he is concentrating on is the only one which exists. And, given a number of usages, it is unlikely that all of them fail to say anything of worth about the reality of international life. In truth, it is not so.

In this inquiry into the role of sovereignty in international relations attention will be chiefly focused on one usage which, while of literally fundamental importance, has received hardly any attention. It concerns the basic issue of the constituents of international relations. Much is nowadays heard about the international role of non-state actors. But even the most progressively minded scholar must allow that states can still be clearly perceived jousting with each other. And he would be hard put to it to deny that their actions and reactions are of considerable importance. But the question arises, what is a state? Or, rather, which of the entities commonly called states participate regularly in the international game? For it is manifest that not all territorial entities which happen to be called states also play a full, or indeed a minor, international role. This implies, and it should cause no surprise, that there is a distinguishing factor which allows some such entities to assume an international part as if to the manner born, while others have no right to venture beyond their home and hearth. The distinguishing factor in question is called sovereignty – the 'essential qualification for full membership'[22] in international society, or, to express the point more comprehensively, the qualification which makes a state *eligible* for full membership. For possession of the necessary requirement does not automatically ensure admission.

The ground for this assertion will be set out in Chapter 2. But it should be said now that it does not rest on the authority of some person of eminence, nor on a tradition of political thought. In fact, although political thinkers have had a fair bit to say about sovereignty, they have, as has been noted, almost always been directing themselves to the domestic political scene. Accordingly, their work has virtually no relevance to international relations, not even to the historical scene, let alone the contemporary one – although many students of international relations have failed to realize this, and so have been led astray in their efforts to relate sovereignty to a state's international capacity and activities. In this inquiry, however, the work of the political theorists will find no place. Instead, what will be focused on is the practice of states, for it is state practice that provides the basis for the claim that sovereignty is what makes an entity eligible for admission to international society. And, as will be seen, the meaning of sovereignty in this context is what states say it is. This is not necessarily the best way in which to organize the international game. But states are in charge, not academics or philosophers, and that is how they choose to run it.

Two further preliminary points should be made. The first is that this is not a historical inquiry. The state practice which will be examined is that of the twentieth century, and especially its middle and later parts. This does not necessarily imply that practice was different at an earlier time. In fact it seems that its essence has been much the same over the whole period of the modern international system, which may be dated from the sixteenth century, although prior to the present century there was much more fuzziness at the conceptual edges and a much greater marginal area containing entities of dubious status. However, that is not the period which is being explored. What will be pursued is the question of how, nowadays, sovereign states give meaning to the word 'sovereignty' when they refer to that which makes them eligible for international life, and how this usage is to be distinguished from others of international relevance.

The other point is that this inquiry is about the basis of international relations, and not its dynamics. Accordingly, it will reveal nothing, except incidentally, about the cut and thrust of inter-state relations. But it is basic in that it has to do with the most important pre-condition of international relations – the identification of far and away the most important actors. States, of course, are doing this implicitly all the time, and occasionally explicitly, when a new state appears at the international door. But they are not very self-conscious about it – it is more a question, for them, of doing what comes naturally. And they certainly do not verbalize, either directly or reflectively, about what is going on. Academics, however, have the task of trying to see if any sense can be made of international relations, of teasing out plausible generalities about the nature of life at the international level. Some may be content to take the international scene as they find it, in that they concentrate on the process of international interchange, drawing attention to regularities in the attitudes and behaviour of states. It is also necessary, however, for questions to be asked about the conditions which are necessary for international interchange to take place at all. Among such conditions is the fundamental matter of the criterion which marks out some territorial bodies as eligible for international life. This inquiry is intended to contribute to an understanding of that issue. It is embarked upon in the belief that, at least in this respect, there is no need for the study of sovereignty to result in a quagmire. States deal with the issue neatly and without fuss. The scholar may need to fuss a bit, as he explores the question's ramifications, but it should be possible for him to convey the neatness of the approach which states have adopted to the relationship between sovereignty and international society. The attempt will be made.

Notes: Chapter 1

1   Mr Geoffrey Rippon, Chancellor of the Duchy of Lancaster, in a debate at the Conservative Party Conference, *The Times*, 9 October 1970.
2   Mr Geoffrey de Freitas, Chairman, Labour Committee for Europe, *The Times*, 22 December 1970.
3   M. Georges Marchais, Secretary General of the French Communist Party, quoted in R. E. M. Irving, 'The European policy of the French and Italian communists', *International Affairs*, vol. 53, no. 3 (September 1977), p. 420.
4   General Salan, quoted in Alastair Horne, *A Savage War of Peace* (London: Macmillan, 1977), p. 419.
5   Quoted in Stanley A. de Smith, *Microstates and Micronesia* (New York: New York University Press, 1970), p. 19.
6   Robert L. Friedheim, 'The "satisfied" and "dissatisfied" states negotiate international law', in R. W. Gregg and M. Barkun (eds), *The United Nations System and its Functions* (Princeton, NJ: Van Nostrand, 1968), p. 391.
7   Quoted in Theodore Draper, *Israel and World Politics* (New York: Viking Press, 1968), p. 108.
8   H. J. Morgenthau, 'The intellectual and political functions of a theory of international relations', in H. V. Harrison (ed.), *The Role of Theory in International Relations* (Princeton, NJ: Van Nostrand, 1964), p. 116.
9   Richard A. Falk, *Law, Morality and War in the Contemporary World* (London: Pall Mall, 1963), p. 29.
10 Professor P. A. Reynolds, *The Times*, 18 February 1971.
11 David Thomson, 'The three worlds of Raymond Aron', *International Affairs*, vol. 38, no. 1 (January 1963), p. 55.
12 Professor A. A. Leff, *New York Times*, 4 October 1968.
13 L. Oppenheim, *International Law, Vol. 1: Peace* (London: Longman, 1905), p. 103.
14 P. Taylor, *International Co-operation Today* (London: Elek, 1971), p. 22.
15 Michael Akehurst, *A Modern Introduction to International Law* (London: Allen & Unwin, 1970), p. 26.
16 In this and the next two paragraphs I have relied heavily on F. H. Hinsley, *Sovereignty* (New York: Basic Books, 1966).

17   Stanley I. Benn, 'The uses of "sovereignty" ', *Political Studies*, vol. 3, no. 2 (June 1955), p. 122.
18   R. Aron, *Peace and War* (New York: Praeger, 1967), p. 743.
19   J. D. B. Miller, *The World of States* (London: Croom Helm, 1981), p. 16.
20   Barry Buzan, *People, States and Fear* (Brighton: Wheatsheaf, 1983), p. 42.
21   C. A. W. Manning, 'The legal framework in a world of change', in B. Porter (ed.), *The Aberystwyth Papers* (London: Oxford University Press, 1969), p. 308.
22   Hinsley, *Sovereignty*, p. 215.

Part One

Quest

2

Definition

The hundred and seventy or so states which engage in international relations have several characteristics in common. Perhaps the most fundamental is that they are all territorially based. Each of them represents a physical sector of the land mass of the globe, and (subject to a few very minor exceptions) at the international level represents it exclusively: the same piece of territory is not the responsibility of more than one state. Thus the world may be imagined as divided into states by frontiers rather as a farm is into fields by fences and walls. A second common characteristic is that all these frontiers enclose not just territory but people also. Their number may and does vary hugely from one state to another, from a few thousand here to hundreds of millions there. But every territorial entity which participates in international relations supports human life. This points to a third characteristic which is shared by the territorially based international actors. It is that, by one process or another, some of the people of a state are designated as its official representatives, as constituting its government. A state, like a university or a club, is not a real person but exists as a person only notionally (which is not to say that it is any the less important for that). It must therefore have a way of establishing who is entitled to speak and act in its name. This applies as much to a state's external relations as to the conduct of its internal affairs. Human persons are the agencies through which a notional person lives, moves, and has its being.

A state may therefore be said to be made up of territory, people and a government. This is often as far as the matter is taken, and for some purposes it is sufficient. But it appears insufficient if one wishes to establish the characteristics which are shared by the states which play a regular and full part in international life. For, while all those players are territorially based, populated, and governed, there are also many governed territories which do not participate in international relations, or do so only on a minimal and occasional basis. The territory of Gibraltar, for example, while only a couple of square miles in extent, has a population which is somewhat bigger than one or two territories which enjoy an international capacity, and is more prosperous than quite a few others. It satisfies the characteristics of statehood which have been mentioned above, yet it has no international part. The same can be said of the territory of Hong Kong, which has a population of about 5 million. The constituent parts of federal states, often themselves called states, also satisfy the criteria of territory, people, and government, but one looks in vain for evidence of their playing a significant international role. Here too the reason certainly cannot have to do with matters of size and wealth. The state of Texas, for example, one of the fifty states of the United States of America, has a gross product greater than that of Australia, Brazil, or Sweden. Its production of oil and cotton is exceeded by only four internationally active states, and only seven such states have a greater number of registered cars.[1] But, like, for example, Ontario in Canada or New South Wales in Australia (both of them provinces of considerable extent and importance) it is inactive on the international scene.

It might be, of course, that the distinction between states which are regular international actors and those which are not is entirely fortuitous and haphazard. It might depend on nothing more than matters of disposition and will. Hong Kong, Texas and the rest might all have decided that they neither wanted nor needed to appear on the international stage. In which case the search for a further common characteristic which distinguishes states which regularly engage in international relations from those which do not would be fruitless. But this is not so. Another distinguishing characteristic can be identified. Some perceive it to lie in the fact that internationally active states enjoy international personality and are subject to international law. The detail of this perception is accurate but it is not one which advances the matter in hand. For the question relates to what it is that results in some states – but not others – having international personality ascribed to them and enjoying rights and having duties under international law. If it is not the consequence of one or more subjective decisions, the states concerned must share an objective feature which entitles them to engage in international relations or at the very least makes them eligible so to do.

Varying usages

The immediate answer to this problem is not hard to find. It is that those territorially based entities which appear regularly on the international stage all refer to themselves and their fellows as sovereign. What they have in common is their sovereignty. It is the characteristic which demarcates them from states which lack an international dimension. Sovereign states are within and non-sovereign states without the international pale. Some, owning a specific endowment which others lack, live at a level which is denied the others. It may be that a good number of those others, perhaps the vast majority of them, have no desire at all to climb the sovereign ladder. There is no necessary reason why they should. But the fact remains that there is a clear line between the two groups and that the distinguishing characteristic of the international group is their unanimous claim to the individual possession of sovereignty.

The mere fact that states with a capacity for regular international action refer to themselves as sovereign, however, does not, in itself, mean very much. It might be that the popularity of the phrase 'sovereign state' in official circles is partly due to its psychological value. For to speak of oneself and one's friends (or one's would-be friends) as sovereign may foster the growth in those so depicted of a sense of their own importance – a characteristic which states, like individuals, are usually glad to cultivate. Then, too, the phrase may sometimes be used by states simply on account of its verbal attractiveness – an alliterative legacy from the days when it was not only customary for internationally acting states to be headed by monarchs, or sovereigns, but also for those sovereigns to rule as well as reign. Another possibility is that the term 'sovereignty' serves as no more than a useful mark of identification, indicating that the states to which it applies are of the sort which, on some quite different ground, have established their right to international actorhood. Yet another possibility is that the term does indeed refer to some attribute which those concerned possess – but an attribute which they just happen to have and which has nothing to do with their capacity to involve themselves in international relations. But in fact it is not the case that the ready association of 'sovereign' and 'state' stems from co-incidence or convenience, any more than it has much if anything to do with a taste for ego-stroking or euphony.

One other and a more substantial preliminary point remains to be cleared away before the heart of the matter can be approached. It has to do with the variety of ways in which the term 'sovereignty' is used. Note has already been taken of this, and what has to be emphasized now is that it is not just academics (particularly philosophers and political scientists) and journalists who ascribe a whole range of meanings to the term. States also use it now in one way and then in another. Nor is this a result of states differing in their settled semantic preferences. Whether of itself or others, the same state is very likely to use the term sovereignty in different ways at different times. It is indeed a very flexible term, and, on account of the almost mystical connotations which often attach to the idea to which it refers, frequently finds convenient employment in a whole range of situations.

It is especially useful as a rallying cry: 'on no account must the sovereignty of the state be infringed' is a theme which, in political circles, only the foolhardy would oppose. If a state is receiving unwelcome attentions from another state or an international organization, the inclusion in a speech of a reference to the need to defend sovereignty can hardly fail to go down well at home. It might even lead to greater caution abroad, for states are always very mindful of the need not to behave in a manner which might later be used against them.

A few examples illustrate very well the difficulty of trying to establish a meaning for the term 'sovereignty' simply by looking at what states say about it. They also show how states will do their best to exploit the convenient malleability of the term. France has been a party to the North Atlantic Treaty since its inception in 1949 and in the early 1950s joined with the other members in building up the military forces of the alliance on a co-operative basis and in establishing an integrated command structure for use in time of war. In consequence there were on French territory the headquarters of two NATO commands and some units of the armed forces of the United States which made use of certain bases and installations. All this, said President de Gaulle in 1966, diminished the full exercise by France of her sovereignty. They must go. In reply the President of the United States said that he had always regarded their presence as a wise and far-seeing exercise of French sovereignty – but to no avail. They went.[2] Two years later the Soviet Union and some of her Warsaw Pact allies sent troops into Czechoslovakia to prevent its government from continuing certain policies which the Soviet Union saw as threatening her dominance in Eastern Europe. This action, followed by a justification published a month later which became known as the Brezhnev Doctrine,[3] led the Western states to charge the Soviet Union with favouring the idea of limited sovereignty. In reply it was said that this was nothing short of slanderous: the movement of Soviet and other troops into fraternal territory was designed above all to defend the full sovereignty of socialist Czechoslovakia.[4] A few years later the debate in Britain on whether the country should join the European Community produced a fine crop of claims about the true nature of sovereignty. Those opposing entry argued that such a step would put a very premature end to a rich history of sovereign statehood going back four hundred years and more, while those on the other side went to considerable pains to argue that entry would present no real threat to British sovereignty, properly conceived.

The conclusion is clear: as states use the term 'sovereignty', it has no single meaning. Nor is there any reason why it should. Words have uses rather than single correct meanings. Hence there is no question of right or wrong about the way in which states use a term such as 'sovereignty'. One need not speak of its misuse, not even when the term is rather obviously being employed for nothing more than tendentious purposes. States, after all, see themselves as having a duty to protect and advance their interests, and may sometimes calculate that they may be able to discharge that duty by a semantic ploy. As a political move it is not unfamiliar at levels other than the international. However, the lack of any overall consistency in the use of the term 'sovereignty' by states does not mean that one must abandon the present enterprise of trying to identify what it is that distinguishes the allegedly sovereign, internationally participating states from others. For the lack of overall consistency in this matter does not mean the lack of any consistency at all. 'Sovereignty' might, for example, be a term which has several accepted meanings. Or at the very least it might have an accepted meaning in respect of the question which is now under examination.

It would be very surprising if it did not. There is, perhaps, no reason in principle why participation in international relations should not be open to any group (or, indeed, individual) which can, as it were, elbow its way on to the stage. But in practice social life in all contexts tends to give rise to the ordering mechanism of categorization. Some are eligible to do this and go there, others not; nationals take this gate, aliens that; sheep on the right hand, goats on the left. Put differently, non-universal groups commonly have restrictive stipulations regarding membership, limiting admission to those of a certain descent, intellectual standard, viewpoint, or whatever. Not every American, Briton, or Russian is eligible to become a Daughter of the American Revolution, an undergraduate of the University of Keele, or a member of the Communist Party of the Soviet Union. Certain qualifications are required, and it may be that there is a further stage at which a choice is made from amongst those with the necessary credentials. It would therefore be odd if at so weighty and protocol-conscious a level as the international there was no criterion governing states' admission. And, given that all of them operating upon it lay claim to sovereignty, it would be odder still if on closer inspection that apparently distinguishing characteristic proved to be of no significance at all.

It has to be said, however, that the making of that closer inspection is not a speedy and straightforward affair. There is no international constitution which can be consulted regarding the relevant meaning of the term 'sovereignty'. What some would regard, with rather suspect accuracy, as its nearest equivalent – the Charter of the United Nations – is not of much help. For what the Charter says is that the organization is based on the sovereign equality of all its member states.[5] In other words, an entity has to be sovereign before it has any hope of getting in, which takes one nowhere if one wishes to know of what that sovereignty, the prerequisite for membership, consists. The lawyers are often of equally little use. In part this is due to the fact that when they write about states in an international context their purposes do not always require that they confine their attention to sovereign states. A varying range of entities is focused upon for, as one writer has put it, ' "State" has no absolute or objective meaning in international law. The range of phenomena covered by the term depends on the definition which a particular jurist prefers to adopt.'[6] Thus they do not always need to look closely at the idea of sovereignty. And when they do deal with this area alone it is very often in the context of a discussion of sovereign rights, meaning the rights which attach to sovereign states – which again, says nothing about what it is which makes a state sovereign and so entitles it to sovereign rights. Non-legal writers, too, contribute remarkably little on this subject. They may well, in talking about one aspect or another of international relations, deal with sovereignty, but only very rarely does their discussion of it have anything at all to do with the question of what criteria must be satisfied before a territorially based entity can regard itself as at least in the running for admission to the international society. And, when it does, they do not often carry the matter very far forward, sometimes because they do not focus on the exact question which is being identified here as the crucial one. One author, for example, says, quite unexceptionably, that a sovereign state is 'nothing more nor less than an entity which participates in the international system on a level of legal or formal equality with all such similar members of the system'.[7] But in so doing he fails, like many others, to address himself to the prior question of what it is about a sovereign state which enables it to participate in the international system alongside others of its kind.

It is indeed remarkable that there has been a widespread failure by writers on international relations to ask this question. For it is in a very real sense the most basic which can be asked about their subject. If one supposes, as is still done very widely, and very reasonably so, that states are the most significant actors on what is generally called the international scene, the first question to ask about them is how they – and not others – came to get there. Even if one takes the pragmatic – and in this respect unacademic – attitude that it does not matter how they got there and that the thing to do is to concentrate on their behaviour, this is still in some pragmatic respects an unsatisfactory reply. For one would wish to know the grounds on which some might come to exclude themselves from the international company and others might put themselves in a position which would fit them for admission. In short, one wishes – more than wishes, needs – to know what it is that qualifies a territorially based entity for international actorhood. The answer to a question directed to this point defines the entities whose activities make up, if not the whole of the academic subject of international relations, at least a very large part of it. And if, as is so, the states concerned prove not to be self-nominating, then one needs to ask what it is that enables them to appear on the international stage, and prevents admission from being just a free-for-all. And, further, if the criterion is something called sovereignty, a close inquiry into its nature (in this specific context, that is) is called for.

This matter has not been wholly neglected, but even when sights have been set exactly on the target the bull's eye seems hardly ever to have been clearly hit. One writer, for example, says of sovereignty that 'At root the term merely denotes superiority. That concept, however, requires a referent. One must ask: superior with respect to what? Applied to a finite government, sovereignty merely is a term implicit of ascendancy established with respect to matters bearing on the government's capacity to function as a going concern. Sovereignty denotes capacity to make and give effect to public decisions. Sovereignty is the situation of being in charge of a domain.'[8] All of which is very vague, for 'ascendancy' and 'in charge' are not susceptible of straightforward and uncontroversial application. And there are many bodies which make and give effect to decisions in a realm which might reasonably be called 'public' but which play no part in international relations, and are therefore to be presumed as lacking in sovereignty. The same writer goes on to refer to 'some of the practical components of sovereignty',[9] such as rulers, allegiance, a common history, the taking of effective decisions, and the undertaking and implementing of obligations. But this list is hardly of much help if one wants to identify the kind of territorial entity which, no doubt displaying such characteristics, is also eligible to do so at the international level.

Another writer defines 'external sovereignty' as 'the claim to be politically and juridically independent of any superior',[10] which is either far too vague or too far-reaching, or both. What, one wonders, is the significance of the words 'claim' and 'superior'? And political independence, unless it is here given a narrow interpretation, is something which hardly attaches to the mass of sovereign states. The same type of comment is applicable to a similar definition advanced by a writer from a different academic discipline, the law, who speaks of the external aspect of the state (which he prefers to call 'independence', reserving 'sovereignty' for the internal exercise of power and authority) as 'the political and legal autonomy of the State, in its not being subject, except with its free consent, to any external direction, interference or control by any like authority'.[11] Even if 'direction' and 'control' are sufficiently precise to allow of the fairly easy application of this definition, 'interference' is hardly so, and 'free consent', too, is a rather murky conception. Similar problems attend another lawyer's definition of independence, which he used synonymously with sovereignty. He said, in his capacity as a Judge of the Permanent Court of International Justice (the interwar predecessor of the present International Court), that an independent state 'has over it no other authority than that of international law' – which leaves open the question of how the entity concerned came to be in that position. He went on to say that as long as legal restrictions on its liberty 'do not place the State under the authority of another State, the former remains an independent State however extensive and burdensome those obligations may be'.[12] This, unhappily, is vague on the crucial point of the exact meaning which is to be given to the word 'authority'.

Another writer (and now we are back in the discipline of international relations) speaks of sovereignty as something which is 'asserted' by the states which participate in international relations. 'On the one hand, states assert, in relation to [their] territory and population, what may be called internal sovereignty, which means supremacy over all other authorities within that territory and population. On the other hand, they assert what may be called external sovereignty, by which is meant not supremacy but independence of outside authorities.' Clearly, much will here depend on what is meant by 'assert', and the author goes on to say that it is both normative and factual. However, he does not elucidate the nature of the normative claim. And with regard to the factual situation, while he allows that it may cover the exercise of supremacy and independence 'in varying degrees', he says that an 'independent [sic] political community which merely claims a right to sovereignty (or is judged by others to have such a right), but cannot assert this right in practice, is not a state properly so-called.'[13] It is not hard to see that the application of this definition, while it may often be straightforward, is going to give trouble at the margin, and it could be a fairly broad margin. For whether a state asserts independence and supremacy in a sufficient degree to be adjudged as actually asserting them 'in practice' is likely to be a very arguable matter.

The matter has been put not very differently by another writer. He suggests that state sovereignty means the 'formal authority to make binding laws and political decisions within recognized territorial limits without interference or control from other bodies and to act externally with a freedom that is limited only by voluntarily-accepted restraints'.[14] One wonders how the last phrase is reconcilable with the obligations of international customary law, which do not come within the immediate meaning of 'voluntarily-accepted'. More substantively, there is the problem here of ascertaining how far through the quotation the qualifying word 'formal' runs, and of attaching an exact meaning to the slippery concepts of 'interference or control'. Like the other writers who have been quoted, this one is certainly aiming in the right direction, but his shot, like theirs, has not made a desirably sharp impact. It could be, of course, that in this matter one cannot obtain a precise result. But this would not seem to be so, for states themselves have very little difficulty in deciding, virtually without controversy, which of them are sovereign, and hence eligible to participate in international relations. If, therefore, as is presumably the case, the quoted writers were striving after a characterization of practice, their definitions fall short of the degree of accuracy which should be possible.

If writers have not on the whole given this matter the attention and care which one might have expected it to attract, the reason could be that sovereign states themselves have made it entirely clear what it is about them, called sovereignty, that results in their being treated on all sides as properly engaged in international relations. Although, even if that were the case, it would still not excuse the writers of general books on international relations from having failed to draw the attention of their readers, usually students, to this fundamental aspect of the international scene. However, as it happens, states too have been surprisingly reticent on this specific point. They are not slow to refer to themselves as sovereign nor to trumpet the term 'sovereignty' whenever it seems useful to respond in this way to some injury or slight. But, when one looks for evidence out of the mouths of sovereign states themselves about what it is that made them eligible to pass through the international gate, one looks in vain. States could hardly regard this matter, literally crucial to their international status, as one of little moment. Nor could they reasonably see sovereignty, meaning that which distinguishes them from territorial entities which do not have an international capacity, as something which is so broad, featureless and widely shared as not to merit attention. The way of international relations may not be particularly narrow but the gate to it is certainly strait. It could be, of course, that the attitude of states towards sovereignty is the same as that, reportedly, of gentlemen towards money: something which is not discussed. Everyone is to be assumed to have it and to be able, in consequence, to maintain an appropriate lifestyle, one which does not involve demeaning calculations and comparisons in terms of pounds and pence. However, even if it was once the case that internationally sovereignty was just taken for granted, an undiscussed given in a group which also shared a wide range of common standards, it would be surprising if the same held true today. The number of sovereign states has more than doubled during the last thirty years, and both new and old states are not renowned for their modesty. The international scene is no longer, if it ever was, one where the prevailing style is that of the understating and urbane English gentleman.

State Practice

Whatever the reason, sovereign states do not spell out what they mean by sovereignty, or by the term they generally link with it to synonymous effect – independence. (In this work, except where the context makes it clear to the contrary, the practice of states regarding the use of the term 'independence' will be followed). And as it happens this does not greatly matter. For the initial thing which the student of international relations needs to know about sovereignty is what it is, rather than what states, or anyone else, choose to say about it. Providing he is asking the question which relates to his purpose, which here is finding out what it is that distinguishes the territorially based entities which play a full and regular part on the international stage from those which do not, the answer can be ascertained, and ascertained most authoritatively, from the practice of states. One can simply look to see what changes take place when an entity secures an international capacity. And, fortunately, in respect of this matter the practice of states is both open and crystal clear. States may not be verbally explicit about the nature of their sovereignty, meaning that which entitles them to seek admission to the international hurly-burly. But their actions make the meaning which they attach to the term 'sovereignty' entirely plain.

Consider what happened in 1978 when two groups of islands in the western Pacific, both of them having formerly been a British responsibility, moved, however minimally, on to the international stage. The Solomon Islands, with a population of about 200,000, had since 1893 been a British protectorate, that is to say, the territory had been in a colonial situation in relation to Britain but had not been in the possession of the British Crown. Following discussions between Britain and the representatives of the islanders, it was agreed that on 7 July Britain's links with the territory should be cut and that it would in consequence become a sovereign state, able, with the co-operation of others, to play such a part on the international stage as it felt desirable and financially possible. A few months later the Solomon Islands was ushered into the United Nations as the organization's one hundred and fiftieth member. The territory, now being sovereign, was eligible to join, had decided to apply, and had been accepted. Equally, the Solomon Islands now has rights and duties under international law, which it did not before 7 July. It may also, by agreement, send ambassadors or high commissioners (a high commissioner being an ambassador sent by one Commonwealth country to another) to other states, and may apply to join additional international organizations. It may be forecast with some confidence that it will not do much if any of these things. But the point is that the Solomon Islands now has the capacity to do them, and much else. It is, in short, in a position to play a part in international relations, whereas prior to a certain time on a certain day it was not. Then Britain acted for the territory in international relations. Now it is a sovereign state and can, accordingly, act for itself.

The significance of the assumption of sovereignty is perhaps made even clearer, in a paradoxical way, when one looks at a second Pacific territory which achieved this status in 1978. The Gilbert and Ellice Islands were a British colony which, until 1975, were administered as one unit. Then they split into two and it was subsequently agreed that the former Ellice Islands should become independent, that is, sovereign, on 1 October 1978, under their new name of Tuvalu. At midnight on 30 September/1 October the British flag was duly run down the flag-pole and replaced by that of the new sovereign state. Britain's responsibility for the islands had come to an end. Now the new sovereign state was in a position to do everything open to the Solomon Islands and all the other states on the international scene. In practice it is likely to do hardly anything, for it is made up of nine populated islands, scattered over half a million square miles of ocean; the land area of these islands amounts to about 10 square miles and the population consists of about 8,000 people. But the point is not what it will do but what it is eligible to do. And, being sovereign, it is eligible to do much. Not everyone chooses to dine at the Ritz, but there is no reason, in principle, why anyone should not do so. Equally, there is no principled objection to Tuvalu playing an active international part. It has in fact joined the Commonwealth (but it came into a special category, then containing one other, even smaller, state, which means that it does not attend Heads of Government conferences). That apart, it may be supposed that it will conduct a very quiet international life. But its status is different from what it was on 30 September 1978. In point of status there is, in fact, now nothing to choose between Tuvalu and Britain, or any other sovereign state.

What happened in both these cases which transformed them from non-sovereign entities to ones possessing sovereignty, and hence gave them international capacity, was a change in their constitutional situation. At one moment the Solomon Islands and the Ellice Islands were a part of the British constitutional set-up. They may have had a measure of self-government, but for them authority lay ultimately with the British Crown, and was exercised by the Crown on the advice of the British Government of the day. In this way it was open to Britain to make itself felt in the internal affairs of each group of islands. Equally, it was Britain who spoke for them in international relations. Final authority lay outside the physical limits of each territory. Then, however, on the basis of decisions of the British Parliament and government, respectively expressed through Acts of Parliament and Orders in Council (the Privy Council, that is), the position of the territories underwent a sudden and far-reaching change.[15] Their constitutional links with Britain were cut (at a specified time on a specified day) and henceforth ultimate governmental authority lies within the territories. It is up to them to reach their own decisions about their internal policies. They may take advice and assistance from outside, and may make promises to other states or international organizations about their internal behaviour. But there is no question of another state taking decisions for them or disallowing their decisions by virtue of that other state's superior constitutional position. Likewise, in international relations it is now up to both states to decide what they wish to do. That is not to say that they, any more than any other, have legal freedom to do what they like. They have obligations under international law, just as they have rights, and they may add to both by treaty. But decisions regarding their international situation are now theirs alone.

The matter may be summed up by saying that for the Solomon Islands and Tuvalu, as for all other internationally active states, the sovereignty on which their international activity is based amounts to constitutional separateness. A sovereign state may have all sorts of links with other such states and with international bodies, but the one sort of link which, by definition, it cannot have is a constitutional one. For sovereignty, in the sense here discussed, consists of being constitutionally apart, of not being contained, however loosely, within a wider constitutional scheme. A territory which is so contained is not sovereign and hence is not eligible to participate on a regular basis in international relations. Once any such connection is severed, the territory concerned has become sovereign and thus ready, if it and others wish it, to join in the usual kind of international activity.

One writer who has both appreciated the nature of the term 'sovereignty' as it is used in this context and given it succinct expression is the late Professor C. A. W. Manning. The way in which he liked to sum it up, in his tantalizingly brief published observations on the subject, was to refer, interchangeably, to a sovereign state being constitutionally self-contained or constitutionally insular.[16] The definition of sovereignty used in this work draws heavily on both the substance of Manning's ideas and the terminology in which he expressed them. However, the phrase which will be used to describe sovereignty is 'constitutional independence'. The meaning of this phrase, it must be emphasized, has nothing to do with what is sometimes called constitutionalism – the conduct of government in accordance with the country's constitution. Whether or not a government behaves properly in internal matters is neither here nor there so far as the independence of its constitution is concerned. Nor does constitutional independence have any connection with a narrower meaning of the term 'constitutionalism': government in accordance with democratic principles. For a constitutionally independent state can have any kind of political complexion, with the most authoritarian of constitutional schemes existing as independently as the most democratic. One further point that must be made is that an independent constitution does not mean that it may be lawfully amended without limit or qualification. The extent to which amendment is permissible will depend on the provisions of the constitution itself. All that constitutional independence means is that a state's constitution is not part of a larger constitutional arrangement. If that is so, one important consequence is that, in accord with current international practice, the state concerned is deemed to be sovereign and therefore eligible to participate fully and regularly in international relations. Moreover, the only territorial actors who may so participate are those which are in this sense sovereign.

International Activity

The reference at the end of the last paragraph to eligibility is a material one. Mention has frequently been made in this chapter to the fact that territorially based entities which play a full and regular part in international relations are distinguished from those which do not by the term 'sovereign'. However, this has obscured the point that it is not a requisite of sovereignty that the state concerned should lead an active international life, or, indeed, any international life at all. Most sovereign states are anxious to make their mark on the international stage and try to do so. But there is no question of a loss of sovereignty if one does not. International activity is not a condition of sovereignty. What sovereignty does is to give a state an international capacity, to make it eligible for international life. It is not necessary that that capacity should be used, that a state should take advantage of its eligibility. The state of Muscat and Oman (now known simply as Oman), for example, played virtually no part in international relations prior to the palace coup of 1970 which replaced Sultan Said by his son, Sultan Qaboos. For much of the 1960s and the early 1970s Burma, although remaining a member of the United Nations, appeared to be doing all she could to opt out of international life. It may also sometimes be the case that a state would like to play an international role, or a bigger one, but is prevented from doing so by the refusal of other states to have dealings with it – probably on ideological grounds. There is nothing improper in this. Sovereignty brings with it no right to participation in international relations; it only fits a state for such participation. For advantage to be taken of that fitness at least one other sovereign state has to respond. Usually there is no problem in this respect, but sometimes a state will meet a difficulty, and perhaps a substantial one. But this is no way affects its constitutional independence, and thus it remains a sovereign state, albeit a frustrated one.[17]

This point has an apparent counterpart, although there is no connection between them. For just as some sovereign states may choose or be obliged not to participate in international relations so it is the case that international participation is not limited to sovereign states. Some non-sovereign states are also to be seen, or may be seen, on the international stage. The component states of a federation, for example, may have a limited treaty-making power, although it may not be described as such. The first Article of the American constitution says that while the states of the Union may not make treaties they may enter into compacts and agreements with the consent of Congress – although a helpful and authoritative distinction between the two categories has yet to emerge.[18] The states of the West German Federation have the right, with the consent of the Federation, to make treaties on matters within their jurisdiction, and the cantons of Switzerland may do likewise on specified matters. The constituent republics of the Soviet Union, too, may enter into agreements with foreign countries, and the Soviet constitution does not expressly require the consent of the federal government for such activities, although 'several provisions assure the overall control of the federal Government' of the foreign relations of the Republics'.[19] It is also the case that some colonies have had a limited treaty-making capacity. And both colonies and the component states of a federal union may sometimes engage in correspondence with foreign sovereign states on a wide range of matters. What all this amounts to is that non-sovereign states may, for certain purposes, act as international persons. But they are not on a par with sovereign states. It is only the latter which are, potentially at least, full international persons. And the basis of this distinction lies in the fact that in the case of a sovereign state its constitutional independence automatically gives it, so far as other states are concerned, full international capacity, whereas the international activity of a non-sovereign state is based on the specific grant or permission of its sovereign superior.

A similar point needs to be made regarding the occasional membership in international organizations of non-sovereign states. If the membership at large is willing to countenance this there is no reason why it should not happen. The non-sovereign state in question then becomes a full member of the organization and to that extent enjoys international personality. However, this has no direct consequences so far as any other international activity is concerned. It does not mean that the non-sovereign member state can act outside the organization as if it was sovereign. It gives it no claim to be considered for membership in other organizations, to exchange ambassadors with sovereign states, to sign treaties and so on. All that has happened is that, doubtless on account of some very specific political circumstances, the unusual step has been taken of admitting a non-sovereign state to sovereign company. The best-known example of this is the presence in the United Nations of Byelorussia and the Ukraine, two of the constituent states of the Soviet Union. This arose out of a deal made in 1945 between the United States and the Soviet Union which began as a Soviet attempt to counterbalance what it saw as the unfair voting advantage which the United States would have in the projected organization on account of its friends in Latin America. After a Soviet claim for sixteen seats in the United Nations (one for each of its constituent republics) and an American comment which mentioned a possible figure for itself of forty-eight (then the number of states making up the United States) the bargaining settled at three seats for the Soviet Union and an option for the United States to ask for three votes (in the General Assembly) for itself. However, news of it was leaked, the American public objected, and the United States relinquished its share of the bargain, leaving the Soviet Union holding on firmly to the promise of membership for Byelorussia and the Ukraine.[20]

Britain make no objections to this proposal, and for a very good reason. When the League of Nations had been agreed upon in 1919 the 'British Empire' delegation to the founding conference had been accorded six seats: one for the mother country, one each for four of the Dominions – Australia, Canada, New Zealand, and South Africa – and one for India. Uncertainty about the constitutional status of the white Dominions was cleared up (more or less) by the Statute of Westminster of 1931 and henceforth they were almost universally regarded as sovereign and independent states, albeit rather unusual ones in that their king was also king of the United Kingdom. India, however, clearly did not become sovereign, nor was it in 1945 when the UN was set up. But the propriety of its becoming a founder member of the United Nations was accepted on all sides. Which put Britain in no position at all to object to the proposal that the Soviet Union and the United States should have three votes in the General Assembly as, in view of India's membership, Britain would, in effect, have two.

In the event the situation did not last for long as a change of government in Britain in 1945 resulted in India becoming independent two years later. By this time one other anomaly regarding United Nations membership had already been cleared up. It concerned the member known in 1945 as the Commonwealth of the Philippines, 'commonwealth' status having been given to this territory in 1934 by its colonial overlord, the United States (this having nothing to do, of course, with the British Commonwealth). Here too the general intention was that, despite its subordinate status, the Philippines should become a founding member of the United Nations and although it gave rise to a question or two this is what happened. However, within a year the constitutional links between the United States and the Philippines had been amicably cut, the Philippines in this way becoming a sovereign state.

Thus it is only Byelorussia and the Ukraine which remain as non-sovereign members of the United Nations. Their presence is testimony to the fact that it is quite possible for non-sovereign states to play a part on the international stage, to enjoy, for specified purposes, international personality. But their presence also testifies to the fact that this is an exceptional arrangement, one which goes to 'prove the rule' that membership in international organizations is normally confined to sovereign states. The membership of non-sovereign states is unusual and stems not just from the willingness of the other members to make a concession regarding the customary requirements of membership but also from the willingness of the constitutional superiors of the non-sovereign states to allow them to play a certain international role. (In the case of Byelorussia and the Ukraine the Soviet constitution was amended in 1944 just to pave the way for the possibility that one or more of the constituent republics of the Soviet Union might be able to obtain United Nations membership.) And in a case of this kind the international role of the non-sovereign state will be strictly confined, both by its super-ordinate state and by other sovereign states, to the purposes for which international personality has been bestowed. By contrast the international personality of a sovereign state suffers no such limitations. It may do what it wishes in international relations, subject only to the general or specific restrictions of international law. Wisdom may suggest that certain things are better left unattempted, and lack of physical or financial means may impose other restraints. But this in no way detracts from the formal capacity of a sovereign state to go its own way in the international arena and to have dealings with any states which are willing to respond. This is not to imply that a sovereign state need take no account in its international activity of what goes on within its own borders. Clearly the state will need to carry its own people (or those of them who matter) with it in its foreign policy. It may also need to act in the light of any restrictions which its own constitution places on its international activity. But these are not issues which are of any direct concern to those other sovereign states with whom it does business. The sorting out of any internal problems to which its international activity gives rise is a sovereign state's private business.

This reference to the details of a sovereign state's own constitution draws attention to one final point of clarification which should be made in this quest for what it is that distinguishes a sovereign from a non-sovereign state. It is to emphasize that what is sought here is an international perspective on the matter, the view about sovereignty which is taken by sovereign states when they are speaking in that – international – capacity. It might be that when a sovereign state is acting internally its own constitutional arrangements oblige it to speak of state sovereignty in a sense quite different from that which it uses internationally. For it could be that the component states of a federation either are regarded by the constitutional theory of the federation as sovereign or themselves assert that they are in this con- dition. The states of the United States, for example, and the cantons of Switzerland claim to be sovereign.[21] Soviet jurists maintain that all the constituent republics of the Soviet Union are sovereign states, [22] and the six states of the Australian Commonwealth have been referred to as sovereign.[23] It was presumably on the basis of this assumption that the legislature of the American state of Mississippi established, in 1956, a state sovereignty commission, the task of which was to publicize and defend the Mississippi version of the southern way of life, then under threat by the idea and policy of racial integration.[24] However, this is merely an illustration of how the term 'sovereignty' can be used in a variety of ways. If a federal state refers to its subordinate units as sovereign, it certainly means something different from what it means when it speaks of its own international situation in terms of sovereignty. Likewise, when a component unit of a federation refers to itself as sovereign that will have no inter- national implications whatsoever. For the criterion of sovereignty which might apply within a state is bound to be different from that which operates internationally to designate some entities as having the capacity to participate in international relations. Such states not only have territory, people and a government. They are also sovereign in the internationally accepted sense of being constitutionally independent, and it is this which gives them the capacity to move on to the international stage.

This is not a historical inquiry. It will not therefore try to ascertain when it became appropriate to speak of sovereignty as constitutional independence. But it is worth just remarking that the principle which constitutional independence expresses, that a state is in ultimate overall control of its own affairs, seems to have been the essence of sovereignty throughout the existence of the system of sovereign states, which is another way of saying throughout the existence of the modern states system. During the Middle Ages the idea of independent states was incompatible with the orthodox theory of the time. The Pope and the Emperor each claimed, were generally regarded as justified in claiming, and up to a point actually asserted a considerable measure of jurisdiction throughout the Christian world. 'In legal theory, the kingdoms and principalities of the late Middle Ages were neither unique nor self-sufficient. The only society which was so was the society of Christendom, a supra-national society of which Christian kingdoms were dependent members.'[25] However, in the view of one authority, even as early as '1300 it was evident that the dominant political form in Western Europe was going to be the sovereign state',[26] with the next two centuries or so seeing the completion of a system of states on this basis. And by sovereignty he means 'independence from any outside power and final authority over men who live within certain boundaries'.[27] Since then there have been changes in the details of this idea and its expression has become more formal and refined, but it seems clear that so far as its essence is concerned there has been some continuity from the sixteenth century to the twentieth.

Put differently, one can say that the political basis on which the world is presently organized, that of distinct territorial entities, has a history which stretches back to the break-up of the medieval system. Nor does this arrangement appear to be declining in popularity. The radical changes in the political map of the world which have had to be made in recent years in response to the successes of the movement for national self-determination provide evidence not of a weakened but of a strengthened overall attachment to the idea of sovereignty. Empires have shrunk but concomitantly new states have been born. There is an opposite process – that of integration – at work, but it has not yet made inroads into the dominance of sovereignty. Not even in Western Europe, where conditions for it are most propitious, has the integration of states proceeded to the point where there is serious doubt as to whether the members of the European Community are any longer sovereign. Indeed as the six of yesterday become the ten of today and look forward to the possibility of becoming twelve tomorrow, the likelihood of the individual member states being submerged seems to become less rather than more. Which is not very surprising. And even if one sovereign state did emerge in place of ten or twelve this would not alter the fact that the world is politically arranged on the sovereignty principle. It would simply mean that in one area local circumstances had produced a reduction in the number of sovereign states, an event which would be exceedingly unlikely to have a snowball effect.

Territorial Dispositions

What has happened over the centuries is that with the spread of European power and influence an increasing proportion of the land surface of the globe has been divided up into sovereign states – an empire being a form of sovereign state. And over the last hundred years the advance of technology together with an increased formalization of international relations has resulted in almost every square kilometre of the earth's land surface being allocated to one sovereign state or another, with virtually all frontiers being tidily delineated and clearly demarcated. Thus to all intents and purposes it is possible to say that, jurisdictionally speaking, there is never any doubt about where one stands, and that one always stands on the domain of a single sovereign state. The exceptions are so small or so literally out of the way as to prove this rule, and now they are even fewer than they used to be.

Until 1980 the largest and best known exception was the Anglo-French South Pacific condominium of New Hebrides – which then became the sovereign state of Vanuatu. The tiny state of Andorra in the Pyrenees has some of the appearances of a condominium, in that it has two 'co-princes' or heads of state: the Spanish Bishop of Urgel and the French Count of Foix, whose functions are now always undertaken by the President of France. But, even if it is so regarded, it is clearly not a dependent condominium but a sovereign state with some very unusual internal arrangements. Prior to 1966 Kuwait and Saudi Arabia shared what was called a neutral zone, but it was then divided equally between them. Another neutral zone used to exist between Saudi Arabia and Iraq, being diamond-shaped and 4,500 square kilometres in extent. But by a 1975 treaty it too was divided equally between the two former joint owners. Another joint regime which has now disappeared is that which was established by the United States and Britain in 1939 with regard to the very small Pacific islands of Canton and Enderbury, this agreement being without prejudice to their respective claims to the two islands. The arrangement was to last for fifty years, but was terminated by a 1979 treaty between the United States and the new state of Kiribati (which had succeeded to the British claim), under which the islands – now no longer needed by the United States for communication and aviation – passed to Kiribati. Finally, a Peruvian proposal of 1976 that Bolivia's longstanding desire for access to the sea be met by the creation of a zone in which sovereignty would be shared by Bolivia, Peru, and Chile came to naught, being rejected by the other two proposed participants.

One case of shared territory which does remain is to be found at the mouth of the Bidassoa River, which at this point forms the boundary between France and Spain. Here is to be found the tiny uninhabited Isla de los Faisanes – or Ile de la Conférence – which is a Franco-Spanish condominium. It must also be noted in this connection that there is no agreed division of the Antarctic continent, the various competing claims to parts of it having, in effect, been put on one side at least until 1991 – the thirtieth anniversary of the entry into force of the 1959 Antarctic Treaty.

It is always possible, of course, for sovereign states to administer territory which does not belong to them. This may happen as the result of war, where, reflecting the ethos of the age (other than in respect of colonial situations), a victorious state may be reluctant to annex the territory which it has taken from the vanquished. Israel, for example, has not annexed the West Bank of the Jordan and the Gaza Strip, which she has occupied since the War of 1967 – and this is not in any way due to the fact that there is widespread uncertainty as to their lawful owners. And her purported annexations of East Jerusalem (arguably, this took place in 1967) and the Syrian Golan Heights (in 1981) have been accepted by no other states. An alternative route to the administration of another's territory is by way of agreement. One such case occurs along the border between Egypt and Sudan.[28] When this frontier was established at the end of the nineteenth century, it was declared to run along the twenty-second parallel of latitude. But it was soon found that in two eastern areas this frontier gave rise to some difficulty with regard to the administration of nomadic tribes. Accordingly, a new administrative boundary was created providing for two enclaves: Bir Tawil, which lay south of the parallel, but was to be administered by Egypt; and the Halaib Triangle, which lay to its north, which was to be administered by Sudan. Nowadays British atlases sometimes show the administrative boundary as the international frontier, but technically this is not the case. Another instance is the American administration of that part of the territory of the sovereign state of Panama which was known as the Panama Canal Zone – regarding which America greatly annoyed Panama in 1946 by including it in a list, sent to the UN, of American-owned non-self-governing territories! Since 1979 the United States has been in effective control of only about 40 per cent of the former zone, including the canal itself, and is due to return all of that to Panama at the end of 1999.

A rather similar situation exists in respect of the New Territories of Hong Kong, which are administered by Britain under a lease from China which expires in 1997. As the British-owned colony of Hong Kong is, in practical terms, dependent on the New Territories (and together they form a single governmental unit), this raised a large question about the future of Britain's presence in this part of the world. At one time there were thoughts that Britain might be able to persuade China that, in return for acknowledging her claim to the whole area, Britain should be allowed to continue administering it. But in 1983 China made it very clear that she found this proposed solution unacceptable, and in the following year Britain's Foreign Secretary allowed that it would 'not be realistic'[29] to expect that Britain would remain in Hong Kong beyond 1997. An agreement providing for the transfer of the colony to China in that year was signed at the end of 1984. In the case of the Falkland Islands, too, the idea that Britain should agree that the territory is Argentinian in return for its remaining under British administration is, as of early 1985, not making any progress. Here both sides think that the lease-back scheme will not do, although it may yet come to have more appeal as the reverberations of the 1982 war over the islands diminish.

Another possibility in some territorial disputes is to leave the question of lawful possession entirely on one side, and to concentrate on *de facto* dispositions. This device was used in the 1954 agreement between Britain, Italy, the United States, and Yugoslavia regarding the Free Territory of Trieste. It provided for the assumption of governmental authority by Italy and Yugoslavia on their respective sides of the agreed new dividing line, but spoke of what had been agreed in terms not of legal finality but of 'practical arrangements'.[30] Not until twenty-three years later did Italy and Yugoslavia feel able to agree, in the Treaty of Osimo, that the provisions which had operated since 1954 should become final.

In all such matters as those so far referred to, however, great care needs to be taken with regard to terminology. For, in discussing the extent of a sovereign state's territory (which it usually but not invariably also administers), the term 'sovereignty' is very often used synomymously with ownership. This usage must be distinguished from 'sovereignty' meaning constitutional independence, which attaches to the state as such, and has nothing to do with whether or not a particular area belongs to this state or that. Thus one might consider whether the sovereignty (in the sense of right of ownership) of the sovereign state of Jupiter extends to the territory known as Pluto. But the answer has no bearing on the status of Jupiter as a sovereign (in the sense of constitutionally independent) state. It concerns only its ambit, and hence the question of whether it may lawfully exercise jurisdiction over Pluto – or allow another sovereign state to do so.

In practice, disputes over a sovereign state's lawful limits – other than minor boundary issues – are rare. (Disputes occur a little more frequently over one state's claims, on other than legal grounds, to some part of another's territory.) This is chiefly a reflection of the fact that the allocation of the world's land surface to sovereign states has reached virtually the ultimate point. Leaving Antarctica on one side as a special case and taking at its face value the widespread view that the sea bed is 'the common heritage of mankind' (the UN General Assembly said so in an unopposed resolution of 1970, and the statement was repeated in the 1982 UN Convention on the Law of the Sea, which has been signed by many states, but neither by the United States nor by the United Kingdom), it becomes clear that expansion into unclaimed territory is no longer possible. Moreover, cases of joint administration are exceedingly rare and insignificant, and international jurisdiction exists only in the realm of ideas. Thus sovereignty is the one and only organizing principle in respect of the dry surface of the globe, all that surface now, to all intents and purposes, being divided among single entities of a sovereign, or constitutionally independent, kind. This condition is regarded on all sides as the one which is necessary if a state is to act on the international stage, and the vast majority of sovereign states wish, and are able, to take full advantage of this opportunity. As territorial actors are still far and away the most important at this level, it is the policies and interchanges of these sovereign states that command the principal attention of the student of international relations.

Notes: Chapter 2

1   See *Newsweek*, 12 December 1977, p. 25.
2   For the texts of the letters which were exchanged on this subject see *NATO Letter*, vol. 14, no. 5 (May 1966), pp. 22–6.
3   See *New York Times*, 27 September 1968.

4 See speech by Foreign Minister Gromyko reported in *The Times*, 11 July 1969.

5 Charter of the United Nations, Art. 2, para. 1.

6 Oliver J. Lissitzyn, 'Territorial entities other than independent states in the law of treaties', in Académie de Droit International, *Recueil des cours 1968*, Vol. 3 (Leyden: Sijthoff, 1970), p. 9.

7 F. S. Northedge, *The International Political System* (London: Faber, 1976), p. 143.

8 Charles Burton Marshall, *The Exercise of Sovereignty* (Baltimore, Md: Johns Hopkins University Press, 1965), p. 3.

9 ibid., p. 4.

10 M. Wight, *Systems of States*, ed. H. Bull (Leicester: Leicester University Press, 1977), p. 130.

11 J. E. S. Fawcett, 'General course on public international law', in Académie de Droit International, *Recueil des cours 1971*, Vol. 1 (Leyden: Sijthoff, 1971), p. 381; cf. J. E. S. Fawcett, *Law and Power in International Relations* (London: Faber, 1982), p. 18.

12 Judge Anzilotti in the Austro-German Customs Unions case (Permanent Court of International Justice, 1931), quoted in James Crawford, 'The criteria for statehood in international law', *British Yearbook of International Law, Vol. 48, 1976–1977* (Oxford: Oxford University Press, 1978), p. 122.

13 Hedley Bull, *The Anarchical Society. A Study of Order in World Politics* (London: Macmillan, 1977), pp. 8–9.

14 P. A. Reynolds, 'International studies: retrospect and prospect', *British Journal of International Studies*, vol. 1, no. 1 (April 1975), p. 6.

15 For a statement of the constitutional procedure involved, see S. A. de Smith, *Constitutional and Administrative Law*, ed. Harry Street and Rodney Brazier, 4th edn (Hardmondsworth: Penguin, 1981), pp. 641–2; cf. Lord Hailsham of Marylebone (ed.), *Halsbury's Laws of England*, Vol. 18 (London: Butterworth, 1977), p. 722, para. 1408.

16 See C. A. W. Manning, *The Nature of International Society* (London: Bell, 1962; Macmillan, 1975), pp. 166–7. See also his chapter 'The legal framework in a world of change', in B. Porter (ed.), *The Aberystwyth Papers* (London: Oxford University Press, 1969), pp. 305–9. The phrase 'constitutional self-containment' had also figured tellingly in Manning's 'Sovereignty for the common man', the proposed publication of which, in the series that included Martin Wight's *Power Politics*, was announced in 1944 but eventually not proceeded with.

17 See further below, Chapter 6, pp. 143–61. And on the distinction between participation and membership in international society, see below, chapter 11, pp. 269–74.

18 See L. Henkin, *Foreign Affairs and the Constitution* (Mineola, NY: Foundation Press, 1972), p. 229.

19 Lissitzyn, 'Territorial entities', p. 35.

20 See Ruth B. Russell, *A History of the United Nations Charter* (Washington, DC: Brookings Institution, 1958), pp. 506–9, 533–9 and 596–8.

21 See P. B. Potter, 'Contemporary problems of international organization', *American Journal of International Law*, vol. 59, no. 2 (April 1965), p. 292, n. 7.

22 See Lissitzyn, 'Territorial entities', p. 37.

23 See leader in *The Times*, 12 November 1975.

24 See James W. Silver, *Mississippi: The Closed Society* (London: Gollancz, 1964), p. 8.

25 M. H. Keen, *The Laws of War in the late Middle Ages* (London: Routledge & Kegan Paul, 1965), p. 240.

26 Joseph R. Strayer, *On the Medieval Origins of the Modern State* (Princeton, NJ: Princeton University Press, 1970), p. 57.

27 ibid., p. 58. For the relevance of this approach to the position of England at this

time, see M. H. Keen, *England in the Later Middle Ages* (London: Methuen, 1973), pp. 202, 219 and 349.

28   I am indebted to Mr Patrick Bannerman for drawing my attention to this curiosity.

29   *The Times*, 21 April 1984.

30   J. C. Campbell (ed.), *Successful Negotiations: Trieste 1954* (Princeton, NJ: Princeton University Press, 1976), p. 159.

3

Explication

The constitution of a state, like that of any human enterprise, consists of the body of principles and basic rules in the light of which it is to be governed. It indicates how, in general terms, the state is to be organized and administered, saying what institutions are to be set up, how they are to be manned, the way in which they are to proceed, what they may and may not do, and how they are to relate to each other. Provision will be made for the amendment of these basic rules so that the constitution can be kept abreast of what are perceived to be the needs of the time. It may well be that, in common with all normative as distinct from scientific rules, the constitution will not always be observed. But for as long as it is generally honoured it will be seen as having validity and will be looked to for guidance as to the manner in which the most fundamental business of the state is to be conducted. It need not be written but, except in the rare case of a country with a long and relatively untroubled internal history, it is difficult to envisage how a modern state could work effectively without a written constitution, or at least without establishing a special category of fundamental laws. In fact, Britain is the only case which springs to mind of a state with a completely unwritten constitution. For, in as much as the constitution gives authoritative prescriptions on matters of great importance, the individuals and groups making up a state will only very rarely be agreeable to decisions on such issues being taken solely on the basis of under-standings and precedents. Usually the requirement will be for a written document, which deals with ultimate governmental matters in a public way and with what might be hoped is reasonable clarity. At the very least it provides a set of fixed reference points in the light of which argument about constitutional questions can proceed.

The function of a constitution is to provide a basis for order as against chaos, for the predictable as against the haphazard. It enables people to know how they stand in relation to each other and to the group to which they belong. In the smallest and most intimate of groups this basic need can be met without formal provisions. But once a group reaches even a very small size or a minimum degree of complexity it will require what is recognizably a constitution. If, for example, a group gives power to notional entities, such as a committee or a council, a constitution appears to be almost indispensable, for it is only from this source that a committee or the like can receive clear and continuing authority to act in the name of the whole. Certainly, where all the members of a group are not able to meet easily and frequently, a constitution would seem to be imperative.

A constitution is therefore the essential foundation for government, at any level. A university or an industrial concern, even a local church or tennis club, will need a constitution. All the more so does a territorially based entity – a state. Indeed, a state and its constitution are inextricably intertwined. For, in working as against mystical terms, it is as difficult to conceive of the state as separate from its constitution as it is to separate a game from the rules which say how it is to be played. The rules may be changed – but to that extent the game has also been changed. Likewise, a state may alter its constitution – and in so doing it alters itself. It may be that in the minds of its people and leaders a state lives independently of its constitutional existence. President de Gaulle certainly appeared to envisage France in this way. But as a going concern, as something which takes daily decisions and is in almost tangible operation, there is a very real sense in which a state is the overall expression of its constitution, so that without a constitution it would, for all practical purposes, be unable to exist.

It is also in respect of a state that the question arises as to whether its constitution is independent. Manifestly, a tennis club, a university and other bodies which exist within a certain territory are subject to the organs of local and national government. But where an entity is territorially defined it is relevant to ask whether its constitution is subordinate to another constitution. If it is, the state concerned, however great its autonomy, is but a subordinate part of a larger state, of a wider governmental scheme. This is clearly a question of considerable importance for the conduct of the state's internal business, for constitutional subordination will almost certainly mean that at least on some issues – and they will assuredly be the larger ones – it will not necessarily be able to get its own way. But it is also of great importance so far as the relation of the state to the rest of the world is concerned. For if a state is subject, constitutionally, to another state, that superordinate state must speak for its dependent territory in international matters. If, however, a state is constitutionally independent this has the consequence that, in the absence of specific arrangements providing otherwise, the state will have to fend for itself externally. No one else is responsible for its affairs and so, just as it has the last word internally, so also it has to provide for the protection and advancement of its interests in relation to other states. Usually there are no procedural obstacles to this activity, for as the world is presently arranged constitutional independence – or sovereignty – is all that is needed to make a state eligible for full participation in international life. And in the normal way such a state can march straight onto the international stage.

A helpful way of envisaging sovereignty is as a kind of shell encasing an appropriately qualified state, but not of the sort which helps to provide a barrier to physical penetration. The existence of such a physical barrier has sometimes been represented as the essence of sovereign statehood.[1] But this is an erroneous conception. For what sovereignty connotes is not a physical but a constitutional shell. It expresses the lack of any links which place the state concerned in a subordinate constitutional position in relation to another state. Using a different metaphor, sovereignty may be seen as a moat, cutting the state off from constitutional subordination to other states and thus expressing the fact of its own constitutional independence.[2] The moat may be bridged from time to time for specific purposes, perhaps making it convenient to leave the drawbridge down almost permanently. But the continued existence of the moat means that the state is not subject in respect of certain constitutional (and hence important) matters to a superordinate state.

Legal

Used in this sense of constitutional independence, sovereignty has three main features: it is a legal, absolute, and unitary condition. The first of these, its legal aspect, is not meant to imply that to be sovereign is lawful whereas a different condition might be unlawful. Instead it means that sovereignty is founded on law in as much as a constitution is a set of arrangements which has the force of law. In consequence, the observation that a state is independent in constitutional terms is an observation about the standing of the state in the eyes of its own constitutional law. It expresses the point that the state's constitution is not subordinate, in law, to that of any other state – and as constitutions are legal arrangements the only kind of constitutional subordination or superordination which one can speak of is the sort which is legal. Just as a sexual relationship can only be one with a physical content, so a constitutional relationship has necessarily to do with the law. This is not to say that the partners concerned, whether individuals in the one case or states in the other, may not also have links of a different kind. But when, as in the case of sovereignty, what is being discussed is a situation which is of a constitutional nature, it is by definition one with a legal content. The distinguishing characteristic of a sovereign state is that it possesses a set of legal arrangements relating to fundamental matters – its constitution – which exists in its own right.

Thus sovereignty is based on law and not physical substance. To achieve this condition a state does not have to meet criteria relating to such matters as the number of people it contains, the extent of its territory, the fire-power of its armed forces, the value of its natural resources, or the amount of its gross national product. What it has to do is to satisfy a specific requirement of a legal nature. It has to show that, in terms of constitutional law, it has no superior, that there is no other state to whose constitutional set-up the first state is subordinate. This is not to say that there are not other, and perhaps more popular, definitions of sovereignty which do place some if not all of their emphasis on size and strength. But the test of sovereignty which must be passed if a state is to play a full and regular part in international relations has nothing to do with these questions. What it has everything to do with is whether or not a state is, in terms of its own constitutional law, an independent entity. Sovereignty, meaning the condition which fits a state for international life, is a matter of law and not of stature. It expresses a legal and not a physical reality.

It is worth underlining the point that the kind of law which is germane to the question of whether a territorially based entity is sovereign is constitutional law. For it is quite widely assumed that, while sovereignty is a legal concept, the relevant law is that which is applicable to states in their dealings with each other: international law. This is mistaken. It is indeed the case that international law applies to sovereign states and regulates their mutual relations. But it is not a provision of international law which has to be satisfied for a state to be ascribed sovereign status, but one which concerns a state's situation in the light of its constitutional law. International law may and does give rise to what are called sovereign rights, but these are the rights given to sovereign states, that is, states which are already sovereign. Thus the position of international law in relation to sovereignty is that it presupposes it. International law makes sense only on the assumption that there are sovereign states to which it can be applied. And those sovereign states are sovereign because they are all independent in terms of their own systems of constitutional law.

A different sort of point which also needs emphasis is that while sovereignty is based on law, and law alone, that does not mean it is unconnected with questions of physical strength and resources. In the first place, the state itself is the legal expression of a physical reality: it represents a certain territorial area of the globe and the people who live within it. Second, the acceptance of a state's legal claim to constitutional independence has consequences so far as physical matters are concerned. It means that other states are not entitled to exercise jurisdiction within the first state (unless they have received permission to do so) nor to speak for it in international relations. A sovereign state's influence and resources can be committed in some international matter only by its own decision. And, third, the acceptance of or continued acquiescence in a claim to constitutional independence may be very directly related to questions of comparative strength. It is not enough for some territorial entity, non-sovereign yesterday, to announce today that it has cut its constitutional links with its superior state and must henceforth itself be treated as a sovereign state. In the absence of agreement with its superior it will have to fight for constitutional independence. Likewise, if one sovereign state is coveted by another, and that other is willing to put the matter to a physical test, it is upon relative physical strength that the outcome will depend. It may be that other sovereign states will come to the aid of the threatened state, partly, perhaps, out of concern for the principle that established sovereignties should be respected. Feelings of solidarity among those who are similarly placed is not confined to trade unions. But this is by no means a response which can be relied upon. Ultimately, therefore, a sovereign state's existence or continued existence will depend upon its ability to keep its enemies physically at bay. The ultimate point is rarely reached but, if it is, the legal claim to sovereignty will be as nothing in the absence of an ability to defend it by force of arms.

There is, therefore, a real sense in which sovereignty requires the consonance of legal and physical realities. It is a legal condition, but its expression in the actual business of government is not only a physical activity but also requires at least the acquiescence of other sovereign states, some of them very muscular. A territorial entity claiming sovereignty must therefore be able to demonstrate that its constitutional independence is meaningful in both legal and physical terms if its claim is to be generally accepted. It must show that it is territorially defined, contains people, and governs them, and also that there is no other state which claims formal authority over it and is providing effective physical backing for that claim.

The physical situation which is likely to provide successful support for a claim to sovereignty will vary with circumstances. A colony of, say, 50,000 people which is distant from the metropolitan country is unlikely, in today's political climate, to have much difficulty in setting itself up as a sovereign state, at least so far as its colonial master is concerned. Indeed, it may very possibly have sovereignty almost thrust upon it. In 1981, for example, the British Associated State of Antigua became sovereign, with a population of 75,000. Two years later, Britain's nearby Caribbean possession of St Kitts-Nevis followed suit, although its population is not much more than half that of Antigua. In 1984 this process reached what might be regarded as the ultimate point, when the Cocos (Keeling) Islands in the Indian Ocean were asked in a plebiscite (supervised by the UN) whether they wanted to become a sovereign state. The total population of the islands is about 600. In the event they declined this option, choosing instead to integrate with Australia. In view of this willingness to countenance tiny sovereign states it is not surprising that when the British colony of Belize became sovereign in 1981 *The Times*, in a leading article, said that it should have happened 'a long time ago'.[3] The territory of which it was speaking, as described elsewhere in the same newspaper, was 'an under-developed, ramshackle chunk of the Central American isthmus with one hundred and fifty thousand people in an area just bigger than Wales and with nothing to maintain it except a little tourism and agriculture and possibly exploitable oil'.[4] Certainly, therefore, there could be no objection to the British Protected State of Brunei becoming sovereign at the start of 1984, for it has all of 200,000 people in its small corner of the island of Borneo. Additionally, however, it has considerable oil and gas resources which make it, per capita, one of the richest countries in Asia. It soon became the 159th member state of the United Nations.

By contrast, a municipality of about 50,000 people set within the metropolitan area of a sovereign state is likely to meet insuperable obstacles if it tries to make a unilateral declaration of independence. No matter how impassioned its assertion that it has cut its constitutional links with the rest of the country or how attractive the home-grown constitution it produces for all to see, it is unlikely to make progress. It is exceedingly improbable that it will be taken seriously abroad and will surely receive short shrift at home from the government of the state from which it wishes to break away. Even if its population is half a million strong, and even, too, if the municipality has a coastal location (which should in theory be a help), its chances of success are still virtually nil, provided always that the population of the state with which it is dissatisfied is appreciably bigger than its own. When, therefore, a small community declares its independence of its constitutional superior – as did the Swiss hamlet of Vallerat in 1982 – its intention is surely focused on publicity for some local grievance rather than on a serious aspiration to international statehood. In this particular case it was the desire of the sixty or so French-speaking inhabitants to be transferred from a German-speaking Swiss canton to one where the predominant language was their own. All this, of course, presupposes that what is at issue is a new claim to constitutional independence. It has no necessary bearing on the maintenance of a physically similar situation which has been sanctified by the passage of time. History may well and often does provide a sufficient justification for the continuation of a state of affairs which would have hardly any chance of emerging in the contemporary world. Of this the best example is probably the continued existence of tiny, land-locked San Marino (with a population of about 18,000) in the Italian peninsula.

What this amounts to saying is that the legal condition of constitutional independence is most unlikely to be achieved (as distinct from maintained) in the absence of an appropriate physical base, what is appropriate being dependent on the physical and political circumstances of the case. There is no theoretical reason why a sovereign state should not consist of an area best measured in acres rather than in square kilometres or square miles, and contain no more than a few dozen people. For the requirements of territory and people (some of whom constitute a government) have no lower limit, not even the most minimal. The existence of the Vatican City is a case in point, a sovereign state of about a hundred acres and a thousand souls, in which, as provided by the 1929 treaty with Italy, there is 'no authority other than that of the Holy See'.[5] But as a practical matter sovereign states are unlikely often to appear in such a minute form, the Vatican City being a very special case. Pint-sized sovereign states are not unfamiliar; but droplet ones, hardly. It bears repeating, though, that this is on account of problems which would arise in the sphere of practicalities and not of principle.

This draws attention to another way in which sovereignty, while not dependent on physical conditions, is closely related to them. It concerns a state's ability to make effective use of its sovereignty. The achievement of this status requires no particular level of area, population, and so on. Nor is it the case that there is always a positive and precise correlation between the influence which a state is able to wield in international relations and the extent of its tangible assets. Small and relatively weak states may be able to make a noticeable impact on their fellows on account of such factors as the skill of their diplomats and leaders, the strategic significance of their geographical situation, and the nature of the overall political context in which they are operating. Correspondingly, larger states may not always have the degree of international success that one might expect from their size. But generally speaking it is the case that if a state wishes to make something of a splash in the world it is more likely to achieve its goal if it is relatively well equipped with the kind of resources which usually count – those of a military and economic kind. Such resources do not bear in any direct way on its being as a sovereign state, but they will usually have a fairly close relation to the effectiveness of its foreign policies.

It remains, however, that sovereignty is a legal condition. Nothing which has been said about its links with physical matters has been intended to qualify that remark. A problem does arise, requiring the application of a further test, when the legal situation regarding constitutional independence is unclear.[6] But that is most unusual, for generally there is no ambiguity about the constitutional position and, therefore, about whether a territorially based entity is sovereign. However, this emphasis on sovereignty being founded on law could lead to the rejoinder that if it is 'only' a matter of law it cannot be of much consequence. The implication is that questions of legal standing relate to a theoretical realm of niceties which are the concern of lawyers and logicians but which hardly deserve the attention of the practical man of affairs or of students who wish to know what is going on in the 'real' world. Blood and iron, sweat and tears: these, it is implied, are the stuff of international relations, and not abstruse questions such as whether a state's legal nature entitles it to be called sovereign.

This line of argument is indicative of a failure to understand the very great significance – in and for the 'real' world – of the legal standing of a person or body. One of the uses of law is to designate in a way which is clear and authoritative for the group concerned who is entitled to do what – and therefore, by implication, who lacks this entitlement. Such a legal determination may not, in practical terms, be conclusive; clubs, rather than law, may prove to be trumps. But commonly it is. If a group's legal procedures authorize a particular person to assume the office of member of parliament, judge, vice-chancellor, or whatever, the consequences of such authorization are generally accepted. On most sides it is taken for granted that by virtue of his new legal standing the person concerned will now be empowered to do many things – often of considerable import – which would not otherwise be open to him. And others, lacking such authority, will not usually try to behave as if they possessed it. Likewise, a municipality or county will, on account of its legal capacity, be entitled to take many decisions, and all of them will flow from the fact that the body concerned – a notional being – has by law been given decision-making capacity. Larger territorially based entities, probably called states, are in a similar situation. And if the legal standing of a state is that of constitutional independence this will have far-reaching implications for what it is lawfully able to do, and what others are not entitled to do on its territory or in respect of its affairs.

It must be said, however, that there is no necessary reason why sovereignty should be based on law. The crucial thing about sovereignty, from an international point of view, is that it makes a state eligible for full participation in inter-state relations. It is the test which has to be passed, the criterion which has to be met if a state is to have any hope of a regular place in international company. There could be no theoretical objection to this purpose being served by a non-legal test, or by a dual test, only part of which was legal in character. It could be, for example, the practice to treat as eligible for admission to the international fraternity only those territorial entities with a population or per capita gross national product of a certain minimum level. As a matter of practice, it is very difficult indeed to envisage the emergence of any such tests on their own, not least because they would encompass territorial entities which are presently part of a larger governmental arrangement. It is very probable that Texas, for example, or Tokyo, would be able to satisfy any such tests. Thus it is highly likely that a legal criterion would be associated with one of a physical nature, so that, continuing the example, regular international activity would only be open to territorially based entities which had, say, a population of at least 5 million and were also constitutionally independent. States which met the legal but not the physical part of the criterion would then have to come to some arrangement with one or more internationally active states regarding the representation of their views to other states and the safeguarding of their external interests. This could be very unsatisfactory in a variety of ways, but it would be a necessary consequence of a physical component to the idea of sovereignty.

However, it happens to be the case that the contemporary criterion for sovereignty is legal, and legal only. Given the formalistic and egalitarian atmosphere of the second half of the twentieth century, this is not surprising. But the point just discussed might also suggest that it would not be surprising if the criterion for admission to inter-state life was found to have something to do with law in any historical period where states co-exist in the absence of government, and thus where there is a question as to how relations between states are to be organized. The advantages of a legal criterion are many, and the practice of states makes it evident that, nowadays at least, the criterion is solely legal.

Absolute

The second main feature of sovereignty is that it is an absolute condition. Nowadays this is often denied, the point being made that even if it was once sensible to think of sovereignty in this way it is no longer so. 'Absolute sovereignty of states is now a myth'[7] is typical of remarks addressed to this question. One writer has gone further, asserting, at the outset of a book which includes the term 'sovereignty' in its title, that the idea of absoluteness can never have been relevant in this context, or indeed in hardly any other. He says, 'the absolute modifier *absolute* applied to sovereignty can well be disposed of at once. Whatever its relevance in the realm of pure ideas, the term usually serves only to clutter up discussion of actual human affairs.' He goes on to say: 'I wonder whether the idea of *absolute*, otherwise than in connection with absolute zero, has utility. I can scarcely imagine any faculty or endeavour wholly untramelled, infinite, or wholly beyond contingency.'[8]

Clearly, therefore, to assert that absoluteness is an essential aspect of sovereignty is to invite trouble or, perhaps worse, passive disbelief. Nor can criticism be averted on the ground that what is being assumed here is something which exists only in the realm of pure ideas – an area which is often thought to be largely if not entirely remote from the day-to-day concerns of men. It may be doubted whether 'pure ideas' are as irrelevant to affairs as is widely supposed (unless, of course, a pure idea is defined as one which has no bearing on life). But in any event the purpose of this study is to examine the meaning and implications of the term 'sovereignty' as states apply it to themselves in their capacity as regular international actors. The concept which it focuses on is therefore one which is ultimately – and fundamentally – concerned with the actual organization of human affairs. It studies an idea, but certainly not one which is pure in the sense of being remote and ineffectual.

How, then, can the implied charge of unrealism in referring to sovereignty as an absolute condition be rebutted? The answer is really very simple. Just as the term 'sovereignty' may and does have more than one accepted meaning, so also is it the case that 'absolute' is used in different ways. It may mean absolute in relation to others, referring to the sort of relationship which is entirely one-sided in the sense that it is totally controlled by one party. There is no necessity about such a situation; it just happens to exist at a particular time. Thus one might refer to one person's absolute control of another. Extending the idea, one might speak of absolute authority, meaning that the governing person or body is subject to no restraints or interference and is therefore unrestricted in its choice of policy. This relationship may have grown out of or lead into one where the authority of those in charge was less than absolute, where they did not enjoy a right or ability to rule in an unlimited manner. But for the time being the position is such that it can appropriately be described as absolute. This was the sense in which the word was used by Lord Acton in his famous dictum that 'power tends to corrupt, and absolute power corrupts absolutely'.

This is, perhaps, the word's more widely used meaning, and on this basis it is easy to see why its association with sovereignty attracts derision. Even in its internal affairs a sovereign state nowadays does well to take some account of the international repercussions of certain sorts of policy. Whatever the legal position (and it is disputed) it has become a fact of international life that in the general area of human rights a state just cannot go its own way and expect other states to take the line that such matters are ones on which they must not say anything. Even if its own population is undisturbed, its fellow sovereign states cannot be relied upon to exhibit this quality. And in the sphere of external relations it makes no sense at all to speak of sovereignty as an absolute condition, in the sense of absolute power. By definition, if only one state is absolute, all the others with whom it comes into contact are not. Such a situation, to all intents and purposes if not formally, would amount to world government, which is incompatible with the existence of a collectivity of sovereign states. It might also be added that in practical terms no one state in the world is in anything like a condition of absolute power. Even the two super-powers, with all their nuclear weapons and their research into the possibility of much more destructive devices relying on lasers and particle beams, are very far from this situation. For, quite apart from the fact that they do not and are unlikely to enjoy absolute sway over each other, they are also by no means in this sort of relationship with lesser states, not even those within their geographical, strategic, or ideological spheres of interest. The United States has its problems in Latin America and in relation to its West European allies. And the Soviet Union's grip on East Europe, while a good deal firmer than anything which the United States exerts, is a long way from complete. Even in relation to the states which have not broken away – those other than Yugoslavia and Albania – she can by no means always be sure of getting her way.

There is, however, a second accepted meaning to the word 'absolute' which is not at all esoteric and which can properly and very helpfully be applied to sovereignty. It refers not to the way in which a person or body relates to others but to whether a person or thing possesses a specified attribute or condition. The attribute in question is either present or absent, and if it is present it may be said to represent an absolute condition. Such terminology is appropriate in respect of the formal standing or status which a person, real or notional, has attained. When someone is appointed as a university vice-chancellor, he holds the office absolutely. There is no question of less or more about it, or being a 70 per cent vice-chancellor, and so on. The person concerned is a vice-chancellor and the man next door is not. It may well be that comments of a critical kind will be made from time to time about the effectiveness of the incumbent. It may even be put about that the effort or skill put into the job may deserve a grade of 70 per cent, or less. But this in no way detracts from the fact that the appointee is fully a vice-chancellor. He may, too, spend time on other tasks but this does not affect his standing in his university office. And he will be no less of a vice-chancellor than others holding a similar position whatever the size or reputation of his university in relation to theirs.

The same line of argument is exactly applicable to sovereignty. Whether or not a territorially based entity is constitutionally independent is a matter of fact which in principle can only be answered negatively or positively. Problem cases may sometimes arise, but even they can usually be placed without too much difficulty on one clear side of the line or the other.[9] For there can be no two ways about whether an entity exists in a condition of constitutional independence. It may approach it very closely, as in the case of a colony where virtually all internal matters are left to the local government, but if it does not actually reach it it has to be adjudged as having fallen short. When, during the First World War, General Smuts coined the phrase 'the British Commonwealth of Nations', he applied it to 'the so-called dominions, a number of nations and states, almost sovereign, almost independent, who govern themselves'.[10] But, although they may have been almost sovereign, they had not reached that condition. From the perspective of establishing which states were sovereign, they fell on the wrong side of the line – absolutely. Contrariwise, a constitutionally independent state is so irrespective of its economic or military weakness. It falls on the right side of the line – and absolutely so. For sovereignty, as the term is used by states to refer to that which makes them – and not others – eligible to participate fully at the international level, is an absolute quality. A state is either constitutionally independent or it is not. In this matter, there can, in principle, be no half-way house, no question of relative sovereignty.

This is not to say that in the light of some other definition of sovereignty it cannot be a relative matter. If, for example, it is defined in terms of power, it would in theory be possible to say that this state was 82 per cent sovereign, another 57 per cent, and so on. Equally, if sovereignty is used to refer to the extent to which a state is legally free to do what it likes, this too could be expressed in percentage terms, a state's legal limitations and obligations reducing its sovereignty below the figure of 100 which would represent total freedom, in law.

The mind boggles at the difficulties which would be involved in any such calculations, and in practice they are not made by those who think of sovereignty in relative terms. Instead, refuge is taken in statements to the effect that as a result of something or other a state has become 'more sovereign' or 'less' as the case might be.[11] More generally, it is asserted that 'sovereignty in practical international affairs is a relative principle'.[12] Such a terminology seems to come to students and commentators with almost infinitely greater ease than one which draws attention to the fact that, from a different perspective, the participants in international relations may be seen as absolutely sovereign. But the fact of the matter is that from such a different perspective, that used by states when speaking of their international capacity, it is necessary, in the interests of accuracy and understanding, to speak of sovereignty as an absolute condition.

The reluctance to use this terminology appears to arise from one of two factors. It seems, in the first place, very difficult for many people to get away from the idea that the phrase 'absolute sovereignty' only refers to a relational context, where its use would indeed be inappropriate in that it implies that the sovereign state concerned is able to manipulate its international relationships entirely in accordance with its own will. This can only be dealt with by getting used to a terminology which has a different reference. The other source of difficulty seems to arise from an either/or fallacy. It appears sometimes to be assumed that if it is allowed that sovereignty is absolute in the sense in which the word has been used here, to refer to a quality inherent in the idea of sovereignty, then there is a degree of awkwardness or even logical impropriety about going on to elaborate the obviously non-absolute nature of such a state's relations with other sovereign states. However, there is no real problem here. To speak of an aspect of a state's nature which is quite independent of its relations with others is wholly compatible with observations about the variety of contacts which a state will have with its fellows – generally deferential towards one, influential in relation to a dozen others on a certain issue, and so on. The state is both absolutely sovereign, in that no qualifications can attach to its constitutional independence, and open to the normal pressures and opportunities of international life. Some states may be thought to be generally important and others generally insignificant, but this is no bar to saying that they all enjoy the same constitutional standing. Just as men may differ in strength, wealth and influence but are all equally and absolutely men, so sovereign states, big, little, and all, are equally and absolutely sovereign.

Unitary

The third, and last, main feature of sovereignty, meaning constitutional independence, is that it is a unitary condition. It may, and does, have different implications in different contexts, so that, specifically, one can speak of the internal and external aspects of sovereignty. But, as the term is used to refer to that which makes a territorially based entity eligible to participate fully and regularly in international relations, its reference is to a condition which cannot be split down the middle, as it were, into two entirely separate compartments. Rather it partakes of the nature of a coin, the sides of which may be different and face in opposite directions but each of which, in the normal way, is found in conjunction with the other and has significance only when so found. One side of a coin is not accepted as legal tender for half the value of the whole, for a coin is not just the sum of its sides but an entity which happens to be dual-faced. It is, indeed, only when it exists as a single whole that it can be spoken of and used as a coin. Likewise with sovereignty. A sovereign state, in the sense in which the phrase is being used here, has two aspects, each of them reflecting, in differing ways, central elements of a unitary sovereign statehood.

This point needs underlining both because of its intrinsic importance and because it is often misunderstood. The reason for this may be that so much emphasis is placed on the different implications of sovereignty that it becomes hard to see or recall that what is being discussed is a single condition. Or the discussion of what is called internal or external sovereignty may proceed in terms which, unlike those used here, suggest fairly clearly that the area in question is autonomous. It then only requires the reader or hearer to assume, falsely, that the phrase 'internal sovereignty or external sovereignty' can have only one meaning for him to deduce that sovereignty cannot be a unitary condition.

It has been suggested, for example, that whereas the internal aspect of sovereignty means final law-making power 'external sovereignty connotes the legal equality of one state with another'.[13] If this is so, the external and internal sovereignty to which reference is made must flow not from a unitary but from separate sources. For that which gives rise to final law-making power within the state does not necessarily give rise externally to legal equality. The two situations are, it is true, entirely compatible. Nor is there any reason why both of them should not be referred to as instances or reflections of sovereignty. But this would be to use the term in two different ways, for there is nothing in the one situation which automatically involves the other. It is quite possible to imagine various types of legal inequality at the international level between entities which are all endowed with final law-making power within their own boundaries. A formal hierarchical arrangement might, as a matter of practice, be very hard to organize, but as a theoretical construct it is entirely conceivable. As it happens sovereign states do proclaim that formal equality is a principle of international life. It is not, however, inherent in the fact that such states are all constitutionally independent. Ultimate law-making power, on the other hand, is an intrinsic aspect of the sovereign condition.

Another source of doubt regarding the unitary nature of sovereignty arises from the way in which the phrase 'internal sovereignty' is often used in connection with an attempt to identify who, internally, is exercising the powers of a sovereign state or, as it is sometimes put, who is sovereign. At one time the answer might simply have been 'the sovereign', and it might still be a sufficient answer in respect of some states, except that the word 'president' would have to be substituted for 'sovereign'. To go to the other extreme, there are probably few if any states which would now deny the theoretical validity of the then revolutionary claim of the Declaration of the Rights of Man (1789) that 'sovereignty resides in the people'. Contemporary othodoxy in constitutional matters is nothing if not democratic. But in practice the situation in most states is more complicated than either of these responses suggests. At different times and in respect of different issues sovereign power generally appears to be exercised by different groups of people, from the periodical expression of an electorate's view down through the broad institutions of government – the legislature, executive, and judiciary – down further through groups within and outside these bodies to small handfuls of people, whether elected or appointed. All of which implies, resoundingly, that internal sovereignty is very far from unitary, with the further implication that sovereignty seen overall is of a like nature.

However, this is to use the term 'sovereignty' in a way which is different from that which this work focuses upon – the one used by states when referring to what it is about themselves that fits them for international life. The exercise of particular powers in the name of a sovereign state is not to be confused with the existence of the state as the kind of territorial entity which is called sovereign. In the one case there are many powers and many exercising them. In the other there is a single state in a condition which is unitary in the sense that it cannot be divided into entirely separate compartments. The state's sovereign powers are a reflection of its sovereignty or constitutional standing. The operation of the levers which control those powers reflects the state's political and social arrangements. The distinction, in short, is between the existence of a unit and its power structure.

A sovereign state, therefore, is all of a piece. External sovereignty, meaning the standing externally of a constitutionally independent entity, is not something which can be divorced from its internal standing, any more than the latter can be divorced from the former. Both are manifestations, in different areas, of the state's constitutional condition, of its sovereignty. For what this amounts to is that, in the formal terms of its constitutional law, a state is master in its own house. This does not mean that it has a completely free internal hand. Quite apart from the limits which its own constitution imposes, other states or international organizations may have been accorded certain rights within the territory of the first state.[14] But they are rights within someone else's establishment, and they flow, almost invariably, from the specific permission of the state concerned. In the absence of such permission no other state or body is entitled to make claims or demands in respect of what goes on within the state in question, let alone take action on its territory. This is not to say that requests and suggestions of a telling kind are never made, or that physical activity by the agents of one state on the soil of another never takes place without the agreement of the 'host' state. But in terms of what is legitimate between states it is wholly clear that without leave no state is entitled to act on the territory of another as if it were its own. And, while this basic rule is sometimes broken, a truly remarkable thing about the relations of states, especially in the light of their huge physical and technological disparities, is the extent to which it is observed. The internal aspect of sovereignty is, for most states most of the time, a reality, their constitutional shell generally being an effective means of keeping outsiders outside. Of course, a state knows that it has to live with its fellows and therefore does well to accommodate their wishes if this can be done without undue inconvenience or cost. But it also knows that, except in the most extreme of circumstances, other states are not going to behave as if its frontiers did not exist. Quite apart from the physical difficulty of doing so, that would in all probability be an exceedingly unpopular move in the world at large. Thus sovereignty has real meaning for a state's internal freedom of action, which is doubtless one reason why in recent times it has been so avidly sought by those who wish to have their affairs in their own hands.

All this is the internal reflection of constitutional independence. It is because a state is constitutionally separate from others that, without its authority, others are not entitled to act in or in respect of its territory as if they owned it. In the absence of constitutional independence there would be some internal matters on which the local government could be overruled, and some on which it would have to accept the decisions of the superior government. But once such constitutional ties are broken, and the local government becomes sovereign, it can then do its own thing without having to take formal notice of anyone else – except, as always, in respect of matters on which it has made promises to other states or given them permission to do certain specific things.

Constitutional independence also entitles a state to take its own decisions externally. Here, too, there may be some areas and issues on which it has agreed to be bound by the decisions of others. More generally, too, there is the consideration that there are certain legal limitations on a state's behaviour flowing from its obligations under international law. No more than internally is a state's legal hand completely free. Political considerations, too, will be sure to impose substantial restraints. There may well be some international matters on which a state knows that the course of wisdom is to hearken carefully to the views of others, or there might be one particular state whose opinions on all issues will, for strategic or economic reasons, be accorded great respect. But the general position regarding external relations is quite clear: that a sovereign state can only be bound on any matter through the giving of its own consent and that its view or decision on any issue can be officially ascertained from it and it alone. Except where it has specifically agreed to the contrary, it speaks with its own voice, and this means that it can offer an opinion or take a decision over a very wide range of international matters. Of course, the extent to which it is listened to, or the import of its decisions, will vary widely from state to state and issue to issue. But that is quite distinct from the point which is being made, which is that in its external relations a sovereign state has the last word. And, moreover, it is only very rarely that it is in the control of a ventriloquist or a puppeteer. Here, as internally, sovereignty usually makes a real difference to a state's position, and there are many who have taken advantage of it over the last generation or so.

The external standing of a sovereign state is, like its internal situation, a clear and straightforward reflection of the fact that it is constitutionally independent. It is because of its constitutional position that it – and not another, superordinate, state – speaks for itself in international relations. Indeed, were it not for its sovereignty it is most unlikely that it would engage in any external activity at all, and it would certainly not do so on a full and regular basis. For it is an almost universal rule that each territorially demarcated area into which the land surface of the globe is divided speaks internationally with just one voice. And that voice, certainly on all significant matters, is almost invariably that of the government which acts for the state as a whole. Thus a subordinate constitutional entity has no international say. But, once it is constitutionally independent, it speaks for itself, for now there is no one else who is permitted to do so on its behalf.

The responsibility of a constitutionally independent entity for its own external relations would exist quite apart from the fact that, as the world is presently organized, such an entity is eligible for full participation in international life. It could be, as has already been noted, that such participation was dependent not only on sovereignty but also on some other requirement, such as a particular form of government – a monarchy, say, or a republic. In which case those constitutionally independent states which did not meet the extra criterion would have to make private arrangements for the protection of their external interests. But it would be their own arrangements which they would be making. No one else would be making them for them (unless any specific agreements to that effect had been made), for constitutional independence means that the state concerned speaks for itself. It also happens to mean that in the normal way a sovereign state can itself look after its external affairs on a day to day basis but this is a consequence of international practice and not of its sovereignty. What sovereignty does is to place ultimate responsibility for external policy, however conducted, into the hands of the state concerned.

The control of both internal and external policy, therefore, flows from the same source: constitutional independence, or sovereignty. By virtue of this condition a state can decide what to do in respect of matters which take place within its own frontiers just as it can decide what line to take regarding events which occur beyond them. No other state is entitled to overrule it or speak for it in respect of either kind of issue (short of specific agreements to that effect) for the state is constitutionally independent. Formally speaking it is in control of its own destiny, both internally and in relation to other states. The absence of a constitutional link with another governed entity means that it is entitled to be left alone both to arrange its internal affairs and to make its moves on the international chess-board. The presence of such links would mean that the superordinate state would be entitled to take certain action in respect of the state's internal affairs and to take all decisions regarding its international posture. Thus the internal and external aspects of sovereignty are inextricably bound up with each other. The one goes along with the other, and the absence of one means that the other is absent too. Their intimate interdependence reflects the unitary nature of the sovereign condition.

A few examples will illustrate the significance of constitutional independence for the conduct of internal and external policy. In June

1978 considerable prominence was given in the British press to the fact that two British subjects had been publicly flogged in Saudi Arabia for selling alcohol. However, no protest was made. Saudi Arabia had not accepted any limitations on her freedom of action in the matter of corporal punishment and thus, as a sovereign state, was entitled to inflict it. Foreigners who placed themselves within her jurisdiction had to take the risk that if they broke the local law they would be treated in accordance with it. Correspondingly, the state to which any such foreigners belonged had no ground for an official complaint, for that would imply either that Saudi Arabia had behaved improperly under international law (which was not so) or that she was under the complainant's tutelage, and hence not sovereign. At one time the punishment of foreigners in a manner deemed to be unduly severe might have elicited a response on the ground that it offended the minimum standards of civilization, but such an approach is now out of fashion. In the future it might be that corporal punishment will be regarded as a breach of human rights of the sort which justifies international attention. But in 1978 the British Foreign Secretary felt obliged to say of this matter that 'It is the right of any sovereign country to determine its own law'.[15]

By contrast, the United Kingdom has, by the 1949 European Convention on Human Rights, bound herself not to impose 'degrading punishment', and in April 1978 the European Court of Human Rights declared that the judicial birching of juvenile offenders on the Isle of Man (for which Britain is internationally responsible and to which the European Convention was extended by Britain) is such a punishment. Accordingly, the Isle of Man has a duty to cease using the birch and Britain has a duty to her co-signatories to the European Convention to ensure that the Isle of Man does so. This, therefore, is a case where a sovereign state has accepted certain limitations upon its internal freedom of action, just as the other signatories to the Convention have accepted similar limitations upon theirs. But by placing a restriction upon her legal freedom as a sovereign state Britain has in no sense diminished her sovereignty – meaning her constitutional independence – which, in any event, as an absolute condition, cannot be reduced other than totally. It might be added that there was no thought in 1949 that the Convention would be interpreted to ban judicial corporal punishment, but that is another story.

A case where one sovereign state tried to treat the territory of another as if it was its own came to the notice of the House of Lords (sitting in its judicial capacity) in December 1977. It concerned certain efforts of the United States to obtain information about a uranium cartel which was possibly in criminal violation of that country's anti-trust laws. In pursuit of this goal the American Attorney-General tried to force some British subjects, on British soil, to testify regarding their knowledge of the cartel's activities. The British Attorney-General said of this that it was 'an infringement of the proper jurisdiction and sovereignty of the United Kingdom' and he was supported by their lordships, one of whom declared that the American action constituted 'an invasion of the sovereignty of the United Kingdom'.[16] In Texas or Utah such action would have been perfectly in order, for here the United States would have been acting within her domain and in accordance with her constitution. But she was no more entitled to take such action in Britain than Britain is in respect of the United States.

Exceptionally, it might be that a state will not make too much of a fuss about another state taking improper action on its soil. When, for example, Adolf Eichmann was seized in Argentina in May 1960 by what were widely presumed to be agents of Israel and removed to that country for trial on charges relating to his activities during the Second World War, Argentina protested. She was supported in this by the Security Council of the United Nations, which called on Israel to make appropriate reparation. However, on no side was there the degree of indignation which might have attended the abduction of a person of lesser notoriety. Israel had claimed that it was the work of private persons but none the less she made a public apology to Argentina and this was accepted as full reparation. It was, however, a very unusual case.

A final instance which attests to the significance of both the internal and the external aspects of constitutional independence can be drawn from the closing stages of the Cuban missile crisis of October 1962. It was agreed by the United States and the Soviet Union that the Soviet missiles which had been emplaced in Cuba should be removed under United Nations supervision. This, however, was to reckon without Cuba, and when the United Nations Secretary-General, U Thant, quickly flew to Havana with a substantial team to make the necessary arrangements he received a frosty reception. It had been recognized all along that Cuba's permission would be necessary for any supervisory scheme, but in a rather casual way. Cuba now made it very clear, as she was fully entitled to do, that the Soviet Union did not speak for her in international relations, despite the close association which had developed between the two countries. Cuba was a sovereign state and was well able to voice her own views on external matters. Furthermore, she refused to have anything to do with the proposed scheme of United Nations inspection, again, as was her right. Being sovereign, only she could agree to United Nations activity on her soil, and in the absence of such agreement neither the United Nations nor any other foreign representatives had the right to be there. She also refused to allow one or two of U Thant's aides to remain behind to constitute a direct link between Cuba and the United Nations, and for good measure refused an alternative scheme for the verification of the removal of the missiles by the International Committee of the Red Cross. U Thant made what was hardly a glorious return, to be met at the airport by what seemed to him to be 'almost the entire press corps in New York'.[17] Meanwhile the two superpowers had to arrange an alternative inspection scheme which involved American aerial surveillance of the ships on which the missiles were removed.

The internal and external aspects of sovereignty are thus bound up with each other. Just as a vice-chancellor or head teacher will have certain powers within the institution of which he is the administrative head and will also, by virtue of the same office, represent his university or school in its relations with other such bodies and with local institutions, so also a sovereign state will have an internal and external role. Both are a consequence of its condition as a constitutionally independent, or sovereign, entity. The application of this concept to cases of a straightforward kind will be considered in the next chapter.

Notes: Chapter 3

1 See J. Herz, *International Politics in the Atomic Age* (New York: Columbia University Press, 1959), *passim*.
2 c.f. Edward Wall, *Europe: Unification and Law* (Harmondsworth: Penguin, 1969), p. 42.
3 *The Times*, 21 September 1981.
4 ibid.
5 *The Times*, 12 January 1929, repr. 12 February 1985.
6 See below, Chapter 6, pp. 153–61.
7 S. K. Mukherjee, *A New Outlook for International Law* (Calcutta: World Press, 1964), p. XI.
8 Charles Burton Marshall, *The Exercise of Sovereignty* (Baltimore, Md: Johns Hopkins University Press, 1965), p. 4.
9 See below, Chapter 5, *passim*.
10 See A. Walker, *The Commonwealth: A New Look* (Oxford: Pergamon, 1978), p. 7.
11 See, for example, Shlomo Slonim, 'American-Egyptian rapprochement', *The World Today*, vol. 31, no. 2 (February 1975), p. 55.
12 Leader in *The Times*, 30 November 1984.
13 F. S. Northedge and M. J. Grieve, *A Hundred Years of International Relations* (London: Duckworth, 1971), p. 343.
14 See further below, Chapter 9, pp. 228–40 and 245–53.
15 *The Times*, 12 June 1978.
16 *The Times*, 2 December 1977.
17 U Thant, *View from the U.N.* (Newton Abbot: David & Charles, 1978), p. 189.

4

Application

Whether or not a state is sovereign in the sense discussed in the preceding chapters is a question which does not usually present any difficulty – provided always that one remembers what is being sought and refuses to be distracted by some other definition of sovereignty. It is simply a matter of examining the constitution of the state concerned to find out whether it is independent or subordinate. If this procedure does not provide a clear-cut answer, one can generally be found by looking at the constitution of the state to which it is thought the first state might be subject. There will be some circumstances in which further inquiries will have to be made, but most cases are quite straightforward. Indeed, in the normal way a satisfactory answer can be obtained without even seeing a state's constitution, as its constitutional practices together with the attitude of other states towards it will make the matter entirely plain.

The phrase 'constitutional practices' must not mislead. It refers strictly to those of a state's activities which are immediately related to its constitutional situation. The making of laws, their interpretation and implementation, the assertion of governmental authority – all these stem directly from the provisions of a constitution. Accordingly, if one state as a matter of course and over a wide range of subjects makes laws which are automatically applicable in another state, that would be a clear indicator of the subordination, in constitutional terms, of the second state, and hence of its lack of sovereignty. The same conclusion could be provisionally drawn if the second state has few or no dealings with those who are regularly on international parade, and that conclusion could be regarded as more or less[1] firm if its territory is spoken for at the international level by the first state. So far as the sovereignty of the first state is concerned, its law-making activity in respect of the second state would be indicative not just of its constitutional superiority but also, in all probability, of its constitutional independence. International responsibility for the external relations of the second state would offer conclusive evidence to this effect. Taken overall, this information points to the one state being sovereign and the other not – this being a reflection of the constitutional assumptions and practices of each and not of anything else. Whether the sovereign state habitually defers, as a matter of political wisdom, to another sovereign state or even takes its line from those in control of the formally subordinate territory is neither here nor there so far as its standing as a sovereign state is concerned, although it could be very germane to some other matters. What counts in relation to sovereignty is whether or not a state, in consequence of legal obligations flowing from an overriding constitution, defers to the authority of another territorially based entity.

Where there is doubt on this issue, and in any event to be sure of an accurate judgement, reference must be made to the constitution itself. There is unlikely to be much ambiguity here. Any statements indicating that the laws of the state shall prevail to the extent to which they do not run counter to those of another, specified, state, or that certain categories of legislation are reserved for the consent of a particular external government, or that specified matters lie in the hands of a governor who is responsible to another state – all such provisions and others of their kind are a sure indication that the state concerned has a constitution which is not independent. Its constitution is subordinate to a wider system of government, and hence the state itself is not sovereign. On the other hand, the absence of any such statements is a very clear sign that the constitution is not connected with any other and, accordingly, that the state is sovereign.

Non-Sovereign Entities

In the vast majority of cases, therefore, no problem arises when the question is asked of a territorial entity, is it sovereign? Some are and others are not, and, sovereignty (as the concept is used in this work) being an absolute condition, there are no in-between positions. One class of territories which falls on the non-sovereign side of the dividing line is made up of colonies. Their constitutional arrangements can vary enormously, from almost complete control by the metropolitan power to almost complete internal autonomy. Southern Rhodesia, for example, obtained self-government in 1923 and until its unilateral declaration of independence in 1965 ran its internal affairs virtually unhindered. However, it was not constitutionally independent, for Britain had the right to veto certain very limited classes of legislation as well as being ultimately responsible for its external relations. Britain also had the right to grant independence at a time of her own choosing. In the Falkland Islands of the South Atlantic, on the other hand, administration was, prior to the crisis of 1982, in the hands of a British governor assisted by a legislative council of eight members, half of whom were elected, and an executive council of six, two of whom were chosen by the legislative council. Between these two extremes there are many gradations, and not too long ago the gap between them was a lot wider as in many colonies the governor exercised considerable powers. In 1945, for example, 'only nine out of fifty-two [British] dependent territories had legislatures with elected majorities'.[2] But the characteristic which all such dependent territories share is that their constitutions are not independent. All such documents indicate, and indicate very clearly, the existence of a constitutional superior, so that the territories are not sovereign.

Colonial possessions are, however, becoming largely extinct, for two reasons. The first is that the ethos of the age has turned against colonialism – the rule, however light, of a territory by a state which is removed from it by an expanse of salt water and often different from it in terms of racial composition. Nowhere has this been made clearer than at the United Nations, where since 1960 the practice has been vociferously denounced time and again by huge majorities in the General Assembly. In itself this might not be a sure pointer to contemporary orthodoxy, for the policies of the small minority of states with colonial possessions are also of considerable relevance in this connection. But as it happens the great colonial empires amassed by some Western European states have been speedily disintegrating over the last generation. Britain, France, Belgium, the Netherlands, Spain and (since the revolution of 1974) Portugal have all been in smart colonial retreat, giving birth in their wake to large numbers of new states. Never before has the political map of the world undergone so drastic a transformation in such a brief time. Thus the colony is a dying breed. There are a few recalcitrant British territories who show no enthusiasm for the sovereign condition. Gibraltar is a case in point. The Seychelles had to be virtually pushed into independence in 1976. Two years later Bermuda received a nudge in this direction from a Royal Commission,[3] but as of early 1985 remains subject to the British Crown. Apart from such cases, however, the only remaining manifestations of colonialism may soon be weak, scattered and tiny islands best known to stamp collectors – Britain's Pitcairn Island, for example.

There is, however, a second reason for the almost complete disappearance of the kind of non-sovereign territory which is generally designated as a colony. It relates to the fact that a number of former colonial powers – but not Britain – have been prepared to alter their constitutional arrangements to provide for the inclusion of loyal outlying territories within the structure of the state on an identical or equivalent basis to the administrative areas into which the metropolitan area itself is subdivided. Such states have in this way transformed themselves from metropolitan states which possess colonial dependencies into geographically dispersed but unitary states. The exact standing within the whole of the outlying territories will depend upon their circumstances, but they suffer no discrimination within the integrated constitutional structure simply by reason of the fact that they are at a distance from the metropolitan area.

Thus in the case of France the Indian Ocean territory of Reunion has become (as long ago as 1947) a department of the republic and, at least theoretically, is administered in exactly the same way and has exactly the same standing as the country's metropolitan departments. The French premier could therefore say to the islanders: 'You are not five hundred thousand Reunionnais lost in the Indian Ocean. You are five hundred thousand of the fifty-five million Frenchmen.'[4] Likewise, the Caribbean territory of Guadeloupe is a French department. In a similar way, lesser colonial possessions have become Overseas Territories of France[5] – New Caledonia in the Pacific, for example. (This kind of device is not, however, proof against demands for sovereignty, as recent events in New Caledonia have shown. There is also an active separatist movement in Guadeloupe.) Spain and Portugal have also altered their constitutions in a like manner, but now the only overseas areas connected to Spain are those which were always sufficiently close to it to be treated as part of the metropolitan state: the Canary Islands, for example, and certain enclaves on the Moroccan seaboard, chiefly Ceuta and Melilla. The situation is almost the same with regard to Portugal, but she does have one former overseas province left, that of Macao (or Macau) on the Chinese mainland. In 1976, following the Portuguese revolution, Macao was redefined as a special territory, and China's sovereignty (in the sense of ownership) over it was acknowledged. But China refused to have it back, and thus it continued to be run by Portugal. Following China's 1984 agreement with Britain regarding Hong Kong, however, it was announced that talks over the future of Macao would probably be held early in 1986. They are expected to result in Macao coming under China's rule at about the same time as Hong Kong.

In the case of the Netherlands, its Caribbean possession of the Netherlands Antilles is part of the Kingdom of the Netherlands, which for certain purposes is governed as a single whole. The Antilles consists of six islands, one of which – Aruba – is scheduled to have a separate status within the Kingdom of the Netherlands as from 1986, existing alongside the Netherlands itself and the (reduced) Netherlands Antilles. The Netherlands government envisages that

Aruba might become sovereign in 1996, but that is subject to further negotiations as the authorities in Aruba do not yet wish to commit themselves to any date. The United Nations has, by and large, accepted that all the constitutional changes mentioned in this and the previous paragraph make sufficient alterations to the position of the territories concerned to take them out of the scorned colonial category – although it must not be assumed that the UN will never wish to reopen any of these issues.

A kind of subgroup of the colonial species is made up of those territories which, although they lack external competence, are in full control of their internal affairs. The Isle of Man (which is nearly equidistant from England, Scotland and Ireland) is a case in point. It possesses one of the oldest legislative assemblies in the world, and, although a British possession, is not subordinate to the British government or Parliament in respect of internal matters.[6] A territory in a similar position is the Channel Islands which, like the Isle of Man, belongs to the British Crown (the only part of the Duchy of Normandy which so remains) but is not part of the United Kingdom. Special arrangements were made with the European Economic Community regarding both the Isle of Man and the Channel Islands when Britain entered the Community in 1973. Denmark also has two outlying territories which possess full internal autonomy. One is the Faroes, a group of islands about halfway between Scotland and the Arctic Circle. It is a part of the Kingdom of Denmark, which is responsible for its defence and foreign affairs, but on internal matters goes very much its own way. The same is now true of the inappropriately named Greenland, the world's second largest island. A Danish colony since the early eighteenth century, it achieved home rule in 1979 and took advantage of this position to negotiate its withdrawal from the European Economic Community, which took effect in February 1985. This has led some commentators to speak of Greenland's sovereignty, but the territory is definitely not sovereign in the sense in which the term is used when designating what is necessary for regular participation in international relations.

These developments point towards a second class of territories which, while possessing many of the attributes of sovereign statehood, none the less are not constitutionally independent and thus must be designated as lacking in sovereignty. It is composed of the component states of federations and, *a fortiori*, a state's less autonomous administrative divisions, such as counties and municipalities. Territories for which a special constitutional arrangement has been devised, such as the Commonwealth of Puerto Rico – a self-governing territory of the United States – should also be included here. The more important of these governmental units, such

as the component states of a federation, will each have its own
legislature, executive and judiciary, and its legislative power may be
extensive. Such a state may also possess much wealth, as has been
noted in the case of Texas.[7] But in all sorts of important ways its
subordination to the federal state will be evident from its
constitution. On matters which are deemed to be of federal concern –
and in cases of doubt it is the judicial system of the federation which,
ultimately, will do the deeming – the federal view prevails. A vivid
instance of this is the way in which, over the last generation, the
United States government has succeeded in undermining the practice
of racial segregation which was so common throughout the country.
Similarly, had the United States Supreme Court ruled, in a series of
1976 cases, that the death penalty was in all circumstances a 'cruel
and unusual punishment', and therefore forbidden by the Federal
Constitution, all the States of the Union would have been obliged to
fall in line, whatever their own views or previous policies on the
subject. (In fact, the Court did not so rule.)

The subordination of a component state of a federation to the
federal state is also clearly seen in the realm of international activity.
For, even if a component state is able to play a certain international
role, that role will be a very limited one. And it will be clear from the
restricted competence allowed to the state concerned that in the
international sphere it is obliged to walk behind and in step with its
superior authority. The Canadian Province of Quebec, for instance,
has hankered after a higher international profile, and maybe much
else, but has not been able to get a lot further than participation in the
federal Agency for Cultural and Technical Co-operation.[8] Nor is it
likely to so long as it remains a subordinate part of the Canadian
federal system. In Australia the running conflict between the states
and the federal government over state rights has threatened to spill
over on to the international scene, but effectively has not yet done so
on account of the states' lack of standing at this level. Queensland is
particularly sensitive on this issue, and has tried to take it up in
Britain, its premier seeking on more than one occasion the assistance
of the United Kingdom government and also of the Queen (in her
capacity as the Queen of Australia). But he was not able to meet
anyone more exalted than an under secretary of state at the Foreign
and Commonwealth Office from whom he received no substantive
comfort, being told that his quarrel was with the Canberra government and so nothing to do with Britain. As this incident illustrates,
the states, for reasons having to do with their constitutional history
and situation, retain access to the British government. But it does not
amount to much and thus underlines their non-sovereign condition –
as does the fact that at about this time and at the request of the federal

government, the agents-general (that is, representatives) in London of the Australian states were stripped of certain privileges and immunities which they had, as a matter of courtesy, hitherto enjoyed. The states were very annoyed but, not being sovereign, were in no position to do anything about it, the conduct of all external matters relating to Australia being in the hands of the federal government.[9]

It should be emphasized that this approach to the standing of the component states of federations is based upon an absolute concept of sovereignty which sees it as a condition which a state either has or does not have. As with measles, there can be no intermediate situation. There may be doubt about its presence but the diagnosis has eventually to go one way or the other. If a different concept of sovereignty is adopted – one, perhaps, which is based on the extent of a state's formal powers – then it becomes possible to speak in terms of degrees of sovereignty. Thus one writer refers to the component states of a federation as 'not-full sovereign-States' and 'part-sovereign States'.[10] Another writer speaks of 'semi-sovereign' states, meaning those which have the competence to act internationally to one extent or another but 'have not a full set of faculties'.[11] But, on the one hand, this terminology does not add anything, for a semi-, not-full, or part-sovereign state is less than a wholly sovereign state. And on the other it is misleading if the term 'sovereignty' is being used to identify those states which are eligible to participate in international relations on a regular basis. For it implies that sovereignty is attained when the powers of the state reach a certain level, that an additional legal competence may just tip the balance in the direction of sovereignty. It reflects a quantitative conception of sovereignty. Whereas, as the term is used by states in this connection, sovereignty is qualitative, something which attaches to the state itself when it attains a particular constitutional condition – a condition quite different from that of a non-sovereign state. Far from being just an extra power, sovereignty indicates a quite different mode of existence, a move from one level to another which involves the crossing of a very distinct and significant divide.

Constitutional independence or its absence, therefore, is usually plain to see in a state's constitution or its day-to-day constitutional practice, from which the appropriate deduction can be made as to whether or not the state is sovereign. What has been said so far, however, relates to a static situation. The question now arises as to whether it is less easy to identify a sovereign state in conditions of flux, at times when states are in the process of birth or death. The answer is that customarily it is not, and that where it is so the difficulty in most cases is of little magnitude.

Acquisition of Sovereignty

Almost all the states which have made their international debut since the Second World War are former colonies or territories in that type of situation, such as trust territories, protectorates and protected states. Thus their accession to sovereignty has not involved the break-up of metropolitan territory. This very largely accounts for the fact that in the vast majority of cases their birth as sovereign states has been without significant pangs. There may have been argument between the metropolitan government and the political leaders in the colony about the pace of the move towards independence or, sometimes, about whether sovereign independence was an appropriate goal. But on the whole there has not been much argument on this last point. Instead the discussion has tended to focus on time-tables, and once this stage has got seriously under way matters have usually moved swiftly. The result has been the disintegration of European empires at a speed which in 1945 would have been almost inconceivable even to the most progressive of thinkers.

Consent, therefore, has been the overwhelming mode by which sovereignty has recently been obtained. In these circumstances there are no problems over the question of whether or not a territory has achieved constitutional independence. Agreement has been reached that the constitutional ties between the metropolitan state and the colony should be severed on such and such a day at such and such a time. The metropole has gone through the necessary constitutional motions to implement this agreement. A ceremony takes place at the appointed hour which marks the emergence of a new sovereign state. No one is in any doubt about the constitutional position and so the fledgling state can be and almost certainly is treated by its sovereign fellows as one of the international brotherhood. From India and Pakistan on 15 August 1947 to Brunei on 1 January 1984 a whole succession of sovereign states have been unambiguously born at precisely identifiable times.

One other way in which sovereign states may be born peaceably is through the break-up of an existing sovereign unit by a process which, if it cannot be designated as consent, amounts at least to assent. This situation is quite distinct from the ending of a traditional colonial relationship in that it involves the disintegration of the home territory itself. An area previously governed as a single whole, laying claim to a single nationhood, and probably existing within a single set of boundaries, undergoes non-violent change and emerges as two or more separate entities. As the parties immediately concerned have agreed on it, however moderate their enthusiasm, there is no problem over deciding whether a new sovereign state (or states) has come into being. The states involved having accepted that their former union is at an end, there is no point in third parties making assertions to the contrary. They have neither any formal ground nor any practical basis for doing so, as those concerned have decided to move in a direction which is entirely theirs to choose and will now refuse, certainly, to entertain representations based on the earlier state of affairs. However, it is not often that the number of sovereign states is smoothly increased in this manner, for such bodies generally display an urgent anxiety to maintain their existing boundaries – at least if the question at issue relates to their possible contraction. Only in most unusual circumstances will a sovereign state allow itself to be subdivided.

The three instances of this process which have occurred since the Second World War exemplify this point, all of them involving the break-up of recently constructed and shaky-looking federations. The shortest lived was the Federation of Mali, which was created out of two adjacent French West African colonies, Soudan and Senegal. It became sovereign on 20 June 1960 but this did nothing to assuage the dissension which had already appeared. The problems centred on the filling of certain key appointments and came to a head when the President of the Federal Government, who was also President of the Soudan Government, attempted to divest the Vice-President and Minister of Defence, also President of the Senegal Government, of his posts. The Senegalese Assembly promptly voted for withdrawal and, aided by the fact that the army was on its side, carried it through without difficulty, its secession dating from 22 August 1960. Now each party to the ill-fated union was constitutionally independent and went its own way, Soudan retaining for itself the historically significant name of Mali. The incompatibility of these two intended partners is perhaps illustrated by the fact that thereafter they took very divergent international paths, Mali adopting a radical posture while Senegal became a leading state in the moderate group of French-speaking African states.

The second instance of this phenomenon is the break-up of the only post-1945 case of two approximately equal sovereign states having come together to form a single entity: the 1958 union of Egypt and Syria as the United Arab Republic. The equality between them was only very approximate, Egypt being more than five times as big as Syria in terms of both population and area, but Syria was sufficiently large and important to be a province to be reckoned with. Moreover, and very significantly, she was geographically detached from Egypt. Thus, when the federal government, inevitably weighted towards Cairo, gave serious offence in Syria, the outlook for the union was poor. The Syrians increasingly felt themselves to be under the thumb of a foreign state rather than part of a single whole, and they took particular objection to the policies of the federation in the sensitive areas of internal security and economics. The Syrian officers in the UAR army were also discontented at what they saw as Egyptian dominance, and at the end of September 1961 an army revolt in Syria brought the federal edifice tumbling down. A tentative attempt to contain the rebellion by military means came to naught and on 29 September President Nasser accepted the fact that the federation was at an end. The constitutional independence of both Syria and Egypt was re-established, although Egypt retained (for a while) the name of the United Arab Republic. The two states which in 1958 had become one were once again separate actors on the international stage, indicating the difficulty of effecting a sudden fusion between states which are sufficiently long-established to have their individual traditions and power structures.

In the cases of Mali and the United Arab Republic the immediate cause of the disintegration of the state was the decision by one of its constituent parts that the situation was so intolerable that the time had come to leave. In the third case, that of Malaysia and Singapore, it was the federal government – of Malaysia – which decided that one of the political units composing the state – Singapore – must be ejected. Thus Singapore did not go; it was pushed. The sovereign state of Malaysia had come into being in September 1963 by the amalgamation of Malaya (which had been independent since 1957) and the British non-self-governing territories of Singapore, Sabah (formerly called North Borneo) and Sarawak. Tension had been present from the beginning between Singapore and the central government and it got worse. The latter's economic measures caused considerable resentment in Singapore, and soon Singapore was charging the government with extremism. In return the government saw the danger of communist influence being introduced into the state through Singapore. Underlying these exchanges was the ethnic issue. In Malaya the Malays were numerically predominant, but there was also a very large Chinese minority, and Singapore was overwhelmingly Chinese. When, therefore, Singapore contended for a Malaysian Malaysia – that is, for the granting of an appropriate degree of political influence to the Chinese element within the state – the Malay-controlled federal government, not surprisingly, saw this as a threat to its dominance. Moreover, the dynamic leader of Singapore was gathering some support in Malaya not only among the Chinese but also among its third ethnic group, the Indians, and was beginning to make very critical remarks about the federal prime minister. All this was interpreted not just in ethnic and political terms but also, on account of the perceived menace of a communist intrusion via the Singaporeans, as a threat to the integrity of the state itself. Some might be talking of an end to the cold war, but in Malaya memories of the pre-independence decade of guerrilla warfare by communist insurgents were still fresh. It was therefore decided that Singapore had to depart; a counter-suggestion that the federal ties be maintained on a looser basis was rejected. The deed was done on 9 August 1965, it being announced in Kuala Lumpur that Singapore had agreed under pressure to secede, and Singapore proclaiming its independence. Singapore's constitution had now to be amended to take account of its unasked-for sovereignty, and its schoolchildren applied the idea of amendment to a ditty which had celebrated the independence of Malaysia two years earlier. In its original version it ran, 'Malaysia, Malaysia, ten million strong'; now it became, 'Malaysia, Malaysia, ten minutes long'. Singapore immediately took the place on the international stage for which, as a constitutionally independent entity, it was eligible.

Renunciation of Sovereignty

The obverse of this process is the loss of sovereignty by consent, where two sovereign states agree to merge and act henceforth as one sovereign entity. From an international perspective it makes no difference whether the states concerned are of roughly the same or very disparate size. In either case, two (or more) sovereign states have become one. Constitutional arrangements have been altered to provide for a reduction in the number of constitutionally independent entities, and hence in the number of those eligible to participate regularly in international life. But whereas the word 'merger' seems appropriate to refer to a union between more or less equal states, in that they are establishing an integrated partnership, 'accession' is a better word to use where the difference between them is such that what appears to be happening is the addition of one state to another. It is probably also more accurate. For when a small sovereign state joins a much larger one it will probably do so on the existing terms and conditions. Thus, while the larger state's constitution will have to be amended to take account of the new situation, from its perspective what is taking place is the addition of a province to those which already exist and on the constitutional basis which is already in operation. A merger between roughly equal states, on the other hand, will almost certainly necessitate the negotiation of a new constitution which takes due account of the interests and strengths of the new partner.

In either event, there will be no difficulty over the identification of the new sovereign entity, nor of those which have surrendered their individual sovereignty. The matter being based on agreement, this change in the political map of the world will have been made in accordance with the appropriate forms and with due public ceremony. It has, however, happened very rarely in recent times. States are far too jealous of their sovereign condition to give it up save in the most exceptional of situations.

One such case has already been mentioned – the merger between Egypt and Syria which was proclaimed on 1 February 1958. This was a reflection of pan-Arab sentiment and the charisma which attached to President Nasser of Egypt, who at that time was riding particularly high. Within a few days a provisional constitution for the United Arab Republic was agreed upon and later in the month the scheme was approved by a plebiscite. Instead of two constitutionally independent entities there was now a single entity with its own independent constitution. Regional councils and assemblies were to play an important part in the government of the new federal state, but in accordance with the revised constitutional set-up there was to be a single national assembly and a single cabinet. Concomitantly, so far as the rest of the world was concerned the two former sovereign states had become one. Embassies in Damascus had at least to be down-graded, as diplomatic representation at this level in the United Arab Republic had now to be based at its capital, Cairo. Correspondingly, the United Arab Republic set about unifying its diplomatic representation in foreign capitals. At the United Nations the number of members went down, by one, for the first time in the organization's history: Egypt and Syria, their flags and seats, disappeared, and in their places came the United Arab Republic.

A rather similar series of events took place some years later in respect of Tanganyika and Zanzibar. Tanganyika had become sovereign at the end of 1961 and Zanzibar, consisting of the island of Zanzibar and its associated islands (all of them lying less than 50 miles off the coast of Tanganyika), followed suit two years later. On 25 April 1964, in a surprise move which seems to have been almost entirely engineered and controlled by their presidents, these two states came together to form a new sovereign state called the United Republic of Tanganyika and Zanzibar (abbreviated later in the year to Tanzania). Once again, United Nations membership went down by one, and once again ideology seemed to have a lot to do with the union. For Tanganyika's President Nyerere was a firm believer in pan-Africanism, and had therefore been very disappointed at its lack of progress during the previous few years. Here at least was one limited chance to break down colonial boundaries. It is also probable that he was worried by the unstable situation in Zanzibar and the possibility of great power intervention which it presented, for Zanzibar had been flirting with the Eastern bloc and alarm bells were ringing in Washington at the prospect of an 'African Cuba'. In Zanzibar calculations seem to have been at a more personal level, in that its president's position was none too sure, with several factions interested in his removal. Union seemed likely to bolster his position.[12]

However, links between Tanganyika and Zanzibar had never been close, and Zanzibar had no wish for them to become much closer. Its former president was still intent on creating a self-sufficient and distinctive community, and successfully insisted on Zanzibar's retention not just of administrative autonomy but also of freedom of action in a range of external matters. Thus, until his assassination in 1972, he continued to play an active foreign role; the island conducts its own trade and has its own central bank; and visitors from the mainland have to go through customs and immigration procedures. Altogether it is a most anomalous situation but, paradoxically, it is almost certainly the looseness of the union which has prevented it from going the way of that between Egypt and Syria. On the face of it Zanzibar is by no means poorly placed to revert to sovereign status. Its island situation gives it a good start; its people do not lack an independent spirit; they number in excess of 300,000; and as the supplier of a large part of the world's cloves and olive oil Zanzibar is not in as poor an economic situation as some states. However, the issue of a return to sovereignty has not been pressed, doubtless because Zanzibar has been allowed so much freedom. Of course, relations with the federal government on the mainland have some-times been strained, and occasionally the latter's international responsibilities for Zanzibar have led to some embarrassment. For some of the often erratic goings-on on the island have had wide repercussions. But the federal government has not been disposed to 'do a Singapore' on Zanzibar. Indeed, in 1983 it proposed some constitutional changes which would have the effect of curbing Zanzibar's autonomy. But they produced a strong reaction on the island, and led to calls for an even looser federation. The abrupt devaluation of the Tanzanian currency in 1984 elicited a similar reaction. All this suggests that at least for the time being things will go on much as before, with the formal situation not being called into question but with an internal arrangement which is a lot looser and more precarious than is usual within a sovereign state. From one point of view the continuation of Tanzania as a single constitutional entity is undoubtedly a surprise. But it reflects unusual circum-stances, and something which has existed for twenty years may yet have a lot more life in it. However, it could be that when Tanzania's long-serving President Nyerere departs from the political scene the whole issue of the relationship between Zanzibar and the mainland will be opened up.

The remaining cases of states voluntarily giving up their sovereignty are all, in one way or another, rather problematical. The first stems from an episode which has already been referred to: the creation of Malaysia in 1963. In as much as one of the four territories which came together to constitute this state, Malaya, had been sovereign since 1957, and more particularly as it was not a matter of the other three joining Malaya but of a new constitution having to be hammered out, the formal position is that Malaya gave up her sovereignty to participate as a founder member of Malaysia. On the other hand, in informal terms the process could be described as, in a sense, the expansion of Malaya. The three other territories had a population between them of only about half that of Malaya, so it was to be expected that Malaya would have a big say in Malaysian affairs. Moreover, steps had been taken to ensure that the dominant ethnic group in Malaya – the Malays – did not find themselves in an inferior position in the new state. North Borneo and Sarawak were in fact only included in it (as, initially, was Brunei) in the expectation that they would provide political support for the Malays against the Chinese, who would be the next largest ethnic group in Malaysia. The new country's constitution also gave Malays certain preferential rights, and the amendment of these provisions was made particularly difficult. It is true that there was a question mark over Malaysia's future relations within the federation with its biggest partner, Singapore, which was not only racially distinct but also go-ahead and relatively prosperous. And in the event these doubts were increasingly seen to be well based. However, the manner of their resolution – Singapore's abrupt expulsion in 1965 – was, from one angle, evidence of the way in which Malayans ran Malaysia: as a kind of greater Malaya. In legal theory Malaya may have disappeared as a sovereign state, but that was not quite how the matter was perceived by Malayan politicians.

The establishment of Malaysia has a footnote which is of some interest to the issue of sovereignty, and also could lend support to the argument that it was not only Malaya who gave up sovereignty to create the new state. It had been planned that Malaysia should be proclaimed on 31 August 1963, but Indonesian and (rather reluctant) Philippine protests at the proposed inclusion of North Borneo and Sarawak led to the UN Secretary-General conducting a speedy 'assessment of opinion' in the two territories. It was a cursory affair and was certainly not seen by either Britain or Malaya as something which would alter the intended course of events. But it did result in a new Malaysia Day being set (when the investigators were less than halfway through their task) for 16 September. However, on 31 August the leader of Singapore in effect proclaimed his territory's sovereignty. Malaya took strong objection to this and pressed Britain to confirm that her remaining powers in Singapore had not been transferred to the locals. Britain obliged. The incident could almost be seen as a prank, but it did have a serious purpose in that it reflected Singapore's annoyance at, in her view, not being sufficiently consulted about the postponement of the original Malaysia Day.

If this was perhaps a case of sovereignty being purportedly assumed out of a jocular intent, another case two years earlier could be seen as the creation of a sovereign state by error or oversight, with that sovereignty being relinquished after five days as part of the process which created a new and larger state. It relates to the establishment of the Somali Republic on 1 July 1960 by way of union between the former Italian Trust Territory of Somalia and the former British Somaliland Protectorate. For some reason, however, Britain's jurisdiction over the protectorate was brought to an end on 26 June so that, technically speaking, the former protectorate was for a brief period a constitutionally independent entity.

Another case of sovereignty being (perhaps) renounced concerns Newfoundland, Britain's oldest colony. At the Imperial Conference of 1917 it had been constituted a Dominion and as such participated in the vague constitutional advance towards sovereignty which these countries made during the interwar period (although unlike the others it did not choose to participate in international relations).[13] The 1926 Imperial Conference declared the Dominions in what was called the 'Balfour formula', to be 'autonomous communities within the British Empire, equal in status, in no way subordinate one to another in any aspect of their domestic or foreign affairs',[14] and this was given legal force by the Statute of Westminster of 1931. It could be argued that at least from this point the Dominions were sovereign states, though doubts still attached to so crucial a matter as whether they were obliged to march together in the waging of war and the making of peace. However, on account of its financial problems Newfoundland's Dominion status was suspended in 1933 and it entered a kind of constitutional limbo, being ruled for the next sixteen years by a commission made up of three members from Newfoundland and three from Britain. In a referendum of 1948 it decided by a narrow majority to join Canada rather than revert to its pre-1933 status, and in 1949 (on 1 April) it became the tenth province of the Canadian Federation. If it is agreed that it did so from a position of sovereignty in suspense, there is a case for the argument that here was a peculiarly sovereign state agreeing to abandon its sovereign condition. It is interesting to speculate on how this decision might have gone if it had been postponed for a decade to the time when the international scene was about to be invaded by a host of new states.

The final possible instance of this process of the voluntary renunciation of sovereignty concerns the former Trucial States of the Persian Gulf – or, to avoid any implication of an Iranian sphere of influence or hegemony – the Gulf as it is now often called. These seven states, of which by far the biggest and richest is Abu Dhabi, were in treaty relations with Britain (dating from the nineteenth century) by which she was responsible for the conduct of their external affairs. However, as part of the process of imperial withdrawal from areas east of Suez, pressure was brought on the Trucial States to bring this relationship to an end. In consequence, on 2 December 1971, six of them came together to form the single sovereign state known as the United Arab Emirates. They were: Abu Dhabi, Ajman, Dubai, Fujairah, Sharjah and Umm al Qaiwain. The seventh – Ras al Khaimah – joined later in the month for want of a better alternative. The question which then arises is whether the individual emirates enjoyed sovereignty prior to this date, and hence were in a position to give it up. It will be discussed later as part of the more general issue of whether protected states are sovereign.[15] All that need be said now is that there is a very strong argument in favour of describing the creation of this new state as an instance of the merging of sovereignties. However, this event in no way weakens the assertion that in the post-1945 world sovereign states are very reluctant to renounce their sovereignty, nor is it likely to have any persuasive precedential effect. For the emergence of the United Arab Emirates was the product of very special circumstances. All the participants were protected states, enjoyed the same protecting power, with whom each of them had a close relationship. Add to this the fact that, although all of them were wealthy, on account of their oil, they were also small (their combined population did not much exceed 100,000) and existed in a region of much larger and wealthier states. These features combined to make a merger much more desirable and acceptable than is generally the case.

A separate point which should be made at this juncture is that the United Arab Emirates, rather like Tanzania, is in some respects a very unusual sovereign state. In the financial realm, for example, the federation's total budget for 1975 was only about one fifth of Abu Dhabi's oil revenue for that year.[16] The same centrifugal pressures were at work in the even more significant area of armaments. Under the original merger agreement the emirates retained the right to have their own armed forces. An agreement on their union was reached in

1976, but the decree to put it into practice was not issued until 1978. Five years later Dubai, the second larget emirate, was still running its own army and air force.[17] Clearly, the process of establishing a common loyalty to the United Arab Emirates which overrides the existing loyalties to the individual emirates still has a very long way to go, and there is some question as to whether the UAE will survive the passing of its two leading statesmen.

But – and it is a very important but – such matters as these have no direct bearing on the question of whether a territorially based entity is sovereign. As has been pointed out, sovereignty is the condition of being constitutionally independent. There is no doubt, on the one hand, that the United Arab Emirates is a state with a constitution which is not subordinate to any other and, on the other, that the constituent members of this state have constitutions which are subordinate to the federal constitution of the United Arab Emirates. This has been widely recognized in such matters as, for example, the United Arab Emirates' membership in the United Nations and its exchange of ambassadors with a number of other sovereign states. Of course, authority could slip away from the centre to such an extent that other states would have to ask themselves whether it is any longer meaningful to treat the state as a single, sovereign entity. But things have to go very far before that point is reached.[18] Sovereignty is, after all, a formal matter, and the substance can move away from the form to a considerable degree without the form having to be called in question. If sovereignty was not based on a legal situation but on the existence of a strong substantive factor, such as an evident overriding loyalty to the state by its people, there would be many states whose sovereignty would be in question, together with much doubt about what degree of doubt held by whom was sufficient to justify not treating a state as sovereign – with all the chaotic possibilities that implies. However, in this connection there is no need to worry about these matters. Sovereignty rests on a certain constitutional situation. Due political account of any centrifugal tendencies which a state exhibits is entirely compatible with the acknowledgement of its constitutional status as a sovereign entity.

Proposed Mergers

Actual and significant mergers of sovereignty have, therefore, occurred only rarely in recent times. More frequently encountered are mere proposals and preliminary agreements to that end, but their failure to come to anything is indicative of the same jealousy about sovereignty which has resulted in so few actual mergers. Such schemes are, in fact, almost always long on ideology (in varying degrees of zeal) and short on practicality. They generally start with a fine rhetorical flourish and then drift away into nothing, often accompanied by bickering amongst the intended partners. It is the Arab world that has given birth to most such proposals, reflecting a perhaps commendable devotion to the pan-Arab ideal but a lamentable grip on reality – assuming, of course, that the proposals were made and accepted in good faith. Bringing two or more hitherto sovereign states into a healthy union is an operation of considerable delicacy and difficulty. Political leaders above all others should know that it involves far more than signing pieces of paper.

President Nasser of Egypt was involved in several of these schemes. The actual three-year union with Syria was extended to (North) Yemen to create an empty Union of Arab States. Another agreement involved Libya and Sudan, and under his successor Egypt put her hand to a tripartite federation with Libya and Syria in 1971. Nothing came of either of them. In 1980 Libya proposed a union with Syria, which promised to seize the outstretched hand – but failed to do so. In the following year Libya announced a merger with Chad, but this was very much a shotgun marriage and was denounced by the Organization of African Unity. In a huff Libya withdrew her forces from Chad before the OAU was ready with its proposed replacement force. During the 1970s the two Yemens – the North moderate and the South Marxist – twice agreed on union and did so again in 1982. The oil-rich but thinly populated neighbour of both of them, Saudi Arabia, naturally has little enthusiasm for the idea and an official publication archly observed that the two countries 'have been discussing unity for the past decade in between border skirmishes'.[19] The presidents of the two Yemens did meet in 1983 to review progress, but it is not unreasonable to suppose that the emergence of a single sovereign state is rather far from imminent. The latest pan-Arab scheme is assertedly a 'union of states' between pro-Western Morocco and left-wing Libya. Proposed out of the blue in August 1984 by the King of Morocco to the President of Libya, it was instantly accepted, and within a couple of weeks had been unanimously approved by Libya's General People's Congress, and received overwhelming support in a referendum in Morocco. However, despite its title it is very far from a union of two sovereign states into one. What has been promised is close co-operation in the political, economic and defence spheres. Whether even that will be achieved remains problematical.

It might be thought that one way around the difficulty of bringing sovereign states together would be, where appropriate, to effect the union while they were still under colonial tutelage. It might be hypothesized that it would be easier to arrange and that the experience of actually living in one administrative unit would augur well for its continuation after sovereign status had been granted. The record, however, does not endorse these ideas. The very early break-up of the French-sponsored Federation of Mali has already been mentioned.[20] Britain too has tried its hand at this sort of enterprise, but without success. Immediately after the Second World War schemes were proposed for a federation of its possessions in and around the Caribbean. It seemed an obvious way to deal with these small and scattered territories, most of them islands. But it was not until 1958 that the West Indies Federation was created, and the hostility of its larger constituents, especially Jamaica, resulted in its collapse in 1962. Almost immediately Jamaica and Trinidad and Tobago became sovereign states, and most of the other former members of the federation have since followed suit.

Britain tried again in Central Africa, bringing the self-governing colony of Southern Rhodesia (now Zimbabwe) and the Protectorates of Northern Rhodesia (now Zambia) and Nyasaland (now Malawi) together in a federal structure in 1953. It lasted a decade, but major differences between its three parts meant that it had to be dissolved before any of them could become sovereign. In East Africa, by contrast, the three former British-controlled territories which became sovereign in the early 1960s – Kenya, Uganda and Tanganyika – looked at one point as if they might merge their newly won sovereignties. For in 1963 their heads of state agreed to establish a federation by the end of the year. But discussion about the detailed terms and conditions gave rise to insuperable problems, and it looked from the way in which Uganda talked as if she had not understood the implications of the earlier agreement, for she wanted to maintain her international identity and membership of the United Nations. Thus the scheme came to naught. Instead, the three states decided to build on the extensive co-operative network which they had inherited from Britain. This too proved difficult, but they established what they called the East African Community in 1967. However, what ensued was 'a long slow process of movement toward total disintegration, culminating, fifteen years after independence in complete disarray with two member states, Uganda and Tanzania, engaged in full-scale war and the shared borders of all three states virtually closed'.[21]

In West Africa, a merger between two former Portuguese colonies was on the agenda for a number of years following their assumption of sovereignty in the mid-1970s. The mainland Guinea-Bissau, with a population of about 600,000, and the islands of Cape Verde, with a population of about half that number and lying 400 miles offshore had several factors in common. One was that Cape Verdeans have long been prominent in the politics and administration of Guinea-Bissau, and another that following independence both states were ruled by the same Marxist party. However, the first of these factors was also a threat to the planned union of the two states, especially as the Guineans are black and the Cape Verdeans half-castes. In 1980 this potential difficulty came to the surface in the shape of a military coup in Guinea-Bissau and a new government composed exclusively of Guinean blacks who were opposed to the merger scheme. Since then all talk of union has been put on one side.

It is, however, immediately to the north of Guinea-Bissau that two sovereign states are working very closely together in what is officially described as a confederation. They are the former French colony of Senegal, with a population of about 6 million, and the former British colony of the Gambia, which has only about one-tenth that number of people. Moreover, the Gambia is surrounded on all landward sides by Senegal, and, being sliver-shaped, goes some way towards splitting its larger neighbour into two. Senegal achieved sovereignty in 1960 and the Gambia five years later, having rejected ideas for association with Senegal. However, one of the first things the Gambia did as a sovereign state was to sign agreements on defence and foreign policy with Senegal and over the next decade a number of other co-operative arrangements were made, without in any sense presaging a merger of the two states. But then in 1980 military disaffection in the Gambia was put down with the help of Senegalese troops, and in the following year an attempted coup was repulsed by the Senegalese army. This concentrated Gambian minds and within weeks it was announced that the two countries would associate much more closely. In December 1981 an agreement creating the Confederation of Senegambia was signed and came into force on 1 February 1982.

The agreement provides that each party shall retain its independence and sovereignty but calls for the integration of the armed and security forces, economic and monetary union, co-operation in communications and external relations, and the establishment of joint institutions. As of early 1985 not much progress has been made in the more difficult of these directions, and Senegalese were reported[22] as accusing Gambia of not wanting the confederation and of deliberately dragging its feet in the negotiations on an economic and monetary union. Obviously there is a very long way to go before there can be any question of whether these two sovereign states have become one. But there is perhaps more promise of that happening here than in most other parts of the world.

It should just be added, however, that aspirations towards a merger have been reported from two other areas. One concerns the neighbouring West African states of Ghana and Burkina Faso (formerly Upper Volta), which adjoins Ghana's northern and north-western borders. In April 1985 the military and radically oriented regimes in both countries announced that, with a view to consolidating their revolutions, plans would be drawn up for the 'political integration'[23] of the two states. It was not clear what, exactly, was meant by this phrase. But it would be not unreasonable to suppose that, even if the aim is far-reaching, the merger of the two presently sovereign states into one is unlikely to come about at an early date.

The other area where there has been discussion along similar lines is the Caribbean, where there is a large cluster of tiny sovereign states and also half a dozen remaining colonial territories, the latter mustering between them about 100,000 people. Six of the sovereign states lying in the eastern part of the region, which have a total population of less than 600,000 and a combined land mass of less than 300 square miles, formed the Organization of Eastern Caribbean States in 1981. Its members are Antigua-Barbuda, Dominica, Grenada, St Kitts-Nevis, St Lucia, and St Vincent and the Grenadines, and they created a straightforward co-operative arrangement between states. In 1983 the organization's members decided to establish a common bank to be used for joint tourism promotions and the joint purchase of imported goods, and it was reported as a 'step towards becoming a single nation'.[24] A few months later domestic developments in Grenada and the perceived need to ask the United States to upset them (which the organization, quite improperly, did – Grenada being absent from the meeting) underlined the fragility of the individual sovereign states of the area, and may have strengthened any existing tendencies towards a merger. The actual creation of a single state out of the six existing ones, however, is most unlikely to take place very quickly, and it would be a bit of a surprise if it ever happened at all. Island communities are notoriously inclined towards individualism, and the giving up of their several sovereignties is unlikely to have much allure, the reasoned arguments in its favour notwithstanding.

Violence, Successful and Unsuccessful

So far, the discussion regarding the birth and death of sovereign states has related to non-violent situations. But even where this process occurs by the threat or force of arms there is not usually much obscurity about it. While a struggle is actually taking place third parties may react cautiously, and be reluctant to acknowledge the arrival of a new actor on the international scene or the loss of an old one – although this is unlikely to be the attitude of those who, although not directly involved, none the less have a stake in the outcome. Such states may well try to influence it by bestowing their blessing on the representatives of the side they support, probably by dealing publicly with them in their asserted capacity as spokesmen for the state over the control of which the conflict is being fought. Other outsiders, however, are likely to stand back until the dust has settled. Then, if a change has occurred, they can take due note of it, although nowadays they may do so more slowly and reluctantly where one state has swallowed up another than where a new entity has appeared out of the possessions or body of an existing sovereign state.

Since 1945 the only case of a state's metropolitan territory being dismembered is that of Pakistan. From its birth in 1947 it consisted of two geographical units separated by more than a thousand miles of Indian territory. Although East Pakistan was the larger in terms of population, the country had always been dominated politically by West Pakistan, which also contained its initial capital, Karachi, its second, Rawalpindi, and its specially constructed capital, Islamabad. The two parts of this single state were divided linguistically, Urdu being the main language of the West and Bengali of the East, and there were also marked racial differences between their inhabitants. In these circumstances it was always questionable whether the common bonds of the Muslim religion and the use of English as the official language would suffice to keep the state together. But, despite difficulties, it was maintained as a single constitutional entity until the 1970s.

The immediate cause of the crisis which then occurred was the country's first ever election, held in December 1970. Nearly all the East Pakistan seats in the new National Assembly were won by the Awami League, which had campaigned for the reorganization of the country as a very loose federation. A postponement of the process which was to transfer power to the Assembly brought the smouldering discontent in the East to ignition point. The government responded by using the Pakistan army to conduct a massive security operation in the East, which involved the banning of all political activity. The East Pakistanis immediately replied, on 26 March 1971, by proclaiming the secession of their part of the state. There followed a violent nine months in which the Pakistan army engaged in what, by all accounts, was a policy of brutal suppression. India became increasingly restive and in December sent her troops into East Pakistan and almost immediately recognized its independence under the name of Bangladesh. Within a couple of weeks the war was over, the Pakistani forces in the East having been driven to the point of surrender. Clearly, the federal government was now in no position to make good its constitutional claim to authority over what had been East Pakistan, and on the other hand Bangladesh had indisputably emerged as a distinct political unit, promulgating its own constitutional guidelines on 15 December 1971, the day before the war officially ended. It was in a chaotic condition but none the less it had constitutional arrangements which were not subordinate to those of any other state. Accordingly, the way was open for other sovereign states to take formal note of the fact that their number had been increased by one, and many of them did. Not surprisingly, it took a little while for (reduced) Pakistan to do the same, but in February 1974 Pakistan and Bangladesh accorded each other mutual recognition. Two years later they established diplomatic relations. A by-product of the episode was Pakistan's withdrawal from the Commonwealth on account of Bangladesh being recognized by Britain and two other Commonwealth countries before the passions of the war of secession had subsided. This, however, is something which may yet be repaired.

The absence of other similar cases is not entirely due to want of trying. Since 1945 a number of discontented groups in various parts of the world have attempted to break away from the states of which they were a part and to set up as independent sovereign entities. Their lack of success is due to two reasons. In the first place, a secessionist-minded group is, almost by definition, likely to be a minority within the state to which it reluctantly belongs. And whatever difficulties it creates for that state by its unwilling and maybe even hostile presence, and however lacking it is in natural resources, the state is most unlikely to agree to its departure. It may well be that the state concerned has but recently come to birth itself, borne to the international shore on the tide of self-determination. But that does not mean that it will be receptive to appeals from within its own boundaries based on this principle, not even if at the same time it is, at the United Nations, proclaiming the principle's validity and urging other states to act in accordance with it in relation to their remaining dependent territories. For, once a territory has acquired sovereignty, those in its charge almost always proceed on the assumption that the principle of self-determination has no further relevance to the area they rule. Empires may be broken up on its basis, but not an established state.

If, therefore, a new sovereign state is to appear out of the metropolitan territory of one which already exists, those who are working towards this end will in all probability need substantial material help from at least one external well-wisher. Even that may not be enough if the home state is well equipped to deal with armed insurrection or is able to obtain physical support from its own friends. But in any event the aid which the secessionists need is unlikely to be forthcoming, for the spirit of the times is hostile to their sort of cause. In most circumstances states are reluctant to assist in the disintegration of one of their fellows, not just because the maintenance of existing boundaries is a principle which they espouse but also on account of the adverse consequences which they themselves might suffer at a later date if they act contrary to it in respect of another state. Such action would make it less easy for them to protest if others assisted secessionist groups within their own boundaries, and it might also encourage those minded towards secession to move more purposefully in that direction. Moreover, there are many states which have at least a latent secessionist problem, especially in Africa and Asia, where boundaries are often relatively artificial constructs in the sense that the people they enclose are not imbued with a strong sense of common nationhood. Thus, a major task for such states is the creation of loyalty to the state, which, reversing experience elsewhere, has been created in advance of the nation. In these circumstances states are anxious to do nothing which might disturb their own process of nation-building or endanger their internal cohesion. For this second reason, therefore, secessionists generally have to fend for themselves, and so find that the path to independence is an almost impossibly difficult one to traverse.

Bangladesh was, therefore, a very special case. Not only was Pakistan unable to bring the full weight of its power to bear on the rebels, on account of the state's geographical nature, but the larger state which lay between Pakistan's two parts was eventually willing to intervene in strength on the side of the East Bengalis. India may well have been partly moved by humanitarian considerations, and also out of the view that she could no longer stand apart from a conflict which was resulting in her border being crossed by millions of refugees. But it is also very possible that she was not unhappy to strike a telling blow at Pakistan, with whom her relations had hardly ever been good. The two had already fought one war, in 1965, and the prospect of an independent state on each of her flanks instead of the same hostile state on both could not but have been pleasing in the eyes of Indian strategists. Divide and rule is not an exclusively imperial maxim.

Elsewhere, however, would-be secessionists have not been able to secure the sort of help which the East Bengalis succeeded in attracting in 1971, and this very largely accounts for their almost uniform lack of success. A good example of this is the attempt by the large and populous Eastern Region of Nigeria to establish itself as the sovereign state of Biafra. Throughout 1966 there had been widespread disorder in Nigeria, including military rebellions and communal violence. Fears in the Northern Region that it and therefore the country as a whole was falling under the domination of southerners found expression in mob attacks on people from the south, especially Ibos of the Eastern Region, with whom the Northerners had some scores to settle. This was followed by the killing of Eastern officers and men by their supposed Northern colleagues in the Nigerian army. The violence spread, and estimates of Eastern deaths ranged from five to fifty thousand. Before long over one million people of Eastern origin had returned to their home region, which, on 30 May 1967, declared itself to be independent under the name of Biafra. For almost a year the region had been more or less governing itself, but now a bitter civil war began.

Initially the Biafrans achieved some military success and there was no doubt that the secessionist government was in control of a good part of the Eastern Region, where it had wide support. It was said to be receiving military supplies from a number of countries, including France, South Africa and China. It also obtained much public sympathy in the West, where newspaper pictures of starving Biafran children made a big emotional impact. However, only one Caribbean and four African states formally recognized the existence of a new sovereign state. In other parts of the continent and also beyond, the official view was that this was an internal Nigerian affair, to which the principle of self-determination had no application. The federal government received arms from, among others, Britain and the Soviet Union, and in due time its superior strength began to show. Early in 1970 the war was brought to an end and the Eastern Region was reintegrated into Nigeria. Despite a number of relatively good omens, an area which by any standard would have constituted a viable sovereign state and urgently wished to do so none the less failed. Metropolitan territory is not easily broken up in the second half of the twentieth century.

Another example of this is the ex-Italian colony of Eritrea, which has a 500-mile coastline at the south-western end of the Red Sea. After the Second World War its disposition was in the hands of the chief victorious powers or, failing their agreement, the General Assembly of the United Nations. They did fail to agree and so the matter passed to the Assembly which eventually decided (after a five-state Commission of Investigation had split three ways) that Eritrea should become an autonomous unit federated with Ethiopia. It did so in 1952, and ten years later was incorporated as a province of Ethiopia. The Eritreans were never happy about this and have been fighting a sporadic guerrilla war since the early 1960s. Latterly, on account of Ethiopia's move into the Soviet orbit, the Eritreans have been receiving some cautious assistance from Iran and Saudi Arabia, but it has been insufficient to counter the growing Ethiopian successes in the field. As of early 1985, sovereignty for the Eritreans looks as far away as ever, as it does for the Kurds, the Basques, and many other such groups.

Insurgent Islanders

On account of the geographical factor, states which consist of a number of islands are perhaps more exposed than most to fissiparous tendencies, but even so islanders of separatist intent have not been very successful. Right at the beginning of its life as a sovereign state Indonesia (the former Dutch East Indies) was faced in 1950 with a revolt by the South Moluccan islands. A United Nations commission which was on the spot offered its good offices, but whereas Indonesia had, during its own fight for independence, welcomed United Nations activity, which it saw as contributing to the Indonesian cause, now it would have none of it. The United Nations was told to mind its own business and let Indonesia settle its internal affairs itself. The revolt died down, but the situation has never been entirely settled, although it now perhaps gives less trouble to Indonesia than to the Netherlands government, on account of the presence in that country of Moluccan activists.

A series of events which was in some respects similar occurred a quarter of a century later in respect of the former Portuguese colony of East Timor, the other part of the island of Timor forming part of Indonesia. Following the revolution of 1974 in Portugal the new left-wing government there planned to give East Timor its independence by the end of 1978. However, in 1975 rival indigenous groups attempted to seize power in the colony and, following a brief civil war, the Fretilin party came out on top. In November it declared the colony to be independent under the name of the Democratic Republic of East Timor. Lisbon refused to recognize the new situation but had little desire or ability to do anything else about it. It could therefore be argued that a new sovereign state had appeared.

However, neighbouring Indonesia had her eyes on the territory. In December 1975 Indonesia invaded, fought a war in which it is said that at least 10 per cent of the local population (of about 600,000) died, and in July 1976 proclaimed East Timor's incorporation into Indonesia. Resistance continues within the territory, and externally the General Assembly of the United Nations keeps the matter alive, regularly passing resolutions which are implicitly critical of Indonesia's action. But Indonesia has no intention of backing down, and evidently no one else is going to make her do so. Thus the people of East Timor join the fairly lengthy list of those who would like to break away from the constitutional entity of which they form a part, but have virtually no chance of succeeding.

An equally unsuccessful attempt to obtain sovereignty, and in the same area of the world, was that of the island of Bougainville, copper from which provides the main export of Papua New Guinea. This very underdeveloped territory became independent on 15 September 1975, but already on the first of the month Bougainville had declared its secession as the Republic of North Solomons. However, it was unable to maintain this position and a year later it accepted provincial status within Papua New Guinea, albeit with a greater degree of autonomy than that which had originally been intended.

As it happened it was Papua New Guinea troops who put down another island rebellion, this time in the neighbouring state of Vanuatu – the former Anglo-French condominium of New Hebrides. A condominium is at best a clumsy governmental device, and it had hardly been at its best in New Hebrides, providing 'a special case study of Parkinson's Law, with a double load of bureaucrats producing a minus form of government'.[25] It has also resulted in the division of the population into francophone and anglophone camps, with the political parties following this division. When, therefore, the anglophone party won the pre-independence elections, the other group declared the secession of the outlying island of Espiritu Santo. Thus Vanuatu came to independence on 30 July 1980 in an emasculated condition. Britain and France would, reluctantly, have been willing to help the central government (with France the more reluctant of the two), but it turned instead to its north-western neighbour. A detachment of 300 Papua New Guinea troops was sent and within a few weeks the dissidents had surrendered without battle being joined.

Away to the north near where the Equator meets the international date-line there was another island problem with secessionist implications. It concerned Ocean Island, or Banaba, which, although distant and geographically distinct from the Gilbert Islands, was included with them for administrative purposes. Thus it was scheduled to become, in 1979, part of the sovereign state of Kiribati, as the Gilbert Islands were to be called. The 2,500 Banaban people, however, had no wish for this, seeking to remain as a British colony and eventually to associate with Fiji. But they were in a peculiar position as, for thirty years, they had not lived on their island but on one belonging to the Fiji group. This was because the mining of phosphate on Ocean Island (which provided much of the Gilbert Islands' wealth) had made it uninhabitable. A remarkably long and expensive legal battle in the British courts (which led in 1976 to a judgment of one hundred thousand words) had not given them the financial compensation they sought, and now they were also to meet political disappointment. For Britain refused to alter the proposed constitutional arrangements. Thus Ocean Island remains with the 50,000-strong Kiribati, and there is nothing the Banabans can do about it.

By contrast, an at least temporary break-up of an island territory has occurred in the Indian Ocean, but in this case the impulse towards separation has not also pointed in the direction of sovereignty. The Comoro archipelago was a French possession lying to the north-east of Madagascar (the Malagasy Republic). It consists of four islands, three of which sought independence. The fourth, however – Mayotte – stubbornly insisted that it wished to remain part of France. Thus, when the Comoros were formally given sovereignty at the end of 1975 (this having been preceded by a unilateral declaration of independence), Mayotte was excluded from the new state and, having reiterated its view, was granted a special status within the French Republic. This has brought France no favour either at the United Nations or in the Organization of African Unity, where the prevailing view is that self-determination can only operate legitimately in the direction of independence. However, it is also strongly held in these quarters that colonial administrative units should maintain their unity when they become sovereign, so Mayotte would probably have received very little support had sovereignty been its goal. Its maintenance of constitutional independence might also have proved difficult if the other three Comoro islands had made a determined effort to reincorporate Mayotte, although its island situation would have worked to its advantage. But as it happens the continued French presence on Mayotte makes it difficult to the Republic of the Comoros to give effective vent to its dissatisfaction. And the continuation of even moral support from abroad for the Comoro Republic was interrupted by a coup which occurred in May 1978, as the new president (who had himself been overthrown three years earlier) was assisted in his comeback by white mercenaries. Such was the offence given by this aspect of the matter that even sympathy for the violation of Comoro's territorial integrity had to be put temporarily on one side, and for a while the geographically incomplete state was ostracized by the Organization of African Unity. These fences have now been mended but as of early 1985 Mayotte remains with France. The 1981 accession to power in France of a socialist government led to some talk there of a possible return of the embarrassing Mayotte to the Comoros – but as yet the words have not been supported by action.

This episode recalls one of ten years before, when in 1967 the tiny Caribbean island of Anguilla, with a population of 6,000, purported to secede from the new associated state of St Kitts-Nevis-Anguilla. At first the Anguillans did not want sovereignty. They just did not wish to be linked with St Kitts-Nevis, and therefore sought some kind of loosely dependent relationship, preferably with Britain. Their wish was granted and for two years British officials assisted the local administrators. But in February 1969 Anguilla proclaimed itself an independent republic, which resulted in Britain sending some paratroops and police to occupy the island – an event which was widely lampooned in the West and attacked in a more straight-forward way in the East. A light colonial-type rule was re-established, and continued – with doubtful legality – for six years. Then a new arrangement was agreed with the islanders by which they were to have a greater degree of independence from the still indignant St Kitts-Nevis than had been planned in 1967, but were not, formally speaking, to be entirely separated from it. However, time did not have an ameliorative effect on the attitude of Anguilla to St Kitts-Nevis, and so at the end of 1980 Britain accepted the inevitable and established Anguilla as a separate dependent territory. (The British Governor of St Kitts-Nevis, however, refused to sign local bills which did not include Anguilla in the title of the territory. He had to be dismissed.) Early in 1984 Anguilla's controversial chief minister, who had dominated its politics for two decades and was the leading spirit behind the 1969 unilateral declaration of independence, said that he did not expect the island to consider independence again for thirty to forty years.[26]

As is also the case with Mayotte, had Anguilla decided from the outset to opt for sovereignty it is perhaps just possible that she might have been able to pull it off. For although sovereign states generally frown on the break-up of one of their fellows they usually refuse to take note of a new factual situation only if it has an unpopular ideological aspect. This was no more present in respect of Anguilla than it was later in respect of Mayotte and Bangladesh. However, there were other factors militating against sovereignty for Anguilla, notably its size and considerable poverty. The situation was also complicated by the fact that it was part of a state – St Kitts-Nevis-Anguilla – which was not sovereign, or not clearly so:[27] it was one of the associated states which Britain had recently established in the Caribbean and for which she continued to bear international responsibility. Anguilla might have been able to deal with the hostility of St Kitts-Nevis, especially as there were others in the area who thought ill of its prime minister. But she was in no position to cope with Britain, even though at one stage she was able to force an under secretary of state from the Foreign and Commonwealth Office to make a most undignified exit.

Another secession from the same state loomed not long after it became sovereign in 1983. For the new constitution with which it was then equipped gave the 9,000-strong Nevis not only a considerable degree of autonomy but also the right to secede from 36,000-strong St Kitts on presentation of six months notice. This was Nevis's price for agreeing both to independence and to support the state's prime minister. In 1984 he called a snap election, and it was generally supposed that had he lost Nevis would have opted for sovereignty. But in the event the ruling party won an easy victory and so, at least for the time being, St Kitts-Nevis continues its hyphenated existence.

Yet 'another Anguilla' had been threatened some years before in the same island group – the Leeward Islands – when plans were made for the independence of the 75,000-strong Antigua. For to the north of the island of Antigua and administratively associated with it is the even tinier island of Barbuda, with a population of about 1,500. The Barbudans, who have long mistrusted the Antiguans and claim to have been neglected by them, refused to sign the constitutional accord providing for Antigua's independence and said that they wished to remain associated with Britain for the time being. As expected, Antigua objected and Britain refused to follow the Anguillan precedent. The whole territory became sovereign on 1 November 1981 and so far the incipient secession problem has been quiescent.

Colonial Struggles

As there has only been one case since 1945 of a sovereign state coming to birth through the contentious break-up of a metropolitan entity, and as that operation was clear-cut and relatively quick, no problems have arisen over the application to such situations of the criterion of constitutional independence. Nor has there been much more difficulty in respect of violent struggles for independence by colonial territories. The reasons for this are threefold. In the first place, colonial powers have generally been very ready to withdraw, so there have been relatively few cases of this nature. Second, where they have occurred and especially where they have appeared or continued since about 1960, some third parties have been more than willing to proclaim the existence of a new sovereign state at the earliest opportunity. For what has been at issue here has been the dismemberment not of metropolitan territory but of empires, and in these circumstances a number of states have had no inhibitions at all about doing what they could to hasten the process. They have held that the principle of non-intervention is inapplicable to imperial possessions, and by emphasizing the specific nature of this exception they have not given any easy hostages to fortune so far as their own well-being is concerned. This has not necessarily resulted in a lot of material help being given. Words are always cheaper than deeds. And the loudest statements of support for those still suffering under the colonial yoke were often made by those least able to supply the wherewithal for its overthrow. However, some physical help was sometimes forthcoming. Diplomatic support, too, in the shape of pressure on the colonialists or on those able to assist their adversaries, was sometimes brought to bear, occasionally with telling effect. And, where the struggle was taking place in territory which was adjacent to a sympathetic state, help of a passive but very important kind could be and often was given, in the shape of sanctuary and bases.

Another form of assistance given by sympathizers to insurgent groups within colonial territories was the recognition, where they existed, of their governments-in-exile. Clearly, such a move could have no direct bearing on the physical progress of the struggle, but it provided a not inconsiderable psychological boost for the insurgents and was a blow of comparable magnitude to the colonial power. It served notice that in the eyes of the states concerned the governmental body which they would look to as the official spokesman for the territory was no longer that of the colonial state or the one which it had established in its colony. Instead, the legitimate voice of the territory was deemed to be found abroad pending the day when the ejection of the colonialists would permit the exiled government to return. Whether this also made it possible to say that a new sovereign state had come into existence is questionable. But it certainly meant that some states, at least, would have no difficulty in perceiving such an event as soon as the government which they recognized was able to exercise effective authority over and from within the territory of which it now purported to be the head.

The third reason why states have not found it hard to see when a colonial struggle has given rise to a constitutionally independent entity is that in all these cases the course and ending of the conflict has not been such as to embarrass emotionally uninvolved third parties. That would have occurred if the struggle had gone overwhelmingly in favour of the rebels, with the colonial power just hanging on in some corners of its supposed possession, or if the colonial authority had been completely ousted but refused to recognize the new regime. In these circumstances there would have been much pressure on outsiders to take formal note of the new position, but to do so would have complicated their relations with the colonial power concerned.

As it happens, however, violent struggles in colonies have not developed into such unambiguous *de facto* situations. In most cases the fortunes of war did flow clearly in one direction but not to such an extent as to support the claim that to all intents and purposes the matter had been brought to a conclusion. Life was made very hard for the colonial powers, but their overthrow was also very difficult. And violence was eventually terminated not by the defeat of the colonial power but by the formal grant of sovereignty to the territories in question, cutting short conflicts which would otherwise have dragged on. This sequence of events made it easy for those states who were not politically associated with the rebels first to distance themselves and then, immediately after the victory of the anticolonialists, to acknowledge the existence of entities whose constitutional independence was not in doubt.

An early instance of this was the struggle for independence of the Dutch East Indies, which had been proclaimed as the Republic of Indonesia at the end of the Second World War. Because Japan had been in control of the East Indies during the war and had encouraged nationalist sentiment, the Dutch found that they started at a disadvantage in 1945 in that they had great difficulty in reasserting control over their colony. Correspondingly, the rebel Indonesian government was never geographically in exile, although the extent of the territory which it controlled varied a good deal during the late 1940s. The Indonesians also had the advantage of continuously receiving a measure of sympathy from most members of the United Nations, which was reflected in the various activities of the organization itself regarding Indonesia. That activity might be described overall as mediation in favour of Indonesia, although on the whole this bias was kept to a moderate level until a late date. But there was little doubt as to its presence, nor as to the fact that Indonesia, like Britain's possessions on the Indian subcontinent, was thought to be in a quite different category from the African territories of the colonial powers. Independence was therefore more or less in sight from the start, and after the Dutch had engaged in a militarily successful but politically disastrous action at the end of 1948 events moved quickly. The Netherlands cut her constitutional links with Indonesia as from 27 December 1949, and the way was now clear for others to take note of the existence of an unambiguously sovereign state.

At this time a colonial war was being fought in the Vietnamese part of the French territories which were collectively known as Indo-China. It had broken out shortly after the Japanese occupiers of Indo-China had been defeated in 1945, and continued until the disastrous French defeat at Dien Bien Phu in 1954. At the subsequent Geneva

Conference France formally withdrew from the area, and two new sovereign states – Cambodia and Laos – took their international bow. A third, however – Vietnam – was divided along the seventeenth parallel for what was said to be a two-year period, until its goverance could be settled by country-wide elections. The elections, however, did not take place and instead a new war developed in which the United States eventually became hugely involved. It was not until 1975 that Vietnam became united, under the regime which had first taken up arms against the French in 1946.

No sooner had France withdrawn from Vietnam than she found herself embarked on another eight-year war in an attempted defence of a colonial possession. This time the fighting was with nationalist forces in Algeria, and very bitter and destructive it was too. The situation was complicated by a substantial and politically important 'kith and kin' factor, one in ten of Algeria's population of about 10 million consisting of people of French descent or origin. Thus France did not feel free to grant independence, as she had done to Algeria's neighbours to east and west, Tunisia and Morocco, in 1956. This move, however, was of great value to the Algerian rebels. In the view of a *New York Times* correspondent, 'but for the aid and protection afforded it by Tunisia and Morocco, the rebellion would have been circumscribed and perhaps crushed before the end of 1957. But as the United States learned in Korea, it is singularly difficult to destroy an enemy enjoying the sanctuary of an inviolable frontier.'[28] It was Tunis which was chosen in 1958 as the seat of the new Algerian government-in-exile, which was soon recognized by the Arab states, China, and the countries of the Soviet bloc – but not by the Soviet Union itself, which did not wish to upset the new French President, de Gaulle, who was taking an agreeably independent stance *vis-à-vis* the United States. In 1960 a majority in the UN General Assembly supported Algeria's right to self-determination, and on 3 July 1962 President de Gaulle bowed to what was becoming inevitable and declared Algeria to be no longer a part of France. All those who had hoped for this event but had not felt able to have formal dealings with the government-in-exile were now in a position to recognize the presence internationally of a new sovereign state, as were those, relatively few, who had little sympathy with the Algerian cause.

The East Indies had been the Netherlands' only substantial colony. France had had huge possessions in Africa, most of which became sovereign without trouble in 1960. In the case of Algeria a distinction had been drawn on account of its ethnic link with France. The other colonial power which fought against independence movements was Portugal, but, by contrast with the other two, this reflected an inflexible ideological position which was applied equally to all its overseas territories. Portugal claimed that each of them was part of a unitary Portuguese state and could look forward to a racially integrated society which was to be reached through the civilizing influence of the Lisbon government. This argument received a frigid reception at the United Nations, which from 1960, in these matters, was very much the voice of the anticolonial movement. But to all its inquiries, denunciations and demands Portugal turned a resolutely deaf ear. Under the long dictatorship of President Salazar it was decreed that while others might be faint-hearted Portugal would remain true to her beliefs, no matter what unpopularity it might and did bring. Only with the fall of the regime in April 1974 did this policy change. Almost immediately, on 9 September, Portuguese Guinea became sovereign under the name of Guinea-Bissau; here the independence movement was both unified and had achieved much success. In the following year the independence of Mozambique was proclaimed on 25 June in the presence of the Portuguese Prime Minister. The road to Angolan sovereignty was harder because of the hostility between three independence groups, but by 22 February 1976 one of them had triumphed sufficiently in the field (with a good deal of aid from Cuba) to enable Portugal to acknowledge the existence of a sovereign Angola. In every case these events enabled the states which had hitherto continued to deal with Portugal as the legitimate authority in respect of Guinea, Mozambique and Angola to take note of the fact that the constitutional situation had undergone a fundamental change and that the former dependent territories were now, being sovereign, eligible to participate in international life.

The obverse of these situations is the loss of sovereignty by violence, by which is meant not the loss of some territory but the extinction of the state as a constitutionally independent entity. However, it is remarkable, in view of the reputation which international life popularly has for being red in tooth and claw, that since 1945 not a single established state, not even a tiny one, has involuntarily lost its sovereignty. Plenty of states have come under the influence of others, in varying and sometimes drastic degree. But none of them has been forcefully erased from the political map of the world. The most recent instance of such a happening took place in 1940 when the Baltic states of Latvia, Lithuania and Estonia, which had become sovereign after the First World War as a result of the collapse of Tsarist Russia and the defeat of Imperial Germany, were overrun by the Soviet Union. Thus they lost their relatively brief constitutional independence and became instead constituent republics of the Soviet federal state.

If action of this kind does take place there will be no objective difficulties over the application of the criterion for sovereignty. When one sovereign state is annexed by another (or partitioned), it has clearly lost its constitutional independence. Being now physically incorporated within one of its fellows, its constitutional arrangements too will be subject to those of the annexing state. It could be that other states who take exception to what has happened will refuse to accord it their formal recognition. If representatives of the former governing regime have established a government-in-exile, some states may even choose to deal with it on all matters regarding the territory of the once sovereign state. They could go further and cut off their own relations with the annexing state. But no such action does anything to alter the fact that a sovereign state has disappeared and is now being ruled and spoken for internationally by another. For political, moral, or ideological reasons others may close their eyes to this fact, but the fact remains.

In practice, unless the annexing state is already enormously unpopular and not of great significance, it is likely that third parties will come to accept what has happened, even if they refuse to give it their blessing. If the concepts of *de facto* and *de jure* recognition had not largely gone out of fashion, it is probable that they would be employed in this connection. Shortly after the end of the Second World War, for example, Britain recognized that the three Baltic states had *de facto* been absorbed into the Soviet Union, but this was not and has not yet been recognized *de jure*. Thus the one surviving diplomatic representative of these states in London is still afforded certain diplomatic courtesies. The witholding of *de jure* recognition also enables a state, if it wishes, to object to the presence in delegations from the annexing state of representatives from the once sovereign territory. But it goes little beyond that. To all intents and purposes *de facto* recognition of this kind of situation is a way of saying that one does not like it but accepts it as a fact of life.

Thus the test of constitutional independence is easy to apply in virtually all circumstances. At any one time it is generally possible to look round the world and identify without difficulty all the territorial entities which are in this condition. If a war is being fought it may be necessary to suspend judgement as to whether a sovereign state has appeared or disappeared. But it should be easy to decide this question once the conflict is over. And in respect of situations which are undergoing change by peaceful means it is unusual for any problem to arise. A day will have been appointed for a merger or a break-up and on that day the constitutional position will alter in a fundamental and significant way. Of course, some states may not want to take note of certain situations, in which case they will be unable to do business on a regular basis with the other states concerned. But that is another matter altogether from the question of which sovereign states exist and, being sovereign, are eligible to participate in international relations.

The ease with which this criterion for sovereignty can be applied to territorially based entities is a reflection of the simplicity of the test itself. All human institutions operate in the light of a constitution, and it is usually a straightforward matter to find out whether a particular constitution is subordinate to another or independent. If it is independent then the territory to which it applies is, in international terminology, sovereign, and hence of the sort which has the capacity to play a full and regular part on the international stage. This illustrates the great advantage of an absolute conception of sovereignty. It can, however, lead to the charge of formalism, to the suggestion that it results in an emphasis on attributes which are sometimes of little importance. But on close inspection this charge usually reveals itself as an illustration of the either/or fallacy. It implies that because constitutional independence is deemed to be important a state's other attributes, such as its size or its power, are unimportant. This, however, does not follow. There is no reason why importance should not be attached both to a state's formal standing in the eyes of its constitutional law and to its power. Nor, in principle, why both should not be thought to be unimportant – although in practice it is hard to see how a state's constitutional situation could fail to be of importance at least to itself. Nor is there any contradiction in saying that a state is both sovereign and generally subject to the will of another. Thus, to say that constitutional independence is the substance of sovereignty in no way means that account cannot also be taken of other and more material characteristics which a state might possess, or not possess, nor that the idea of an insignificant sovereign state is a contradiction in terms.

In any event, whatever this or that analyst may think of the use of the term sovereignty to mean constitutional independence, practice reveals that this is how states use it when they refer to that which makes them eligible to participate in international relations. And with good reason. For it is difficult to see how this purpose could possibly be served by anything other than a formal or absolute test, especially in a formal age such as the present. If there was, as one study has suggested, a problem as to 'the adequacy of independence and sovereignty which a territory must possess to be considered as a [sovereign] state'[29] the problem would indeed be huge, giving rise to endless argument and not just in the context in which the observation was made – that of very small territories. There would be enormous scope for controversy as to whether a particular state displayed, and continued to display, an adequate amount of whatever it was that was necessary for it to play an international part. As it is, however, the ground for any such controversy is removed by states universally working on the uncomplicated premiss that the territorial entities with which they may do business without procedural difficulty are those in a condition of constitutional independence.

All this is not to say that there are never problems over the application of this test in conditions other than those of international or secessionist war. But usually such problems arise on account of a lack of rigour in applying the test, which in turn is generally due to the issue being clouded by the intrusion of other conceptions of sovereignty. Such matters will be considered in Part Two.

Notes: Chapter 4

1 See further below, Chapter 5, pp. 104–9.
2 S. A. de Smith, *The New Commonwealth and its Constitutions* (London: Stevens, 1964), p. 45.
3 See *The Times*, 3 August 1978.
4 *The Times*, 7 November 1978.
5 Art. 72 of the French Constitution of 1958 declares that 'The territorial units of the Republic are Communes, Departments, and Overseas Territories'.
6 Although Britain may be held internationally responsible for what goes on there, which could be embarrassing; see above, Chapter 3, pp. 55–6.
7 See above, Chapter 2, p. 14.
8 *Canada Handbook*, 46th edn (Ottowa: Canadian Government, 1977), p. 170.
9 See *The Times*, 13 December 1974, 29 January 1975 and 30 January 1975.
10 L. Oppenheim, *International Law, Vol. 1, Peace*, 2nd edn (London: Longman, 1912), pp. 109 and 115. The terminology is exactly the same in the 8th edn (1955), ed. H. Lauterpacht.
11 D. P. O'Connell, *International Law*, Vol. 1 (London: Stevens, 1965), p. 345.
12 See Martin Bailey, *The Union of Tanganyika and Zanzibar. A Study of Political Integration* (Syracuse, NY: Syracuse University, 1973), ch. II.
13 See Joe Garner, *The Commonwealth Office* (London: Heinemann, 1978), p. 121.
14 K. C. Wheare, *The Constitutional Structure of the British Commonwealth* (Oxford: Clarendon, 1960), p. 12.
15 See below, Chapter 5, pp. 100–3.
16 See *The Times*, 31 March 1976.
17 See *The Times*, 16 November 1983.
18 See further below, Chapter 5, pp. 123–9.
19 *International Saudi Report*, vol. 2, no. 33 (17 May 1982).
20 See above, p. 66.
21 Werner J. Feld and Robert S. Jordan with Leon Hurewitz, *International Organizations* (New York: Praeger, 1983), p. 173.
22 See *The Times*, 4 April 1985.
23 *The Times*, 11 April 1985.
24 *The Times*, 26 October 1983.
25 Robert Whymart, *Guardian*, 30 July 1980.
26 *The Times*, 9 March 1984.

27 See below, Chapter 5, pp. 104–9.
28 Quoted in Alastair Horne, *A Savage War of Peace* (London: Macmillan, 1977), p. 130.
29 United Nations Institute for Training and Research, *Status and Problems of Very Small States and Territories* (New York: UNITAR, 1969), p. 135.

Part Two

Quandaries

5

Doubt

The situations where the application of the test of sovereignty may sometimes give rise to difficulty, in the sense of not immediately providing an unambiguous answer, fall into three categories. In the first place there are those cases where problems arise on account of the status of the territorial entities in question, in that they are out of the usual run of sovereign states but are also not obviously lacking in sovereignty. Second, there are problems which have to do with smallness of size, in that a good number of observers feel that if a territory's population falls below a certain, vaguely defined, level it can hardly be counted as a full or proper sovereign state. And, third, there are problems relating to authority, as the condition of some allegedly or possibly sovereign entities gives rise to the question, can it really be said that here is a sovereign state?

Formal Problems

The first set of complications may be subdivided into three, one having to do with states which are formally designated as protected states, another with those which are termed associated states, and a third with those states which, although apparently sovereign, are not, formally speaking, in full control of their own constitutions. What the states in all three subcategories have in common is that there is no uncertainty regarding the details of their constitutional position, nor about their international situation. Everyone knows what they may or may not do at the international level, and about the exact nature of their relationship with the sovereign state which gives protection or with which the entity concerned is associated or has a special constitutional link. What can give rise to doubt is whether the condition of such entities, seen overall, amounts to constitutional independence and, hence, whether they may be counted as sovereign. This question is purely theoretical, in that the answer has no bearing on how these states should behave or how other states should behave towards them. Nevertheless it is not for that reason wholly unimportant. For, quite apart from such merit which it may have as an academic tidying-up operation, the clarification of the position of such states in relation to the concept of sovereignty will in turn help to highlight the exact nature of the concept itself.

The precise arrangement which gives rise to the status of a protected state or protectorate (in international, but not British, terminology the two are synonymous) can vary from one case to another. But the essence of the situation is that in consequence of a treaty one state places itself under the general protection of another. This almost always involves giving the stronger state the right to control and conduct the foreign relations, including the defence, of the weaker state. The 'protection' so afforded is therefore not just or even, necessarily, at all a matter of what happens in practice. Rather it is the expression of a particular legal relationship – one which used to be not very uncommon. Tunisia and Morocco stood in this position *vis-à-vis* France for many years. For a brief while at the beginning of the century Korea was under the protection of Japan. And Britain made a number of such treaties, as the result of which Zanzibar, Bahrain, the Trucial States and Tonga, to name but some, were for a long time British protected states. Now the status of all these and also all the others has been changed. The egalitarian spirit of the age has choked over the formal inequality represented by a treaty of protection. Accordingly they have been terminated. There is, however, no reason in principle why such an arrangement should not be revived.

The question of whether a protected state is sovereign may profitably be approached through the distinction, peculiar to British practice, between such a territory and a protectorate. The latter is a territorial entity which, while not formally part of Her Majesty's Dominions, is treated as if it were. To all intents and purposes, therefore, a British protectorate is in the position of a colony. It may have had an independent constitution prior to its effective incorporation within the domain of the Crown, but subsequently it clearly does not. A protected state, by contrast, not only is constitutionally independent before it assumes that status – as is indicated by the fact that it becomes a protected state by way of an international treaty; it also persists in that condition thereafter, as the independence of its constitution is unaffected by the treaty of protection. It has not become part of a wider constitutional set-up but has just entered into a rather special treaty relationship with another state. From which it may be concluded that it remains a sovereign state – and a fully sovereign one at that, there being no half measures in this sphere. It has voluntarily chosen to restrict the exercise of its sovereign rights in a certain area, allowing another to act on its behalf.

But in respect of areas not covered by the treaty of protection it retains its complete freedom of action and, if appropriate, may make treaties on such matters. It may also be open to a protected state to exchange diplomats with other sovereign states, a practice which 'historically . . . has been a common occurrence'.[1]

This line of argument is by no means without support. In Britain the heads of protected states have always been afforded a full measure of immunity in respect of legal processes, in exactly the same manner as the heads of sovereign states which are not the beneficiaries of (or afflicted by) a treaty of protection. On a viceregal visit from India to the Persian Gulf in 1903, Lord Curzon told the sheikhs of the Trucial States that 'We have not seized or held your territory. We have not destroyed your independence but preserved it . . . The peace of these waters must still be maintained; your independence will continue to be upheld, and the influence of the British Government will remain supreme'.[2] Of course, in this context, a British spokesman is hardly the most reliable witness. But the International Court of Justice is on record as saying that 'Morocco, even under the Protectorate, has retained its personality as a State in international law . . . [It has] remained a sovereign state but it made an arrangement of a contractual character whereby France undertook to exercise certain sovereign powers in the name and on behalf of Morocco.'[3]

Many commentators, however, find it difficult to accept this conclusion. One writer says that while Morocco and Tunisia, when protected states, were subjects of international law, 'no one would assert that [they] were sovereign'.[4] The legal adviser to the State Council of Bahrain has referred to that country as only a 'quasi-sovereign' state, its full sovereignty having been 'partially suppressed for the duration of protection'.[5] And a leading textbook on international law speaks of protected states as 'half-sovereign'.[6] It is not hard to see how these views might be reached. They reflect a conception of sovereignty as an accumulation of sovereign rights, which can therefore be subdivided. But it is probable that they also reflect something else, as it is doubtful whether the renunciation of the exercise of any sovereign right would be regarded as chipping away part of a state's sovereignty. Thus in this particular type of case what is renounced is seen as having a special importance. The management of one's own international relations is clearly thought to lie close to the heart of sovereignty, so that a sovereign state which deprives itself of this function has engaged in a significant act of self-mutilation. It can no longer be unambiguously designated as one of the elect.

There is no reason at all why the test of sovereignty should not be the conduct by a state of its own international relations – although in that case it is not clear why a state which has asked another to look after all or the more important of its international concerns should even be called a half- or quasi-sovereign state. If it is not in full possession of that which amounts to sovereignty, it might seem appropriate simply to term it a non-sovereign state. There are, after all, many territorial entities which, as it were, dabble in international relations, having some international contacts on matters for which they are immediately responsible.[7] However, such a test says nothing about what makes a territorial entity eligible to participate fully in international life. Such participation is not haphazard, as there is an established criterion which is the basis of the most fundamental use, by states and commentators, of the term 'sovereignty'. In the light of that criterion of constitutional independence a protected state appears as sovereign, but one which, unusually, has chosen to let another speak and act for it at the international level. This is in no way improper. It would, it is true, look rather odd if a majority of sovereign states opted for protected status, as the whole object of identifying sovereign entities is to find out which territorial units have what is needed for playing a full and regular part on the international stage. But there is nothing in sovereignty which necessarily calls for a great deal of international activity. An internationally busy state is one which is sovereign, but it does not follow that a sovereign state is required to lead a busy or indeed any kind of external life. The status of a protected state is, therefore, not at all incompatible with the possession of sovereignty; indeed, protected states are sovereign states which have decided to accept the formal protection of one of their fellows, and they remain sovereign during the currency of the treaty of protection.

As the terms of treaties affording protection may vary a good deal, the mere existence of such a treaty is not necessarily an infallible pointer to the existence of a protected state of the sort which has just been discussed. The Himalayan states of Bhutan and Sikkim are contrasting cases in point, with the South Pacific state of Samoa having gone through a rather similar development to that of Bhutan. By a treaty of 1910 all Bhutan's foreign relations were placed under the supervision of the government of British India, which led some, but not other, observers to speak of it as a protected state. Two years after India's independence in 1947, Bhutan signed a treaty with India by which she agreed to be guided by India's advice in regard to her external relations. This suggested that Bhutan was a protected state, but subsequent developments pointed in the opposite direction. For in the 1960s Bhutan began to play a more independent role, and this culminated in her successful application to join the United Nations in 1971. Three years later a joint Indian-Bhutan announcement said merely that they would continue to maintain 'regular consultation and close co-ordination'[8] in their foreign policies, which is a very different situation from one country being guided by another. Clearly, whatever Bhutan's status may once have been, it is not now a protected state.

A roughly similar experience was undergone by Western Samoa, as it was then called. On attaining sovereignty in 1962, it signed a treaty of friendship with New Zealand whereby the latter agreed to defend Western Samoa and represent it overseas where and when necessary. For a number of years Western Samoa relied totally on New Zealand in external matters, and did not even become a formal member of the Commonwealth until 1970. But then it began to assert itself internationally, and entered the United Nations in 1976, where it identified itself as a Third World and non-aligned country. The new posture is perhaps reflected in the change of its name to plain Samoa.

Sikkim, on the other hand, was under such extensive British protection that there was some doubt as to whether its degree of autonomy was sufficient for it to be placed in the same category as other protected states. Its maharajah only rated a fifteen-gun salute under the British raj, whereas the heads of the more important princely states of India were accorded twenty-one guns, and he also sat in the Chamber of Princes in New Delhi, unlike the more independent King of Bhutan.[9] Thus it could be said of Sikkim that it had 'never acquired any international identity'.[10] After 1947 India assumed the British role, saying it was a 'regrettable necessity',[11] and by a treaty of 1950 bound Sikkim closer to her side. India assumed responsibility not only for Sikkim's foreign relations and defence (in connection with which she posted troops in the kingdom) but also for its communications and currency. Subsequently the ruler of Sikkim, spurred on, it is said, by his young American wife, assumed a more ambitious lifestyle and made it clear that he wished the trappings of authority to be accompanied by a greater degree of actual independence. This led, in 1973, to riots which, according to some reports, were inspired by India. They certainly had the consequence of establishing an even more intimate link between the two countries, as India restored order and appointed an administration. In the following year, in accordance with the wishes of its parliament, Sikkim became an 'associate' of the Indian union (with more autonomy than the other states of India). And in 1975 the office of ruler or Chogyal of Sikkim was abolished, and, again in response to the wishes of the representatives of its people, Sikkim became a state of the Indian union on the normal basis.

While, therefore, the evidence is neither clear in itself nor in its implications, it does seem at least open to doubt whether Sikkim, despite its treaty with India, had been a sovereign state since 1950. And certainly it has now disappeared from the map of sovereign entities. If it was sovereign immediately prior to its embrace by India, it has to be identified as one of the few sovereign states which have disappeared since the Second World War, although whether it extinguished itself voluntarily is much harder to say. Probably the majority of its people welcomed the change, being of Nepali origin and Hindu religion, and therefore distinguishable from the Tibetan minority from which the ruling house was drawn. But it also seems probable that without Indian pressure the change to majority rule would not have taken place. Possibly, therefore, Sikkim is a lone post-1945 case of a sovereign state being swallowed up by a neighbour, although it seems a doubtful conclusion on several grounds. What can be said with assurance, however, is that the brief episode of association with India through which Sikkim passed on its way to full union is quite unrelated to the concept of association now to be discussed.

An 'associated state' is for many practical purposes in exactly the same position as a protected state. The essence of this idea of association, which was introduced in the 1960s, is that while the foreign relations of the territory in question are the responsibility of the state with which it is associated its internal affairs are almost entirely in its own hands.[12] The only limitation on its internal freedom is the reservation by the stronger state of such legislative power and executive authority as is necessary for the discharge of its external obligations regarding the territory. In all this the situation of the typical protected and the typical associated state is virtually identical. In one other respect the associated state is in a more formidable position, in that it has the right to terminate the association unilaterally. The consequence of this would be that thereafter it would have complete control not only of its internal but also of its external affairs. There is no reason in principle why a protected state should not also be given this right, but in practice such arrangements have followed the general rule relating to the termination of treaties – that the only lawful way of bringing them to an end is through the agreement of all the parties.

However, it does not follow that an associated state is sovereign. The one argument in favour of it being so is that to all intents and purposes it has total control over its own constitution. It has power to alter any of its provisions, including any entrenched clauses. The only limitation on its power of amendment is the obvious one that it cannot change the details of the association relationship without the consent of the other party. It can end the association unilaterally, but not tinker with it. This points to one argument against the proposition that an associated state is sovereign – that such lesser constitutional changes are dependent on the agreement of another. But a more substantial argument is that the other party to the association is also able to bring the relationship to an end on its own account. Both sides have the right of unilateral termination, which means that the constitution of the associated state can be altered in a fundamental way by an outsider. This hardly amounts to constitutional independence. Moreover, there is no doubt that the typical associated state was not sovereign prior to the association arrangement. It was in some kind of colonial subordination, and while the new arrangement would only have been introduced following full discussion, none the less it would have become operative in respect of the associated state only by virtue of an act of the state with which it is associated. There is no question here of a treaty between equals, as in the case of a protected state. Rather it is a case of one, superior, country legislating for another. And that legislation does not provide for constitutional independence, even though it may open the way to it. Thus an associated state is not a sovereign state. It has an option on sovereignty, but while the association relationship subsists it is not in a sovereign condition.

The rather technical argument giving rise to this conclusion is reinforced by the circumstances which gave birth to the concept of association. It was in fact an attempt to adapt the idea of protection to those very small non-sovereign territories which were seeking greater independence but which seemed insufficiently strong to take a place on the international stage as sovereign states. The hope was that this new status would remove the stigma of colonialism while continuing to provide some of its more important benefits, making both parties happy and also satisfying the world at large, especially as manifested in the United Nations. The first experiment in association seemed to do so. The Cook Islands were a dependency of New Zealand, which had a population of about 20,000 on fifteen islands scattered over half a million square miles or so of the Pacific Ocean. In 1965 New Zealand won an immediate good mark by inviting the United Nations to watch over the electoral process which could lead to associated status, the first time the world organization had been allowed to supervise a colony's decision regarding its future. Association was chosen and the United Nations gave its blessing. Since then the Islands – where the crew of the Bounty started plotting mutiny in 1789 after Captain Bligh had ordered them to sail away – seem to have been very satisfied with their status, and have shown no real desire to opt for sovereignty. Nor is this a reflection of the absence of democracy. In 1978 a brisk election campaign was fought between the leader of the party which had been in power since 1965 and its rival led by the grandson of a Welsh sea captain and a Polynesian princess. He had had a brilliant medical career in the United States – but appeared to be less successful at politics, for the party in power came out on top. However, this was later adjudged to have been due to malpractice, government money (derived from the sale of postage stamps) having been used on a large scale to bring supporters home from New Zealand to vote. In consequence of this ruling, certain seats changed hands, the government was brought down, and the Polynesian Celt took office as Prime Minister. Later he fell from power, but regained office in 1983.

This experiment in association was extended in 1974 to the tiny New Zealand dependency of Niue, which, with a population of about 4,000, is geographically part of the Cook Islands but administered separately. The only other area where associated status has been tried has proved less hospitable: the British West Indies. Britain's original idea here had been to bring almost all her possessions to independence as a single sovereign state but the colonial federation which she had established was dissolved in 1962 on the very day on which it had been destined for sovereignty, Jamaica and Trinidad deciding to go it alone. Britain tried again, but negotiations for a federation among the 'little eight' collapsed with the decision of Barbados to opt for independence. Now there were seven. In 1965 associated status was proposed for six of these: Antigua, Dominica, Grenada, St Kitts-Nevis-Anguilla, St Lucia, and St Vincent and the Grenadines. Two years later it was implemented for the first five of these territories, the sixth being excluded for two years on account of the alleged irresponsibility of its regime. However, the United Nations refused to accept that they had been properly decolonized, to Britain's considerable chagrin. Moreover, Britain was becoming more mindful of the problems of associated status – of which she had been warned by experienced colonial administrators in the mid-1960s but to which she had then paid no heed. Now, however, she realized that if she tried to exercise her right to intervene on the ground that internal developments jeopardized the proper fulfilment of her external responsibilities she would face a hostile reception, both locally and at large. And in the West Indies the prospect of the need for such an intervention could not be regarded as wholly hypothetical.

Accordingly, associated status in its original form has not been tried elsewhere and in the West Indies it has come to an end, local politicians developing a thirst for sovereignty partly on account of association having turned sour. By the close of 1983 all the former associated states had opted for independence, although one part of one of them – Anguilla[13] – had returned to the colonial fold. From one angle the West Indian story is symptomatic of the current view that even for the smallest territories nothing less than sovereignty is acceptable. No matter how great their impoverishment or how poor their prospects, territories feel – and there is a good deal of external pressure encouraging that feeling – that the only proper position is one which puts them on a formal par with the great majority of the territorial units into which the world is divided. In face of this movement, one wonders how long the Cook Islands, at least, will feel able to remain in a status which from one perspective can be seen as the last spasm of the spirit of colonialism.[13a]

A few attempts are still being made, however, to square the circle. Several of them concern the Trust Territory of the Pacific Islands – about one hundred islands and island groups scattered over an ocean area of about the size of the United States, but with a small land area which contains only about 100,000 people. At the end of the Second World War they were taken from Japan by the United States but administered in accordance with a trusteeship agreement which the United States signed with the United Nations. Subsequently the United States divided them into four areas: the Northern Marianas to the north, the Marshall Islands to the east, the Federated States of Micronesia (the former Caroline Islands) to the south, and Palau to the south-west. In 1975 the Northern Marianas elected to become a commonwealth of the United States, a status which, as in the case of Puerto Rico, in the Caribbean, combines many of the advantages of self-government with the benefit of American citizenship. Negotiations about the future of the other three areas (which had long been in train) continued, and in the early 1980s resulted in all of them signing a compact of free association with the United States.

Like the earlier experiments in association, these agreements provide for complete internal self-government and also state that the arrangement may be ended either by mutual consent or by the unilateral action of either signatory. They also provide for the United States to have authority for security and defence matters. However, they differ from the previous association arrangements in that these associated states are to be given the right to conduct their own external affairs and, no doubt, partly for this reason, it is said that they will be sovereign. For the reasons which have been given above, it may be doubted whether they do in fact satisfy the criteria on which the international society has hitherto been working. And there will certainly be some well publicized argument about the matter, for the United States is now finding itself hoist with its own forty-year-old petard. For at the end of the Second World War, on the insistence of American service chiefs and with a view to getting a firm American hold on the Pacific Islands, a special category of trust territory was established by the United Nations Charter to cater for what were called strategic areas. The trusteeship agreements regarding such areas were to be supervised not by the UN Trusteeship Council but by the Security Council, where decisions are subject to the hazard of a veto from any of the council's permanent members. As it happened, only one trust territory was designated as a strategic area – the Pacific Islands – and the United States was, of course, the trustee.

This scheme has so far worked very well for the United States, but now she is running into a problem. In 1983 all three areas of the Trust Territory of the Pacific Islands voted in UN-observed plebiscites in favour of the compacts of free association. But even before the plebiscite was held in the Marshall Islands the Soviet Union had entered the lists. It charged that the United States was aiming at the 'dismemberment and de facto annexation of the islands', that it wanted to turn them 'for ever into [its] colonial appendage'; that the status being 'foisted' on them was 'nothing but an unlawful attempt to decide the fate of people by methods which are characteristic of the worst times of colonial pillage'; and that the United States was 'employing the most refined methods of diktat and blackmail' to frustrate the 'inalienable right' of the islanders to 'their self-determination'.[14] Clearly much more will be heard along these lines when the United States comes to the Security Council seeking its consent to the termination of her trusteeship agreement regarding the islands. It seems unlikely, therefore, that, formally speaking, the islands will reach associated status. In this way the Soviet Union may do many other states a service by relieving them of the necessity of having to decide whether to accept the doubtful American claim that its type of associated statehood also creates a sovereign state.

The one other attempt to revive the concept of associated statehood concerns the French overseas territory of New Caledonia, which lies about one thousand miles to the east of Australia. Of the population of 145,000 slightly less than half are indigenous Kanaks, being outnumbered by French settlers, Polynesians, and other groups. Towards the end of 1984 militant pro-independence Kanaks began to engage in violence. This led, early in 1985, to the proposal by a special governmental envoy from Paris that New Caledonia should become 'independent' as from January 1986 – but under a contract of association with France by which the latter would retain responsibility for the territory's external defence and internal security. The capital, Noumea, where most of the whites live, would have a special self-governing status in the form of a long-term lease from the territory's government to a special mixed committee. It was further proposed that this arrangement should last for a 'lengthy but limited period of perhaps five or ten years'.[15] Altogether it amounts to a package which seems to promise something less than sovereignty.

Even this, however, was thought to be probably too much for a majority of the population, who seemed to have no wish to weaken, let alone cut, any of the territory's existing links with France. Accordingly, while accepting its envoy's scheme, the French government tried to avoid a rebuff by postponing a New Caledonian referendum on it until not later than the end of 1987. By then a general election will have been held in France, so that the nub of the problem will not only have been postponed but may also have to be dealt with by a quite different government.

Undoubtedly, however, the concept of association is much more in accord with contemporary orthodoxy than that of protection. It may, therefore, reappear in connection with plans for the future of the handful of tiny colonies which remain scattered about the globe. The term may also conceivably be used by those who are trying to sell secession to their people and their constitutional superior, in an attempt to obscure the extent of the break which the achievement of sovereignty would entail. One instance of this is the referendum held in the Canadian province of Quebec in 1980, in which the electorate was asked by its provincial government to express a view on the idea of 'sovereignty–association' for Quebec. From material issued by the Quebec government it is clear that they wished the province to break away from Canada to become a sovereign state, constitutionally independent and therefore in control of taxation, communications, cultural affairs, foreign relations, and so on. The possibility of separate Quebec armed forces was envisaged, as was participation in the North Atlantic Treaty Organization as a full member. In this way the government intended that the people of Quebec would be able to express their own distinct identity. The 'association' side of the proposed status referred to co-operation with Canada in appropriate areas, not excluding defence, and certainly including a number of key economic issues, so that both states could continue to benefit from the existing integration of their economies. It would be 'a union not unlike the European Common Market'.[16] However, all this meant that it would have been a co-operative arrangement between two sovereign states, and therefore fundamentally different from the kind of associated status which has been chiefly discussed in the preceding pages. (It should also be made clear that the present discussion has nothing to do with the situation which results from a sovereign state having associated status within European Communities, of which there are now more than sixty cases.) As it happened, however, the people of Quebec rejected the idea, the 'no' vote attaining a majority, albeit a narrow one, even among French-speaking Quebeckers. Accordingly, the Government of Canada, which was strongly opposed to the idea, did not have to consider it in a formal way. Nor does it look as though it will be troubled by the matter in the immediate future. For by 1985 the ruling party in Quebec, which had led the campaign for an independent state, had decided that it was in its electoral interest to shelve the issue.

The third subcategory of states that can give rise to formal doubts regarding their sovereignty consists of those which, although to all appearances sovereign, none the less do not seem fully to meet the test of constitutional independence. The reason for this is that all or part of their constitutions can be amended by a foreign state. It is arguable that in principle this is true of all former British possessions, as their independence and their constitutions stem from Acts of the British Parliament or Orders of the British Privy Council. In British constitutional practice any Act or Order, whatever it says to the contrary, can be superseded by a later Act or Order and therefore, in theory, Britain could revoke the independence of a former colony, or legislate for it. But, as has been observed by a former Lord Chancellor, any such argument 'is theory and has no relation to realities'.[17] And there is no doubt how the courts of the state to which any such legislation was addressed would react. They would take the line that a grant of independence cannot be unilaterally withdrawn.

However, until recently, part of the constitutions of two Commonwealth countries could only be amended by an Act of the British Parliament. One is Australia. Its constitution, which is contained in a schedule to a British Act of 1900, makes no provision for the amendment of its first eight sections, which deal with the establishment of the Australian federation. In consequence, it would only be possible for the federation to be legally abolished if an Act to this effect were passed by the British Parliament. In 1985 it was agreed that this anomaly should be ended. The other state which used to be in this kind of position is Canada. Its constitution, too, was contained in an Act of the British Parliament, the British North America Act of 1867, and it contained no provision at all for amendment. All amendments had therefore to be made through British legislation, although such Acts were always passed at the request of both Houses of the Dominion Parliament, with individual provinces generally being consulted as a matter of courtesy when the proposed legislation affected their particular rights. In 1949 this situation was changed, Britain giving Canada (at its request) the right to amend its own constitution, except on certain matters which chiefly had to do with the exclusive powers of the provincial legislatures and the use of the English and French languages. Finally, in 1981, the Canadian Parliament and nine of the ten provinces (Quebec being the exception) agreed on an amending formula to cover these matters and also on a charter of rights. The package was presented to the Westminster Parliament, passed, and then proclaimed in Ottawa by the Queen of Canada on 17 April 1982. At last Canada had custody of its own constitution.

Strictly speaking, therefore, it might appear that until 1982 the constitution of Canada was not fully independent and that, accordingly, Canada was lacking in sovereignty, with Australia still in that condition. But this would be an unreal conclusion. The limitations on the power of these two states to amend their constitutions were and are purely nominal. The British Parliament would always respond speedily and positively to a request made in the proper form – and if it did not it would be quickly ignored. In these matters Britain is no more than a cipher. It is, therefore, not even necessary here to resort to the argument that Canada and Australia were the exceptions which prove the rule. The reality of the constitutional situation is that both these countries had control over their own constitutions. It just happened that, for one reason or another, the mechanism for amendment had in certain circumstances to involve recourse to an extraterritorial agency. However, both countries had the whole operation effectively in their own hands. They were, therefore, constitutionally independent and, from an international point of view, sovereign – no less so than any other sovereign state.

Small States

The second group of territories about the sovereignty of which some observers are doubtful consists of those with very small populations – and it often happens that such entities are also very small in terms of area. 'Mini-states' or 'micro-states' is the phrase which, nowadays, is generally used to refer to them. A study which was published in 1969[18] listed ninety-six entities with a population of 1 million or less, smaller, that is, than Birmingham or Glasgow. Of these, three-quarters were less than 20,000 square kilometres in extent, which is about the size of Wales. About half of the ninety-six were eligible for sovereign status in the sense that they were then neither sovereign nor in some other condition which made a progression to sovereignty unlikely, such as being integrated with a metropolitan state. And during the following fifteen years more than half of those which were so eligible lost their subordinate status, most of them becoming, allegedly at least, separate sovereign states.

This, however, is precisely the sort of development which in some arouses feelings of annoyance, despair, or disbelief. As early as 1954, at the fifth unofficial Commonwealth Relations Conference held at

Lahore, 'a United Kingdom delegate thought that a prospective [Commonwealth] Member needed to have a firmly established parliamentary system and sufficient size and resources to support the responsibilities of a sovereign state: "bogus nations" were not wanted within the Commonwealth community'.[19] Ten years later it was suggested that independence 'is an extravagant and improvident recipe for the remaining small territories'.[20] But none the less states continued to appear which 'existed only by virtue of the movement of decolonization to its illogical conclusion',[21] and did not 'match the level of capabilities traditionally attributed to states in the century and a half after the Congress of Vienna'.[22] How many UN members, asked a veteran of the League of Nations, are 'really sovereign'? He answered his own question: 'few of the small ones can be counted as such'.[23] That, it should be noted, was a comment made when the United Nations was less than half its present size. And before the 1960s were out a leading scholar was observing that the world was made up of 'so-called sovereign nations, most of which are not even able to take care of their internal affairs'.[24]

To the extent, however, that this kind of comment implies that very small states are not or cannot be sovereign, it is in error. As has already been argued,[25] there is no reason in principle why the tiniest territorial unit should not exist in a condition of constitutional independence, and hence be eligible to participate in international relations. The acquisition of sovereignty in 1978 by the diminutive island state of Tuvalu is a case in point. In Europe the land-locked state of San Marino in the northern part of the Italian peninsula traces its history back to the fourth century, and is but one of a small handful of European mini-states. It has a population of only about 20,000, but this has not deterred it from sometimes acting in a manner which has displeased the 50-million-strong state by which it is surrounded.

Even smaller sovereign entities are conceivable. The phosphate-rich Pacific island of Nauru, with a population of about 6,000, has been independent since 1968. In principle, the same path could be trodden by Christmas Island, population 3,000, in the Indian Ocean; Norfolk Island in the south-west Pacific, which is less than half as populous; and even by Pitcairn Island in the South Pacific, the population of which does not quite reach three figures. Viewed in a lengthy historical perspective, this kind of development might seem less strange than it sometimes does. For, 'immediately before the French Revolution, Europe swarmed with diminutive states'.[26] And in those days it was also 'considered quite normal to let small and insignificant states participate in world conferences' such as the Congress of Vienna of 1814–15, where 'innumerable minor powers were represented, including scores of independent German and

Italian mini-states'.[27] However, there is no need for very small states to be active in international relations to any considerable degree, and, clearly, the limited extent of their interests and the relatively high costs of involvement together suggest that they are unlikely to seek a prominent international role. Moreover, it is possible for their essential concerns to be looked after in a manner which is partially or wholly indirect. Monaco, for example, which is on the Mediterranean but is otherwise surrounded by France, is by treaty under the latter's general protection, a situation which does not make her a protected state in the usual sense of the word as she still conducts her own foreign relations. And when Western Samoa became independent in 1962 it was agreed that New Zealand, her former superior, would, when asked, act for her on an agency basis – which is what Switzerland does for Liechtenstein.

Western Samoa joined a few international organizations which were of special interest to her. But she did not apply for membership of the United Nations, which brought approving comments from a number of quarters. Later, however, she changed her policy in this respect and joined in 1976 under the name of Samoa. With a population of about 130,000 she was not the smallest member, but none the less this highlighted the aspect of the mini-state question that had particularly troubled a number of observers since the 1960s. With all members represented in the General Assembly, and each member having just one vote, there was much apprehension about the effect which the rapid advance of decolonization might have on the Assembly's shape and behaviour. The prospect of a large increase in the number of very small members, all making a minimal contribution to the budget, brought with it a picture, if not a spectre, of a body which would increasingly combine unmanageability with irresponsibility. The only remedy seemed to be the imposition of admission requirements which would have the effect of restricting entry, or entry as full members, to those who were adjudged capable of behaving in a proper manner, or, in less offensive terms, of discharging in an adequate way their obligations as United Nations members.

But of course this was a nettle which no one wanted to grasp. In the Security Council the representative of the United States did go so far as to observe that the principle of the sovereign equality of members was both valid and necessary, but that it would remain valid only as long as it was not carried 'to an ultimate extreme'.[28] However, a committee of experts which was appointed to study the problem failed to come to any agreement, and the matter was allowed to lapse.[29] By the end of 1984, with the United Nations continuing to admit virtually all qualified comers, membership had risen to 159, more than three times the original membership, with the most recent arrival having a population of about 200,000, and the most recent but one of about 45,000. It is arguable that this development has not had the dire effect on the organization that many predicted, and also that such predictions might have been thought at the time they were made to be somewhat exaggerated. Be that as it may, two points deserve notice.

The first is that, in so far as there is a problem here for the United Nations, it is basically one of political will. If the organization wished to put a stop to the admission of mini-states it could do so, and could have done so at any time. An applicant can be rejected by the negative vote of any one of the five permanent members of the Security Council, or of one-third of those present and voting in the General Assembly. It would not be too hard for such negatively voting states to justify their action by reference to that part of the United Nations Charter which says that membership is open to states which, in the judgement of the organization, are able and willing to carry out the obligations of membership. And in any event there is no shortage of precedents for membership in the United Nations being dealt with on entirely political grounds. The League of Nations certainly took a clear line on this matter at the outset of its life, refusing admission to Liechtenstein in 1920. The stated reason was that she had passed over some of the attributes of sovereignty to another state and would therefore be unable to discharge all the obligations of League membership, but one student has suggested that it was really on account of her smallness.[30] This decision led to Monaco withdrawing her application and to San Marino bringing her preliminary inquiries to an end. In principle there is no reason why the United Nations should not have followed suit, or even do so now at this late hour. Although, with so many small states already in the organization, and with members generally being anxious not to give offence against the egalitarianism of the times, it is not hard to see why nothing has so far been done and why any such action is most unlikely.

The second and, from the perspective of this study, the more important point is that the decisions which the United Nations or other international bodies take about mini-states really have nothing to do with the question of their sovereignty. Some may feel that certain small states should not have been given sovereignty, but any dispute along those lines is now of historical interest only. The fact of the matter is that constitutional independence has been accorded, making the states concerned eligible to move on to the international stage. It may be felt that to refuse admission to the United Nations will cast doubt on that eligibility, for, in a rather undefined way, admission is now fairly widely seen as a form of confirmation of a state's sovereignty. But this is woolly thinking. Membership in the United Nations is indeed a sign that one is sovereign, but the reason for this is that it is (in principle) open only to sovereign states. Thus sovereignty is what a territorial entity needs to make a meaningful application for admission. But the consideration of applications is conducted in the light of quite different criteria, and it is not at all to be assumed that a refusal says anything about one's sovereignty. As the League of Nations committee which dealt with admissions said in 1920, 'there can be no doubt that juridically the Principality of Liechtenstein is a sovereign State'.[31] Equally, by admitting states not much larger than Liechtenstein, the United Nations has shown that it has no doubts about the sovereignty of such tiny territorial entities.

This line of argument has not gone unchallenged. One writer says that the League of Nations' observation about Liechtenstein's sovereignty is 'legal reasoning of the most unfruitful kind'. She adds: 'It is more in conformity with the facts to come to the conclusion that sovereignty is a relative concept; and that while [diminutive] states may possess its attributes for limited participation in world events, they do not possess it for comprehensive participation.'[32] If sovereignty is seen as a bundle of attributes, this conclusion could follow. But when states use the term to refer to that which makes them eligible to participate in international relations they are referring to the constitutional condition in which they exist – something which is possessed as a whole or not at all. Accordingly, there can be no question of a sovereign state only being qualified to participate internationally in a limited way. This is quite compatible with saying that some such states may, on account of their interests, desires, finances, or expertise, follow a very restricted international life. And that others may also not play much of an international part on account of some of their fellow sovereign states choosing to have little to do with them, perhaps preventing their entry to some international organizations. But all this has no bearing on the sovereignty of the states concerned. For 'sovereignty in international usage, like the degree of doctor in university usage, is a label which covers wide differences of capacity'.[32a] Some constitutionally independent entities may be tiny, insignificant, or obscure. But this has no effect whatsoever on the fact that these states are sovereign – as little and as much so as the biggest states in the world.

Problems of Authority

The third set of states about whose sovereignty a question mark may sometimes be raised are those in which there is substantial doubt about the extent or effectiveness of their internal authority – so much so that it can be seriously asked whether it still makes sense to speak of the continued existence of single sovereign states. This group falls into three subcategories. In the first place there is the theoretical possibility that a group of sovereign states may co-operate with each other to such an extent, channelling that co-operation through increasingly important institutions, that at some point a real question arises as to whether the many have become one. The situation envisaged here is unclear because it does not involve the signing of a formal document announcing the inauguration of a new sovereign state. There is no constitutional convention from which a changed state of affairs can be conveniently and accurately dated. Instead it is a matter of trying to decide whether the interweaving of policies and the operation of common institutional structures has extinguished the constitutional independence of a number of formerly separate entities and brought a larger sovereign state into being. The taking of such a decision will rest not only with third parties to the changing situation, with academic analysts playing the role of a chorus, but also with the co-operating states themselves. For in this kind of case the possibly vanishing states will be well able to speak for themselves and will have ample opportunities to do so.

The second subcategory consists of those states which appear to be breaking up into fairly clearly defined parts. If such a process is taken through to an actual break-up, the result is clear for all to see and respond to. But prior to that point complications may arise. It may be that the state concerned is geographically divided by land or water, and that the part which does not contain the headquarters of the central government is very much going its own way, albeit without, maybe, formally declaring its secession. Or a federal state may be very loose, with its several parts seeming to be more important and powerful than the theoretical whole. Or rebels may be in control of substantial areas of a state's territory. In all these circumstances the central government will almost certainly continue to claim that it speaks for a united state. But, if it is manifestly unable to exert its authority throughout the land, doubt will in time arise in the minds of third parties as to whether formal note should be taken of the emergence of one or more new sovereign entities.

The final subcategory is a variant on the second, consisting of states which, while theoretically subsisting, have in reality collapsed or appear to be on the brink of doing so. The breakdown of the institutions and assumptions of government will at least have produced something approaching chaos, and while a formal governmental voice may still be heard it will be almost wholly without effect in any quarter. Faced with this situation, outsiders, both official and non-official, can hardly fail to ask themselves whether there is any point in continuing to act on a basis which now seems to be without substance. However, they may find that the position is, for them, more complicated than it appears, in that abandoning what is little more than a pretence may open up a far more alarming prospect than continuing to connive at an unreality.

There is only one instance of the first type of development, and it has not yet progressed to the point at which there is any real question as to the continued sovereignty, in the sense of constitutional independence, of the participating states. It is that of the close institutional co-operation which has developed in Western Europe since the early 1950s, and which has given rise to what is now generally called the European Community. This consists of three separate arrangements. In 1951 the original six states – France, West Germany, Italy, Belgium, the Netherlands and Luxembourg – signed the European Coal and Steel Community Treaty. Six years later, after the still-birth of the European Defence Community, they moved further ahead on the economic front, signing the European Economic Community Treaty and the European Atomic Energy Community Treaty. In 1973 the six were joined by three new members, Britain, Denmark, and Ireland; a potential tenth, Norway, decided at a late hour not to take this step. In 1981 Greece did make the number of members up to ten – with Spain and Portugal poised to take the membership up to twelve in 1986. In the earlier days of the Community it was often described as supranational, a term which appeared in the Coal and Steel Community Treaty. However, it was deliberately omitted from the two later treaties, not because they were in a different vein from the earlier ones but because of some political reservations about the idea. And the practice of the Community over the last twenty-five years, while it has become highly complex and quite far-reaching, is generally thought to have been marked by a decline in its supranational elements. As it is this aspect of the Community which might pose a threat to the sovereignty of its individual members, the potential effect of supranational institutions on state sovereignty has in recent years become much less of a live issue.

None the less, it remains an important theoretical question and could yet have significant practical implications. However, especially in view of the way in which the Community has developed, it is perhaps more conveniently considered in detail as an aspect of the jurisdictional concept of sovereignty.[33] Accordingly, no more will be said at this point about supranational institutions, except to emphasize one thing. That is that the general point which has been made regarding the failure of the European Community to undermine or erase the sovereignty of its members relates only to the use of the term 'sovereignty' in the sense of constitutional independence. There is no doubt that adherence to the Community brings with it legal obligations of a substantial kind. It also brings rights and opportunities, but it remains that by joining the Community a state becomes far less legally free than it was before. If, therefore, as is often the case – and not least in the West European context – the term 'sovereignty' is used synonomously with legal freedom, it is certainly true to say that membership diminishes one's sovereignty. It is also true to say that in a more general way membership involves a state in a process which, short of departure, puts certain political limits on the lengths to which it may go in the almost continuous negotiations which are such a prominent feature of the Community. This, too, is sometimes described as a limitation on sovereignty. But neither in theory nor in practice does either of these limitations necessarily affect a state's constitutional independence, and the European Community has certainly not had such an effect so far. It is in this last sense of the term 'sovereignty', therefore, and no other, that the assertion is made that the members of the Community are still sovereign states. Whether or not they may have set out on a slippery slope which will bring them to a sovereignty-less condition is something which will be considered later. But so far, at least, they remain constitutionally separate one from another, co-operating intimately in certain respects, but each maintaining its own identity and its own role on the international stage.

The second subgroup, consisting of states which, *de facto*, have split into two or more parts, provides more illustrations than the first, although such an occurrence is not always clear-cut. One possible instance of it concerns Tanzania, where the former sovereign state of Zanzibar, separated from the mainland by the Zanzibar and Pemba channels, has often seemed to be going its own way during the twenty years of the state's existence. There has been no declaration of independence (not, at least, as yet), but the writ of the central government based in Dar-es-Salaam has frequently seemed rather flimsy in the offshore islands.

Similarly, in the United Arab Emirates the individual emirates have often seemed more weighty than the sovereign state in which, purportedly, they are united. But here too the single state, as of early 1985, continues to subsist. In these circumstances there is no formal problem for third parties. They may well, in their dealings with the states concerned, take account of the internal situation. Thus they may decide not to enter into arrangements which the divided state might have difficulty in honouring, or which might put their nationals beyond the protection of the divided state's central government. But for all outward purposes they will almost certainly continue to work on the assumption that there is only one state in the territory concerned, and that the government of the state is the only one which is entitled to speak for that territory in relation to the rest of the world.

The situation could be somewhat more difficult for outsiders where rebel groups are clearly in control of substantial parts of a sovereign state. Here a distinction needs to be drawn between a group which is trying to take over the government of the whole country and one which is attempting to divide the country – to secede. The situation in Angola since its attainment of sovereignty in 1976 is one instance of the former situation, and is of the sort which can cause problems for third parties. However, disputes over who is to speak officially for an existing sovereign state are not germane to the present stage of this inquiry, which concerns the problems which can arise where a group is able to make something of a case in support of its claim to have broken away from an accepted entity and set up as a sovereign territory on its own. The best example of this since 1945 is that of the Eastern Region of Nigeria which attempted to establish itself as the sovereign state of Biafra during the civil war of the late 1960s, and went some way towards doing so. A rather similar case is that of East Pakistan from its announcement of secession in March 1971 to its successful emergence as Bangladesh at the end of that year. Another is the province of Katanga, which declared itself independent of the Congo (the former Belgian Congo, now known as Zaire) in July 1960 and maintained a more or less autonomous existence until it was, in effect, suppressed by the United Nations Force in the Congo in January 1963. And in Cyprus the government has not been in control of the northern third of the state since Turkey's invasion of 1974. A Turkish Federated State of Cyprus was declared there in 1975, which, despite its name, did not claim to be a sovereign state but only an autonomous administration. In November 1983 it was replaced by the Turkish Republic of Northern Cyprus, which does purport to be sovereign.

In all these instances there was for a while more than one authority claiming ultimate power within the boundaries of what were, supposedly, single sovereign states, and this is still the case in Cyprus. In one case, that of East Pakistan, a violent civil war was raging throughout the relatively brief period of its disputed independence, and was not brought to a conclusive end until the intervention of the armed forces of India. Here, therefore, there was hardly any opportunity for outsiders to decide whether they should accept the allegedly new state as one of themselves. Katanga was incomparably more peaceful and had a government which ruled effectively over people who inhabited a clearly defined territory. Moreover, the central government, sitting in what was then known as Leopoldville (now Kinshasa), was in no position to resist its claims to constitutional independence. Thus Katanga presented a fair representation of a state governing itself on its own constitutional assumptions and largely untroubled by the constitutional claims of the central government. Yet not a single sovereign state took official note of Katanga's existence. Belgium, the former metropole, was for a while very sympathetically inclined, but even she refused to take this step. And likewise in Cyprus no state except Turkey had anything to do with the Turkish Federated State. The same fate is likely to befall the new Turkish Republic of Northern Cyprus. The day after its declaration of independence its recognition was announced by Bangladesh. But then, doubtless following representations from third parties, Bangladesh declared that its recognition was provisional, and would have to be ratified. Nothing more was heard about it. Thus only Turkey has recognized, and exchanged ambassadors with, Northern Cyprus. At a less formal level, however, this little Muslim state is by no means without friends, as is shown by the very sympathetic reception given to its president by thirty-nine co-religionist states at a summit meeting of the Islamic Conference Organization in January 1984.

The immediate reasons for this cold-shouldering are not hard to find. The events in Cyprus are seen as a thinly disguised annexation by Turkey, which offends one of the fundamental norms of the international society. Additionally Cyprus is a member of the Non-Aligned Movement, which helps her a lot (in diplomatic terms), whereas Turkey, albeit Muslim, is a member of NATO, which does her cause little good in the wider world. In Katanga the rebel government had what might have been thought of as the advantage of being undeniably black. But as against that it was very widely seen, and correctly so, as having close links with external groups of a kind which put it doubly beyond the pale. First there was Belgium, the ex-colonial overlord, which was regarded as trying to control the richest part of the Congo through the country's back door. Here, then, was the spectre of neo-imperialism. And, second, Katanga was receiving assistance from the agents of capitalism. For its considerable mineral wealth was being mined by the Brussels-based company Union Minière, with which the Katangan government had cordial relations. It is not surprising, therefore, that no state would extend even a chilly formal hand towards Katanga. In the case of Biafra, by contrast, none of these obstacles were present. The rebel government controlled a sizeable portion of Nigeria and did so for a lengthy period of time. It clearly had wide popular support in the Eastern Region and at first acquitted itself successfully in battle. It was, it is true, receiving some material support from outside, but so was the Nigerian government. There was ample ground, therefore, for third parties to acknowledge, maybe provisionally, that here was a sovereign entity. Yet only five states, four of them African and all doing so at a relatively late stage, took formal note of the *de facto* division of Nigeria.

The shunning of Biafra is indicative of a response which nowadays is fairly general amongst sovereign states when they are faced with the division of one of their fellows. It was also at work in respect of Katanga and Northern Cyprus, and would almost certainly have had a big influence on attitudes to East Pakistan had its revolt taken a longer course. It reflects the fact that states are very reluctant to do anything which might seem to encourage the involuntary disintegration of one of their own kind. If a state breaks up amicably, that is acceptable. But a group or area trying to set up as a sovereign state against the wishes of the central government of the state concerned must, in most circumstances, expect little sympathy. The doctrine of self-determination is indeed one of the most popular and influential of the post-Second-World-War period. But it is only deemed to be applicable to appropriate territorial units, such as colonial territories. For any part of an existing sovereign state, on the other hand, it is regarded as highly inappropriate. If, none the less, such a break-up does clearly occur, third parties are unlikely to refuse to recognize what has taken place – unless there are some ideological or legal circumstances which are deemed to taint the new state. Katanga, had it succeeded in maintaining its independence, would probably have run into this kind of difficulty, as does Northern Cyprus now, whereas it is likely that an unambiguously sovereign Biafra would soon have been welcomed into the international society. In the case of Bangladesh third parties fell over themselves in their haste to recognize the new state, which no doubt was partly due to their sympathy for the recent sufferings of the people of East Pakistan at the hands of the Pakistan government. But, prior to the undoubted disintegration of a sovereign state, rebel forces are usually very much on their own, no matter how much emotional support may be felt for their cause on humanitarian grounds.

This approach is understandable and not inherently unreasonable. In part it reflects a natural caution. Even if there is only the slightest doubt about the finality of a secessionist revolt, third parties will, in the normal way, be reluctant to risk doing official business with it. To do so at that stage would be sure to incur the considerable displeasure of the state against which the revolt is directed, and its wrath may have repercussions for some time to come. Moreover, if the rebels are eventually suppressed, the states which acted precipitately may well be seen as having a certain amount of egg on their faces. But beyond such particular considerations as these there is also a more general point. It is that all sovereign states have something of an interest in discouraging secession, and in very many of them there are fissiparous tendencies which make this a very lively interest indeed. This type of concern is not confined to the new states of Africa and Asia, where, especially in Africa, the cultivation of loyalty to the state is necessarily a considerable governmental concern. In the old and supposedly stable states of Western Europe such problems also arise, whether in the Celtic fringe of France and Britain, the Basque region of Spain, or in Belgium on account of the division between the Flemings and the Walloons. It is not quite a question of all states having to hang together for fear of hanging separately. But it is the case that among sovereign entities there is something in the nature of a trade union, which takes the inviolability of present frontiers as, probably, its most basic principle. This is not to say that there are never circumstances in which one or more states discover an over-riding interest in acting in a contrary manner. But such occasions are rare. In the second half of the twentieth century would-be secessionists are almost always finding that their movements will be acknowledged by established states only once they have achieved complete and unambiguous success.

There is no necessary reason why states should follow this line. It would be possible for them, or some of them, to try to pinpoint the moment at which a rebel group was in effective control of a more or less clearly defined area. They could then announce that, as the constitution under which the central government was operating was without force in the rebel territory, that territory must be seen as in a condition of constitutional independence. In other words, the old sovereign state had suffered truncation and a new state had emerged on part of its former territory. Two courses would then be open to the states making such an announcement. They could do nothing further about the matter, other than making it clear that they would hold the new state responsible for its actions and would not regard the state from which it had broken away as having responsibility for the rebel-held territory. This would be entirely consistent with the acceptance of the fact that a new sovereign state had come into being, as sovereignty carries with it no right to participation in the regular business of the international world. But it would also be possible for states to announce not just that a new entity capable of full participation in international life had appeared. They could go further and invite the new state from the wings on to the international stage itself. Ambassadors might be exchanged and arrangements made which held out the prospect of mutual profit. In this way the new and perhaps still shakily based state would be treated as an equal member of the international fraternity.

However, these possibilities are based on the willingness of states to come to a conclusion about the break-up of a sovereign state in advance of its irretrievable occurrence. This would require a decision which would not only be politically hazardous but would also present considerable technical complexity. A fine judgement would be needed to ascertain exactly when a secessionist movement had reached the point at which it could be declared to be a sovereign state. And, the situation being fluid, that decision might later call for revision, and then further revision. It is perhaps not surprising that the current practice of states avoids such complications. Instead of setting out on the difficult and dangerous path of trying to recognize a new sovereign state immediately there is just sufficient warrant for such a decision, states have decided to play safe. Generally they will have nothing to do with the appearance, within a state, of a second centre of fully autonomous authority unless and until it has established its constitutional independence beyond all possible doubt. Prior to that point they will continue to deal with the government against which the revolt is directed, and proceed on the formal assumption that its authority runs throughout all the territory which is in theory under its control. Of course, they will have a clear mental understanding of the actual situation, and it may well affect the nature of their dealings with the troubled state. But on the surface all will continue as hitherto until there is no question that a final split has occurred.

The third subgroup of states in which doubt regarding the location or effectiveness of central authority may give rise to questioning about their sovereignty are those which appear virtually to have collapsed. In such a state the governmental apparatus is no longer in operation throughout much if not all of its territory, and the more or less habitual obedience on which government depends has seeped away. The result is that the state resembles a shell which is partially if not wholly empty. Burma in the late 1970s was a possible candidate for this category, as the government's authority was said to run over only about one half of the country. All the land entry points from its five neighbours were unsafe on account of insurgents or under their control. However, as the government had consolidated its hold on the heartland of the country, where the main ethnic group lives, the state was perhaps not in an obviously different situation from a number of others which are beset by an insurgency problem at a distance from their centre of power. Another and perhaps stronger case is that of Laos. Since the Geneva Agreements of 1954 brought the colonial war in Indo-China to an end the Laotian government seems hardly ever to have been in control of all its country. An article written in 1978 began, 'Laos has become a country in name only', and went on to assert that Vietnam, Russia and China had carved the country into 'three separate satrapies'.[34] Only the capital, Vientiane, was under the control of the government, and some observers doubted even that. By 1985, however, one close observer of the scene was reporting that Vietnam had secured control over virtually all of Laos, having a garrison of about 70,000 troops there, with Laotian auxiliaries under their command. He said, further, that Vietnam had placed advisers at key points within the Laotian government, and their advice had to be taken.[35] (If this is indeed so, Laos should now be regarded not as a collapsed but as a puppet state.)[36] Yet another candidate for a collapsed state might be Iran following the overthrow of the Shah early in 1979, when there was much internal confusion and a lack of authority at the centre. *The Times*, for example, complained eighteen months after the Shah's fall that 'it is still not clear whether Iran has a government'.[37]

But the two best known cases of collapsed states since 1945 are probably the former Belgian Congo immediately following its independence in 1960 and Lebanon since the start of the civil war in 1975. The Congo came to independence with a speed which was quite unparalleled even in the post-1945 period, which was itself notable for the haste with which imperial possessions were off-loaded. For half a century Belgium had ruled this huge African colony – about the size of Western Europe – in a paternalistic spirit, and saw no reason to change its policy just because almost all around were changing theirs. Thus when one of Belgium's colonial experts proposed in 1955 that the Congo should become independent in thirty years time he was widely regarded as a radical. But then at the end of the 1950s, following political riots in Leopoldville (the Congolese capital), Belgium panicked. A conference was called in January 1960, to which Belgium went proposing independence in four years. It came out of the conference having agreed that its constitutional ties with the Congo should be cut on 30 June of the same year – this in respect of a colony which had no experience of self-government, in which there was little education above the age of 14, and where hardly any Congolese held positions of executive or operational responsibility. It was estimated that thus far the population of about 14 million had produced thirty university graduates at most – there being some dispute about the exact figure.

Had the Europeans occupying the middle and higher administrative and virtually all the professional posts stayed behind, a gradual Africanization of the governmental machine might have been possible. But within a week of independence the *Force publique*, which combined the functions of an army and a police establishment and which was entirely officered by Europeans, had mutinied. Disorder spread, property was destroyed and some whites were killed. The centrifugal forces of tribalism, regionalism and political rivalry were given a free rein and a substantial proportion of the European population fled across the nearest border. Violence and chaos followed this administrative decapitation and the state seemed about to tumble into anarchy. It was saved only by the United Nations, which mounted its largest peace-keeping force to date to assist the government pending the creation of an effective national security force, and also what, for the United Nations, was a massive civilian operation designed to put the country's public services back on their feet. But there is no doubt that for a while the Congo could accurately be described as in a collapsed condition.

Lebanon, by contrast, had since 1945 been a prosperous and well run state which also, except for one hiccup in 1958, enjoyed political calm. However, the country was based on a fine balance between several varieties of Muslims and Christians, the confessional cleavage being reinforced by those of ideology. The result was that its inhabitants tended to see themselves primarily as members of a particular clan or community and only secondarily as Lebanese. The intrusion into this situation of more than a quarter of a million Palestinian refugees did nothing to enhance its stability. Nor did the fact that from the early 1970s south Lebanon became the permanent base for the Palestinian armed struggle against Israel – and the only place in the Arab world where Palestinian military activity was not curtailed. Eventually, in April 1975, the country's precariously based equilibrium fell apart. A civil war broke out between, principally, the Muslim and Christian elements, who could also be roughly characterized as left and right respectively. A year later, on 1 June 1976, Syria intervened in strength, sending in some 25,000 troops in an effort, essentially, to preserve the balance of forces in Lebanon. At first this seemed to have been a fairly successful move. But within a year intra-Lebanese clashes were recurring with some frequency, and the Syrian army of occupation (dressed up semantically as the Arab Deterrent Force) was finding itself in a situation on which it was apparently unable to exert a positive influence and from which it could withdraw only at very considerable political cost. It is still there, notwithstanding the fact that its mandate from the Government of Lebanon has expired.

Meanwhile, in the southern part of the country Israel has come and gone twice. First Israel invaded in 1978 in a move against the Palestinian guerrillas. Under strong pressure from the United States it quickly withdrew but left a puppet regime in the southernmost part of Lebanon under a renegade officer from the Lebanese army, Major Haddad. In 1979 he declared the area to be the Republic of Free Lebanon and for the next few years was a serious thorn in the side of the UN peacekeeping force which was trying to take control of southern Lebanon prior to handing it back to the Lebanese government. The troublesome Major died early in 1984. By then, however, Israel had invaded again, in 1982, and this time advanced northwards right up to the Lebanese capital, Beirut. In 1983 it made a partial withdrawal but remained firmly entrenched right across southern Lebanon. Early in 1985 plans for a withdrawal were announced and implemented by the middle of the year – although it was reported that several hundred Israeli troops and intelligence agents were continuing to operate in southern Lebanon.

Throughout these events the Government of Lebanon sat in the capital, still nominally exercising authority over the whole of the country, but in reality doing so only over a very small part of it. For, quite apart from the presence of two foreign armies, the civil war continues. The chief Muslim groups, the Sunnis, Shias and Druze, are at odds with each other as well as with the government, which has for a long time been seen, realistically, as mainly representative not of the country as a whole but of the Christian Maronites and their extremist political grouping, the Phalange. An attempt by several Western states, led by the United States, to bolster up the authority of the government by despatching a multinational force to Beirut in 1982 was unsuccessful. Instead, the force came to be perceived as just an additional partisan element, and the American contingent in particular suffered heavy losses. The whole force withdrew early in 1984. A bilateral American-Lebanese agreement whereby the United States was to retrain and re-equip the Lebanese army (echoing a similar attempt by Syria in 1977) was also built upon sand, the army disintegrating along confessional lines as soon as it was put to the test. At the political level, too, all talks aimed at national reconciliation proved unsuccessful.

Thus Lebanon, as one state, can truly be said to have collapsed. Its numerous communities continue to show remarkable resilience, and in effect govern themselves – often with considerable sophistication. The inner resources to which this points, together with the communities' strong instinct for survival, may yet result in them coming together and producing a viable scheme for the restoration of some reality to the concept of the Lebanese state. But the ideological and religious zeal which they all display, together with the hardening of their divisions in the violence of the last decade, does not encourage optimism about this possibility. The firing continues, and the government speaks without national authority. From numerous third (or, more accurately, thirteenth) parties come statements proclaiming Lebanon to be at least in abeyance. 'The Lebanese state is in eclipse, the economy paralysed, and society disintegrating'[38] was one early verdict. An aide of the Lebanese president was later quoted as saying, 'Today the President speaks for nobody but himself . . . the head of a state which no longer exists.'[39] This view was echoed by a leading newspaper, which declared that 'the Lebanese state . . . has in fact long ceased to exist'.[40] A social anthropologist and philosopher declared that Lebanon is 'one place where the state really is withering away'.[41] A more recent comment to the same effect is that 'As a nation state Lebanon no longer exists' but is 'now a mosaic of armed communities'.[42]

It might be thought that, faced with this kind of situation, the chief complication for other states would be deciding on the exact point at which to announce that in their considered opinion a sovereign state had gone out of existence. And that while some cases, such as Burma and Laos, might present considerable difficulty from this point of view others, such as the Congo and Lebanon, would be less of a problem. Yet in none of these cases, nor in any other during the last thirty or so years, has any such announcement been made, not even by a single state. Here, too, as with the previous subcategory, states would appear to have decided not to make life unnecessarily awkward for themselves.

It is not hard to see why this course has been followed. The alternative of declaring a collapsed state to be extinct would run up against what might also be regarded as natural instincts. A decision by a state to change a well established view or position always requires a certain amount of effort, and so has to overcome the substantial opposing tendency to inertia – which is greatly reinforced in this type of instance by the consideration that what is at issue is so important and sensitive a matter as the very existence of a fellow sovereign state. Moreover, there is always the possibility that the collapsed state might revive, in which case the premature announcement of its demise would have embarrassing consequences. This reluctance to burn boats finds encouragement in the fact that no matter how great its disorganization a state will almost always produce one (or more) claimant to central authority. Outsiders can therefore deal with those who purport, with some measure of conviction, to be the legitimate spokesmen for the state, even if it is tacitly accepted on all sides that their voice does not carry very far. This was so even in the case of the Congo, as it continues to be in respect of Lebanon, and makes it a lot easier not to take the far-reaching step of declaring that a state has ceased to be.

But the avoidance of such a decision is not just an easy way out of a difficult situation. There is also a lot to be said for passivity. For the declaration that a state no longer exists would have implications of a very serious kind. It would mean that from the point of view of the state adopting this view the territory of the former state was now there for the taking. Such a state would not be entitled to complain about any predatory action of this sort, and it might be that its declaration would actually encourage such behaviour. For it could be cited as a precedent by those who, with the intention of clearing the way to the exploitation of a favourable opportunity, were also anxious to take a similar step but wanted to avoid being the first to do so. There might well be several such states, quite apart from indigenous groups which saw themselves as ideally suited for all or part of the succession. It could be that outsiders with designs on the carcass would, in keeping with the spirit of the contemporary age, abjure outright annexation, aiming instead at the installation of a regime which might be expected to hearken carefully to their wishes. But in any event it is clear that the developments which might flow from the official death of a state could very well be of a destabilizing nature, perhaps to a substantial degree. Quite apart, therefore, from its convenience, a refusal to conclude that collapse means extinction also serves the cause of international order, in which all states have an interest, even though it may vary in intensity.

There is one other factor pointing in the same direction. It is that there is nothing in the assumptions on which international relations rest which encourages a state to see in another's collapse a ground for announcing that that state is no longer a member of the international society. Rather the contrary. The ineffectiveness or even disappearance of a government has no necessary bearing on the constitutional independence of the territorial unit in question, and it is constitutional independence which makes an entity eligible for international activities as a sovereign state. From the external point of view, therefore, sovereignty is unimpaired by internal disorder, provided always that the situation does not result in the state becoming subject to another's constitutional embrace. The state may be unable to make much of a contribution to international life, but it still has every right to be on the international stage. It is, to change the metaphor, as if the ship of state was drifting on international waters on account of its lack of a firm helmsman, but none the less it remains recognizably a ship, and one which may soon take a more purposeful course. There is always the danger of it breaking up on rocks, running ashore, or being taken over by a foreign crew and incorporated into their navy. But until the occurrence of any of these contingencies there is no call on any other navigators to proclaim that the ship is in fact merely a bundle of timber which anyone may salvage.

In the case of collapsed states, therefore, as of most of the other instances discussed in this chapter, the doubts which can arise over the application of the test of sovereignty are fairly easily dispelled. Supranational arrangements could present a real problem, but that is for the future. The other apparently difficult areas fall quite clearly on one side of the line or the other, some by a direct comparison of their nature with the criterion of constitutional independence and others through an examination of state practice. Thus it can be asserted that whereas associated states are not sovereign, protected states are, as are those states where the process of constitutional amendment involves the assuredly automatic participation of a foreign legislature. Small states, however small, are not by virtue of that characteristic to be regarded as lacking sovereignty, although their size might very well result in their playing a limited international part. States apparently on the point of break-up do not give rise to serious problems on account of the understandable reluctance of their fellows to take formal note of the process of disintegration until it has clearly gone beyond recall. And the same political caution influences the attitudes of outsiders towards collapsed states, encouraging them not to alter their official view that a sovereign state exists. Additionally, in this type of situation, there are wider considerations relating to overall international order which point strongly in the same direction.

Thus, many of the quandaries in which states and analysts might have been thought to find themselves when trying to decide whether a particular entity is sovereign, prove, on close examination, to be unreal. By sticking to the criterion of constitutional independence and, in respect of states in deep internal trouble, taking note of state practice regarding their continued existence as single territorial units, it is not at all difficult to say, at any one time, which states are sovereign and which are not. In consequence it is possible to determine which entities are eligible to participate in international relations on a full and regular basis, although note will also have to be taken of the fact that a few of them may have voluntarily surrendered that right to another, and that others may choose to make little use of it. There are, however, some territorial entities which clearly exist as distinct units and which also give every sign of being constitutionally independent but which meet strenuous opposition from at least some states when they claim that they are eligible to take a place on the international stage. The opposition to their claims stems largely from ideological considerations, but is often expressed in terms of reservations about their sovereignty. In contemporary practice, however, sovereignty has nothing to do with ideology, which could place the states that purport to see a deficiency in an entity's claim to sovereignty in a rather embarrassing situation. Certainly, the weak and woolly arguments which have to be used to support their case might be thought to reflect intellectual embarrassment, or at least to deserve it. It is to the nature and details of this quandary that attention will now be directed.

Notes: Chapter 5

1   Albert A. Forgac, *New Diplomacy and the United Nations* (New York: Pageant, 1965), p. 21.
2   James Morris, *Sultan in Oman* (London: Faber, 1957), p. 161.
3   International Court of Justice, *Reports 1952*, pp. 185 and 188.
4   Raymond Aron, *Peace and War* (New York: Praeger, 1967), p. 741.
5   Husain M. Albaharna, *The Times*, supplement, 16 December 1970.
6   L. Oppenheim, *International Law, Vol. 1, Peace* (London: Longman); the same phrase is used in both the 1st, 1905, edn at p. 138 and the 8th, 1955, edn (ed. H. Lauterpacht), at p. 192.
7   See above, Chapter 2, pp. 26–30. For a discussion of the international appearances of the provinces of Canada, see P. R. (Roff) Johannson, 'Provincial international activities', *International Journal*, vol. 33, no. 2 (Spring 1978), p. 12.
8   Government of India, Ministry of External Affairs, *Foreign Affairs Record*, vol. 20, no. 12 (December 1974), p. 231. See also T. K. Roy Choudhury, 'The India–Bhutan relationship: some new trends', *The World Today*, vol. 37, no. 12 (December 1981), pp. 476–81.
9   See *Newsweek*, 24 June 1974.
10 *The Times*, 15 July 1974 – although in its obituary of the last ruler of Sikkim, *The Times* spoke of India having 'annexed' the country: 1 February 1982.
11 Werner Levi, 'Bhutan and Sikkim: two buffer states', *The World Today*, vol. 15, no. 12 (December 1959), p. 493.
12 See William C. Gilmour, 'Requiem for associated statehood?', *Review of International Studies*, vol. 8, no. 1 (January 1982), pp. 11–12.
13 See above, Chapter 4, pp. 86–7.
13a Early in 1986 it was reported that the Cook Islands had declared its 'neutrality' – an action which impliedly severed the association agreement with New Zealand. See *The Times*, 30 January 1986.
14 UN Document No. A/38/340 and S/15927, 16 August 1983.
15 *The Times*, 5 January 1985.
16 'Sovereignty-association: a new partnership with Canada', published by the Quebec Ministry of Intergovernmental Affairs, May 1978; see also a declaration by the Quebec Prime Minister before the Quebec National Assembly on 10 October 1978, available from the Quebec Office in London.
17 Lord Sankey in *British Coal Corporation v. The King*, Appeal Cases (AC) 1935, p. 520.
18 United Nations Institute for Training and Research, *Status and Problems of Very Small States and Territories* (New York: UNITAR, 1969), pp. 31–4.

19 S. A. de Smith, *The New Commonwealth and its Constitutions* (London: Stevens, 1964), p. 18, referring to N. Mansergh, *The Multi-Racial Commonwealth* (London: Royal Institute of International Affairs, 1955), p. 124.

20 David W. Wainhouse, *Remnants of Empire* (New York: Harper & Row for the Council on Foreign Relations, 1964), p. 133, quoted in Patricia Wohlgemuth Blair, *The Ministate Dilemma* (New York: Carnegie Endowment for International Peace, 1968), p. 3.

21 Richard E. Bissell, 'The "Fourth World" at the United Nations', *The World Today*, vol. 31, no. 9 (September 1975), p. 376.

22 James Fawcett, 'The law and international institutions', in Avi Shlaim (ed.), *International Oranisations in World Politics, Yearbook 1975* (London: Croom Helm, 1976), p. 101.

23 Salvador de Madariaga, 'Blueprint for a world commonwealth', in Carnegie Endowment for International Peace, *Perspectives on Peace, 1910–1960* (New York: CEIP, 1960), p. 51.

24 Hans J. Morgenthau, 'Organization of a power system: unilateralism and the balance of power', (US) *Naval War College Review*, vol. 20, no. 7 (February 1968), p. 7.

25 See above, Chapter 2, pp. 22–5, and Chapter 3, pp. 41–3.

26 Stanley A. de Smith, *Microstates and Micronesia* (New York: New York University Press, 1970), p. 7.

27 UNITAR, *Status and Problems*, p. 1.

28 UN Information Office, London, Weekly Summary, 2 September 1969.

29 See Michael M. Gunter, 'What happened to the United Nations ministate problem?', *American Journal of International Law*, vol. 71, no. 1 (January 1977), pp. 111–12.

30 See Michael M. Gunter, 'Liechtenstein and the League of Nations: a precedent for the United Nations ministate problem?', *American Journal of International Law*, vol. 68, no. 3 (July 1974), p. 499.

31 Quoted in ibid. at p. 498.

32 Rosalyn Higgins, *The Development of International Law through the Political Organs of the United Nations* (London: Oxford University Press, 1963), p. 35.

32a W. K. Hancock, *Survey of British Commonwealth Affairs. Volume 1: Problems of Nationality, 1918–1936* (London, New York, Toronto: Oxford University Press, 1937), p. 261.

33 See below, Chapter 9, pp. 245–53.

34 'Laos: remote control', *Newsweek*, 22 May 1978.

35 See Dennis Duncanson, 'Fruits of victory in Vietnam', *Times Higher Education Supplement*, 17 May 1985.

36 On puppet states, see below, Chapter 6, pp. 139–40.

37 *The Times*, 2 September 1980.

38 Frank Stoakes, 'The civil war in Lebanon', *The World Today*, vol. 32, no. 1 (January 1976), p. 8.

39 See Geoffrey Boweder, 'Lebanon in turmoil', *The World Today*, vol. 34, no. 11 (November 1978), p. 428.

40 *The Times*, 15 June 1978.

41 Ernest Gellner, 'State and revolution in Islam', *Millennium*, vol. 8, no. 3 (Winter 1979/80), p. 198.

42 Patrick Cockburn in a special report on 'The crisis in Lebanon', *Financial Times*, 17 February 1984.

6

Aversion

The quandary in which states sometimes find themselves over the application of the test of sovereignty arises not from the straightforward factual situation with which they are presented but from their attitude to it. For, whereas circumstances may occasionally make it hard to discern whether what is before them is or is not a sovereign state, at other times the position seems to be fairly clear – but states are reluctant to draw what appears to be the obvious conclusion. They are not so much in doubt as to what they see as averse to say that they see it. This is because, for one reason or another, they have some reservation about the territorial entity which on the face of it measures up to the requirements for sovereignty. They are therefore unhappy or unwilling to acknowledge that it is a sovereign state for fear that this will somehow imply that they approve of it, or that they disapprove of an assertion made about it by one of their friends. Yet it remains that in the general practice of states sovereignty is linked with the existence of particular facts, and nothing else. If a territorial entity has a constitution which is independent of any other constitution, that is usually deemed to be a sufficient indication that it is sovereign. No further questions need be asked, or conditions satisfied, as sovereignty has only to do with the presentation to the world of a certain constitutional appearance. In the cases about to be discussed, therefore states have found it necessary either to blur the issue or to add a requirement which has not hitherto been insisted upon. If blurring is their object they may ignore the specific question of sovereignty and instead make much of a refusal to recognize the entity in question, of a denial of its claims, of its inherent iniquity, or of the impropriety of its very appearance on the face of the earth. In these ways it is hoped that no doubt will be left in the eyes of the uncommitted as to the illegitimacy of the state concerned, so that even if in some minds the nagging thought remains that perhaps it is after all a sovereign state it will nevertheless be unlikely to benefit from all the consequences which usually flow from that condition.

The entities about which there may be this kind of aversion fall into five categories, which are not mutually exclusive. First there are those which have been created in an illegal manner, probably by way of a unilateral declaration of independence. The problem here for third parties is whether entities which are able to carry through such an enterprise should benefit from their constitutionally improper behaviour by being accepted as sovereign states. The second category consists of states which are deemed to be living an illegal existence on the ground that another state has properly made an exclusive claim to the territory which they rule and possibly also to the name they bear. Those who accept the lawfulness of such an exclusive claim must also, logically speaking, deny the mantle of legitimacy to the state which assumes the appearance of a competitor. Third, there are those entities which, although apparently independent in constitutional terms, are perceived to exist as such only in a notional way. Really, it is said, they are puppets or stooges, merely part of other states' governmental structures. In these circumstances it is sometimes denied that such entities can be spoken of or treated as separate, sovereign states. The fourth category consists of tainted territorial units, in the sense that they are ones which have been created for what is deemed to be an objectionable reason. Thus, although they exist and appear to satisfy all the necessary criteria, it may be thought that they do not deserve to be regarded as sovereign states. Fifth, and finally, are those states which give rise to the same reservation on account of the principles on which they operate. It is not the circumstances surrounding their creation to which exception is taken but the manner in which they exist, the political philosophy on which they are based. Such objections could, more particularly, relate to the states' external policy, but so far the entities which have in this way fallen foul of a sense of moral outrage have done so on account of their internal arrangements.

Misbegotten States

Illegally created states might be expected to run up against some difficulties when they try to mix with the established members of the international society, but in fact they rarely do so. For, generally speaking, states do not allow the mere fact of illegitimate birth to stand in the way of their acceptance of a new state as sovereign. Provided the entity which has broken away from a larger state is clearly independent, in practical terms, of its former superior, others will usually be willing to take formal note of its existence and to do business with it. Of course, the state from which it has seceded is unlikely to be in an equally generous mood, and some time may well elapse before it feels able to come to official terms with what has happened. It may also be able to persuade some of its close friends to take a frosty view of the situation. But for those without an emotional or political stake in the matter the appropriate course of action is likely to be clear and straightforward. This does not imply that they condone constitutional wrongdoing, particularly such a grave act as secession. It is, rather, a reflection of the fact that, broadly speaking, the international political scene is ultimately based on the principle of effectiveness, as is, for that matter, the domestic. Accordingly, if a state has clearly established itself in the international firmament, there seems no point, other things being equal, in refusing to take account of its presence. Other things will not always be equal, as will be seen in respect of the last two categories. But, if they are, states are not in the habit of making what they would regard as an unnecessary problem in respect of an event which is indeed illegal in terms of the constitutional law of one of their fellows, but is also an instance of the working of a time-honoured mechanism for securing fundamental change at the international level.

There are not many examples of this sort of happening since the end of the Second World War, not least because, as has been noted, there has been a general hostility to the involuntary break-up of the metropolitan territory of existing sovereign states. The only clear-cut case is that of Bangladesh, which, once clearly separated from Pakistan, received widespread recognition without any difficulty at all. The emergence of Algeria as a sovereign state might fall in here at the margin – but at the end of the day she had sovereignty formally bestowed on her by France. Had Biafra been successful in the Nigerian civil war she would very probably have had to be added to the list. The Turkish Republic of Northern Cyprus, proclaimed in 1983, is not regarded by states as a genuine case of secession but of annexation – and this, external, type of illegality is one which states do find almost impossible to stomach. Moreover, it results in the creation of a puppet state. It will therefore be considered later, in the third section of this chapter. Nor, technically speaking, is the refusal of the United States and a number of other states to have anything to do with mainland China after the success of the communists in 1949 an instance of what is being discussed, as what was at issue was the recognition of a new government and not of a new sovereign state. The American attitude was also influenced much more by the nature of the new regime than by the route along which it came to power. The same is true of the almost universal negative reaction to the illegal appearance and life of what, arguably, was a new sovereign state: Rhodesia. It therefore falls to be discussed in the fifth category and not the first.

Divided States

Problems do arise, however, where one state splits into two and at least one of the successor regimes asserts that it is the legitimate heir to the whole patrimony. For in the eyes of that state and also, therefore, in the eyes of its close friends the other regime is living an illegal existence, governing territory to which it has no right and, in all probability, passing itself off under a name to which it has no claim. Ruritania and all the Ruritanian people are deemed to have but one legal representative, the legitimate Ruritanian government, which unhappily is for the time being ruling over a state which is less extensive than it should be. Those who do business with it, however, will almost certainly be required to accept its claims, which means that they cannot also take official note of the existence of the rival Ruritanian government. Correspondingly, those who do enter into formal relations with that government will suffer an equal likelihood of being made unwelcome at the other Ruritanian court. Thus, even if one of the successor regimes is willing to live and let live, the tougher line of the other will be enough to create problems for third parties.

This kind of issue is particularly likely to occur at a time of ideological ferment. The splitting up of one's state is at any time likely to be regarded as little short of a catastrophe – something which is not to be lightly accepted. But if, additionally, the errant half is seen as having fallen into the hands of the children of darkness, the split will probably be regarded with nothing less than abhorrence. And the fact that it is one's own kith and kin who are in charge across the artificial divide is likely to make the situation seem even worse than if part of the state had been annexed by an external power, even an ideologically hostile one. Knavery is what one expects of foreigners, but when those of one's own nationality both turn their backs on the legitimate organs of authority and embrace a sinister creed it is hard not to see them as having doubly committed treason. In these circumstances the chances of the situation being viewed with resignation are not good and the prospect of reconciliation is even gloomier.

Yet the fact remains that a state has been split into two and that, whatever one side might say about the illegitimacy of the other, that other side exists as a territorial entity which appears to satisfy all the requirements for sovereignty. Especially if, as is likely, it is accepted as such by a number of other sovereign states, it make no sense to pretend that it does not exist, and little more to say that it is not sovereign. The obvious way out of this dilemma is to distinguish between a sovereign state's existence and its international acceptability, which in turn determines its ability to participate in international life. A state will only be able to join in international relations to the extent to which others are willing to do business with it, but even if it is boycotted on all sides this makes no difference to its being as a constitutionally independent entity. However, sovereignty is an emotive term, and will not therefore willingly be used of an enemy who is also deemed to be illegitimate, for that may be thought to give it some gratuitous international standing. Indeed, the whole issue of sovereignty is likely to be obscured and refuge taken in denunciation on other grounds. And it may also prove that even in respect of divisions which have produced much bitterness time may have an emollient effect. In which case there will be some advantage in not having to eat any words which unambiguously indicated that the same state with which one is now coming to international terms could in no way be regarded as sovereign.

A number of states found themselves split into two in the wake of or soon after the Second World War, and all of them reflected not just a local political conflict nor even just the competition of larger powers but also the great ideological divide of the time. Indeed, in two cases the local split was entirely artificial, being a consequence of the larger conflict. One such case was Germany. Here the three occupation zones administered by the victorious Western allies, Britain, France and the United States, were brought together as the German Federal Republic in 1949, and in 1955 this entity emerged as a sovereign state. A similar process took place in the remaining, Soviet, zone of occupation, a good deal of power being handed over to the communist-led German Democratic Republic in 1949 and the remainder six years later. On the face of it, therefore, two sovereign states had appeared on territory which prior to 1945 had made up just one. But, although the Democratic Republic, or East Germany, was willing to adopt this approach (perhaps being assisted towards it by the fact that, diplomatically speaking, it was in the weaker position), the Federal Republic, or West Germany, would have none of it. Backed by its NATO allies, it asserted that Germany must still be thought of as a single entity and that West Germany alone was entitled to speak for the whole. The communist regime in the east was said, rightly, to have been foisted on the people, and, questionably, therefore to have no claim to international acceptance in view of the Federal Republic's existence as the sole legal representative of Germany.

Whatever the merit of this argument, for some years it carried a considerable amount of political weight. Accordingly, East Germany went officially unnoticed by many, although that did not stop such states from taking due notice of its existence for purposes other than protocol and representation. After all, it was manifestly governing certain defined territory on a basis of constitutional independence and, although it may have suffered from considerable restrictions on its political freedom, they were not appreciably greater than those of the other states within the Soviet sphere of influence in Eastern Europe. Moreover, it was recognized by a number of states, notably by the other communist states. An accurate representation of its situation, therefore, would have been that it was a sovereign state which was widely unacceptable on account of the fact that a much more popular and influential state contested its right to exist. But this would have been too plain for Western comfort. Not until the passage of time and the growth of East–West *détente* had produced, in the 1970s, a softening of attitudes could East Germany be referred to by the NATO powers as, simply and unqualifiedly, a sovereign state.

Korea, too, became a divided state after the Second World War. Russian troops entered the country in August 1945 immediately following the last-minute Soviet declaration of war on Japan, and Korea was partitioned along the thirty-eighth parallel, American troops taking over the southern area. It was said, of course, to be only a temporary arrangement, but the cold war was largely instrumental in it assuming a marked air of permanence. The south, following UN-supervised elections, was declared independent as the Republic of Korea in 1948, and the United States was able to withdraw in the knowledge that it was leaving a sympathetic regime behind. Similarly in the north, an independent, communist-led, state was proclaimed in the same year – the Democratic People's Republic of Korea – and Soviet troops departed. However, the then Western-dominated United Nations refused to recognize the legitimacy of the northern regime, declaring that the only lawful government in the country was the one which had emerged in the south, and ever since the West has refused to recognize the north. But, unacceptable though it may be, it clearly exists as a sovereign state.

A reconciliation between North and South Korea along German lines would probably be widely welcomed – but is unobtainable on account of the mutual antipathy of the two Korean regimes. The third divided state – Vietnam – has displayed another pattern. Here France fought a colonial war for eight years in an effort to re-establish her control after the Japanese occupation during the Second World War. In 1954 she was forced to give up, the Geneva Agreements of that year leaving the country divided along the seventeenth parallel, with a communist regime to the north and a Western-inclined one to the south. It had been agreed that this arrangement should last only for two years, when elections would be held for a reunified Vietnam. However, largely on account of southern apprehension that it would lose, the plan was not followed, and a war developed in the south which eventually involved massive American participation. Here, too, there were, effectively, two sovereign states and again the West refused to take formal note of the existence of one of them. But in this case the ending was different, the country being forcefully unified by the north in the mid-1970s following America's ignominious withdrawal.

A rather similar case is the existence, since 1949, of two governments claiming to represent China. Each of them has its own clearly defined territorial base – the communist regime on the mainland and the nationalist regime on the island of Formosa, or Taiwan. Almost the only thing they have agreed upon is that there is just a single state called China which at the moment happens not to be wholly under the authority of its rightful government. Until the 1970s, both received fairly wide recognition and so, annoying though it doubtless was to both, the argument that a lack of recognition meant a lack of legitimacy could not be pressed too far. But the events of the 1970s have changed this situation. Recognition has now been overwhelmingly shifted to the People's Republic on the mainland, and states dealing officially with Peking can no longer use the name China in respect of Taiwan. However, Taiwan continues to insist that it must be addressed as China, which has resulted in it now being recognized by nobody. The consequence, according to one legal writer, is that its statehood (by which he means what this work calls sovereign statehood) 'is generally denied'.[1] The logical reasoning by which this conclusion is reached is quite clear, but it seems very strange to see Taiwan referred to as an effective territorial entity which is none the less not a state. It certainly fulfils all the criteria for sovereign statehood which are applied in other contexts. It would be more realistic to draw upon the distinction between a sovereign state's existence and its participation in international life. Taiwan could then be described as a sovereign state which is unable to play an international part on account of its insistence on being referred to by a name which others are not free to use. However, although China has been taking a noticeably moderate line towards Taiwan, it has not wavered in its emphasis on the integrity of China's territory. Accordingly, it would not smile on a terminology which carried any implication to the contrary. This means that, at the official level, the present unsatisfactory situation regarding references to Taiwan is likely to be continued, although there is no reason why students of international relations should necessarily follow the official semantic line.

A somewhat analogous situation to the one where two governments claim to be the sole standard-bearers for the same state and where each secures some recognition exists when a disputed territory is said to be subject to a government-in-exile. During the Second World War, for example, a number of such governments had their headquarters in London following the occupation of their homelands by the Axis powers. Subsequently, reluctant decolonisers sometimes found themselves faced by insurgents who claimed to be the arm of the territory's legitimate government, which perforce had to sit in its margins or in a sympathetic foreign state. In both kinds of situation some third parties may choose to work on the assumption that a sovereign state exists and that its true government is the one in exile. It may well be that there are strong arguments in favour of the legitimacy of such bodies. What is harder to accept is that they represent sovereign states. For where a state has been overrun and is formally governed by an invader it no longer exists as a constitutionally independent entity. And where a colonial power is still in substantial control of a territory it is difficult to argue that the territory has become constitutionally independent. None the less, political factors may lead some states to ignore the existing facts in the hope that this may assist in their actual alteration. Guinea-Bissau, for example, was treated as a sovereign state by keen opponents of Portugal's rule before the colony was given its formal independence. And in 1976 Palestine was welcomed as a full member of the Arab League – with a Palestinian state still apparently very far off. Such decisions are not to be discounted, but they reflect the view that it is desirable that the entities concerned should become sovereign states rather than a considered opinion about their actual status.

Puppets

The third category of states whose alleged illegitimacy may well lead to a reluctance to style them as sovereign or even to a refusal to do so are those which attract the designation 'puppet states'. They do so because their relationship with another and more powerful state is regarded as so close that it justifies their treatment as mere appendages of the larger state, entities which move at its will and only at its will. It is this last phrase which is the important one here. There are many states which in varying degree, or on this issue or that, are dependent on another. They may habitually eschew certain action so as to avoid the other's displeasure, or even be accustomed to following its line on a wide variety of matters. But in these circumstances there is at least some reality in the statement that the dependent states are taking their own decisions. They deem it wise to cultivate the continued favour of another and so easily find themselves falling into step. This is distinguishable from the situation where it seems that the steps which states take are not really theirs. They may exist as formally separate states, with their own independent constitutions, but they are also seen to be subject to the detailed control of another, making their moves only in response to the movements of the puppeteer's hands.

The line between a dependent and a puppet state may not always be easy to draw.[2] It has been suggested that the criteria for the latter include illegality of origin and lack of support from most of the population, but in themselves these factors have nothing to do with the question at issue. Nor is it enough to point to the fact that a state customarily acts in a way which another finds pleasing, for, as has been argued, there is a significant difference between compliance and control. The crucial element is the staffing of all the key positions in a state's decision-making apparatus by nationals of another state, those nationals being known to be there for the purpose of seeing that the will of their state is done. The key positions in this sense will not, of course, necessarily be those with the greatest outward importance. It will be enough if those who formally take the decisions do so on the advice of nationals of the dominant state who are always at their side.

So extended and manifest a system of dominance is nowadays out of fashion. It is arguable that one or two such cases arose in the inter-war period out of Britain's Middle Eastern policy. Egypt, for example, 'was proclaimed independent, in 1922, but remained a British fief just the same'.[3] And Iraq, which became independent in 1930, 'really remained a British puppet', being 'effectively run by British advisers'.[4] It was also this period which gave rise, in the Far East, to the best known instance of a puppet state. The Chinese province of Manchuria was invaded by Japan in 1931, and on 1 March of the following year was set up as the supposedly independent state of Manchukuo. However, its independence was widely seen as a 'transparent fiction'. For its government was 'essentially a Japanese one, with a Chinese facade . . . The non-Japanese members, from the emperor downwards, were under the constant surveillance of their Japanese masters; they went nowhere and did nothing without the Japanese at their elbow, especially in any matter which involved contacts with foreigners'.[5] Other instances occurred during the Second World War, when Albania was Italy's puppet, the Philippines Japan's, and Germany set up two puppet states in territory which it occupied: Slovakia in 1939 and Croatia in 1941. Germany also established a puppet state in northern Italy in 1943, under Mussolini after he had been deposed in Rome and a new Italian government had signed an armistice with the allies. But, in the nature of things, none of these regimes outlasted the defeat of their controllers.

Since 1945 just three instances have occurred of what, arguably, are puppet states, although they also exemplify the difficulty of distinguishing between puppets and dependent states. One is the state which used to be called Cambodia, but which in the 1970s changed its name first to the Khmer Republic and then to Kampuchea. In 1975 the government was overthrown by the Marxist-Leninist Pol Pot, who established a regime which turned out to be the most bestial of the postwar period. Even conservative estimates allow that he slaughtered or starved to death 2 million out of the country's total population of 7 million, while other observers speak of the massacre of 3 million people. Kampuchea's institutions were systematically destroyed and its currency abolished, being replaced by barter. When, therefore, neighbouring Vietnam invaded at the end of 1978 and defeated Pol Pot it might have been thought that few would mourn.

But not so. For Pol Pot was supported by China, whereas Vietnam's Great Power friend was Russia. Furthermore, other states in south-east Asia were worried about the traditionally assertive Vietnamese, and had their anxiety confirmed when Vietnam established the compliant Heng Samrin as head of the Kampuchean government and left 200,000 troops in the country to ensure that he did not become less compliant. Vietnamese advisers were established at every level in both national and provincial government, and although a number of them were later withdrawn the impression remains that Kampuchea is still firmly under Vietnam's thumb – so much so as to justify regarding it as a puppet state. (Laos might also, on this reasoning, be regarded as Vietnam's puppet, as its government is 'backed' by the presence of about 70,000 Vietnamese troops). As against that, Vietnam argues that it – or, rather, a band of volunteers of its nationality – is just helping a friendly government which is beset on many sides – which it certainly is, there being about thirty or forty thousand anti-government guerrillas in Kampuchea, about three-quarters of them left-wing supporters of Pol Pot, and most of the rest on the right wing. Vietnam adds that all its helpers will be withdrawn once the security of the state is assured,[6] by which it means, of course, assured in its own direction. In mid-1985 Vietnam announced that this position would be reached by 1990.

Another state which might now be designated as a puppet is Afghanistan. For at the end of 1979, with a view to safeguarding its left-wing regime, the Soviet Union intervened in strength, sending in about 100,000 troops. Babrak Karmal was installed as president and still needs the support of about the same number of Soviet troops, who are harried at many points by the numerous, but far from united, opponents of the Soviet presence and its Afghan associates. However, this is not just a military occupation, for operational control in nearly all governmental ministries has been assumed by Soviet advisers. Indeed, it has been said[7] that in most cases they have taken over the top positions, with Afghans not even formally in control but relegated to the role of deputies. The president is surrounded by Russians, the Afghan newspapers are edited by Russians, and 10,000[8] young Afghan people are studying in the Soviet Union. All told, it sounds like a full-blown process of sovietization, going far to justify the inclusion of Afghanistan in the category of puppet states.

The third probable instance of a puppet state is the Turkish Republic of Northern Cyprus, which was proclaimed in 1983 after nine years of *de facto* separation from the state of Cyprus. This attempt by the Turkish-Cypriots to upgrade their status may not have pleased the mainland Turks. But Turkey was in no position to withhold continued support for its cultural compatriots, for quite apart from other considerations it was Turkey which had prised them apart from the authority of the state of Cyprus by invading the country in 1974. Effectively, the new state depends on Turkey in almost every respect, and it may therefore be assumed that Turkey will have a very big say in its government. It is therefore reasonable to categorize it as a puppet state.

Whether third states do business with a puppet state depends very much on the circumstances. If it has been created out of the territory of another state it may well be widely shunned, as the breach of territorial integrity which this entails offends what is probably the most basic canon of the contemporary international society. But if a puppet government has been imposed on an already existing state the attitude of third parties will be much more varied. Those in close relations with the controlling state will almost certainly give speedy acknowledgement to the new regime. Others may take a frostier line, but will be reluctant to break off relations with the puppet regime, for that can have a number of inconvenient consequences. However, the politics of the situation may point in this direction, especially if there is an alternative regime waiting in the wings.

Thus in the case of Afghanistan, although the Soviet presence has been condemned by very large majorities of the General Assembly of the United Nations, the Karmal regime sits in Afghanistan's UN seat, and its formal right to speak for the state is generally accepted. By contrast, the Samrin regime has been denied the Kampuchean seat, and the Pol Pot grouping – attemptedly sanitized through the creation of a coalition government-in-exile with an earlier ruler at its head – continues to speak in the United Nations for Kampuchea. This has enabled a number of other states who do not wish to offend China or the lesser states of the region to ignore the Vietnamese-backed government, something which is facilitated by the fact that Kampuchea is neither of much diplomatic moment nor at an international crossroads. The creation of Manchukuo evoked a broadly

similar response in that it received no international acknowledgement at all except from the states with whom Japan was closely
associated during the late 1930s and the Second World War. It is also
more than likely that the Turkish Republic of Northern Cyprus will
be almost completely ostracized.

This last kind of reaction provides a ground for the claim, said to be
'established',[9] that puppet states cannot be regarded as sovereign.
This, however, is an unsatisfactory position, both on account of the
unlikelihood of universal agreement as to whether or not a state falls
within the puppet category and because political considerations will
lead to even the most blatant of puppets being treated as sovereign by
some members of the international society. Furthermore, the fact of
the matter is that, by definition, a puppet state has *not* been formally
incorporated into another's territory. Accordingly, as well as
demarcated territory, subjects and a government, it will have an
independent constitution. It is therefore far more satisfactory to
classify puppet states as sovereign. This both enables the established
formula to be applied consistently and is not contrary to state
practice. It can also be justified by reference to the distinction
between sovereignty and participation in international relations. It
may well be that a puppet state is not able to do much international
business on account of the lack of willing partners, and even those
who do enter into relations with it will know full well that it is controlled by a third state. But that does not affect its status as a
constitutionally independent and hence a sovereign state. This status
may be much more of a formality than in most cases. But sovereignty,
while it does not usually end in formalities, always starts there.

Offspring of Apartheid

The fourth category of states whose sovereignty may be doubted or
denied on account of their alleged illegitimacy consists of those to
whose mere existence strong objection is taken. The circumstances
attending their conception and birth are thought to be so improper
and unseemly as to put them irrevocably beyond the pale. This is not
just a matter of illegality. Indeed, it may be very hard, using only the
normal criteria, to show that they are in any way illegal, although, as a
matter of form, the best available argument to that effect will doubtless be advanced. But the real complaint about them is of a different
order. It is that such territorial entities suffer from a peculiarly
objectionable form of original sin, from the kind of congenital
deficiency which leaves all right-minded states in no doubt as to their
response. The wrongdoing of the fathers must be visited on their

conniving sons. It matters not that the entities in question appear to satisfy all the requirements for sovereign statehood. Exceptional circumstances call for exceptional measures, and the company of the tainted must be entirely shunned.

The territorial entities which have most clearly elicited this response are those which have emerged out of the body of South Africa to provide independent homelands for certain tribal groups. In accordance with South Africa's policy of apartheid or separate development, nine such homelands (or Bantustans as they used to be called) have been designated and four have already been given independence. The nine make up about 13 per cent of the land area of South Africa, and the plan is for each member of the large black African majority (about 19 million as against 4 million whites) to be allocated to one or other of the homelands. It is not expected that they will all be able to live there, as many if not most of them will continue to be able to find employment only within the white areas, where they will officially be strangers within the land, foreigners with few rights and subject to many restrictions.

From one point of view this policy can be seen as an imaginative and commendable attempt to give political rights and identities to the black majority in a way which is compatible with the established system of white rule. The area governed by whites will become marginally less, but the essence of their position will be untouched. At the same time, the blacks will have control over those parts of the country that are said to be traditionally theirs, which, at least on paper, will be a considerable advance on their previous political situation. From another point of view, however, the policy appears as an empty institutionalization of the principle of racial discrimination, divide and rule in an especially iniquitous form. The homelands are, with good reason, expected to be heavily dependent on South Africa, and the position of many of their nationals – those living within the white republic – to be no better than before, and maybe worse. And this is the view which, at the official level, finds universal endorsement outside South Africa. Moreover, it is endorsed with considerable enthusiasm. For racial discrimination is considered to be one of the major evils of the modern world, and South Africa its only living exponent – at least on any noticeable and significant scale. Accordingly, much energy can be and is devoted to its condemnation and to the urging of its eradication, by which is meant the replacement of the white regime in South Africa by a black one.

It follows that the world at large has not taken kindly to South Africa's statements that when the homelands are given independence they are no less sovereign than any other state on the international stage, and therefore fit to be welcomed into the international society.

Those which have so far been given separate constitutional existence have therefore met with a very chilly, indeed hostile, reception. The first was Transkei, the homeland for the Xhosa-speaking people, of whom there are roughly 3 million (about half of them actually living in the tribal areas), which on 26 October 1976 was declared to be an independent state. It consists of one large area, which has a coastline on the Indian Ocean and for some distance shares a frontier with Lesotho, and two smaller areas entirely surrounded by South Africa. In vain did South Africa point out that Transkei was bigger than twenty-two members of the United Nations and more populous than 34 per cent of the membership, and that its gross national product was higher than that of a third of United Nations members. No other state chose to attend its independence celebrations, which had to be given an international flavour by the invitation of a collection of foreign dignitories of right wing persuasion. Nor was the world moved when its first prime minister, Chief Matanzima, on accepting the transfer of ultimate power from South Africa, declared that 'We reject utterly the racial discrimination which has been characteristic of so much that is South African'.[10] Instead the General Assembly of the United Nations, by one hundred and thirty-four votes to none, with just one abstention – the United States – immediately declared its independence to be null and void. Not even Transkei's severance of diplomatic relations with South Africa in April 1978 over an unsatisfied territorial claim could cause any other state to change its mind, nor yet Transkei's subsequent abrogation of its non-aggression pact with South Africa. Transkei is an offspring of apartheid, and as such cannot be treated as other than a pariah.

The other independent homelands have met a similar international response: Bophuthatswana in 1977, Venda in 1979, and Ciskei in 1981. Even South Africa's 1984 security agreements with Angola and Mozambique are not going to change any outside attitudes towards the homelands policy. Undoubtedly, this is a disappointment to South Africa which, with a keener eye for the intellectual component of the policy than for its political and emotional impact, hoped that it would provide a way out of its huge racial problem. Thus there was talk of all homelands being independent by the mid-1980s. But now the policy has been slowed down, and the financial cost of maintaining the homelands 'has become a severe embarrassment'.[11] It is hard to see the policy being abandoned, for, so far as the black population is concerned, South Africa has nothing else to offer which the whites find politically acceptable. But it may be less emphasized in future.

In any event, the question arises as to whether the homelands which have been proclaimed independent should be regarded as sovereign states. Certainly they are weak and are likely to be heavily dependent on South Africa in several important ways. But weakness and dependence are no bar to sovereignty. If they were, doubts would arise about the status of a large number of states which presently appear on the international stage – and which in fact move on it without even the hint of a challenge from any quarter. Other grounds for raising a question mark about these entities can be found by those who care to look for them. Britain, for example, keeping company with its European community partners, loftily announced that Transkei did 'not fulfil our well-established criteria for recognition as an independent state'.[12] Much the same was said of Bophuthatswana, although here the more specific point was also made that there were doubts about 'its ability to conduct its own foreign and defence policies'.[13] One wonders how closely, say, the nearby states of Lesotho and Botswana were scrutinized under this particular micro-scope. Both are very weak and closely linked with South Africa's economy, the former is an enclave within South Africa, and the latter has long boundaries with both South Africa and South West Africa or Namibia – which, as of early 1985, is still effectively under South Africa's rule. As against these points, it can be said that they each have territory which is clearly demarcated, a government, people, and a constitution which is separate from all others. Thus they satisfy the current requirements for sovereignty – and neither experienced any difficulty in securing recognition as such. But it is equally the case that the four independent homelands also satisfy these requirements.

There can, in fact, be little doubt that had Transkei not been linked with South Africa and brought to birth in consequence of its policy of apartheid it would have been welcomed into the collectivity of sovereign states. And but for what its leader likes to refer to as an accident of history this might very well have happened. For the land of the Xhosa people was annexed towards the end of the nineteenth century by the old Cape Colony, and then incorporated with the rest of the colony in the Union of South Africa in 1910. It could just as easily have been taken over by Britain as a protectorate in the way in which she assumed jurisdiction over Basutoland (now Lesotho), Bechuanaland (now Botswana), and Swaziland. Moreover, the dream of an independent Xhosaland predates South Africa's Bantustan policy by a good many years – so on this extra ground, too, the credentials of Transkei as a potential sovereign state would have been very good. It is also very possible that the other black homelands would have been deemed internationally acceptable had they pos-sessed a more orthodox provenance. A state consisting of more than one geographical unit and divided by the territory of another – which is Transkei's condition – is not uncommon. The United States,

Pakistan (until 1971) and Angola are all cases in point. To consist of six scattered units, which is Bophuthatswana's inheritance, or one large unit and a number of outlying pieces of land, which is how Ciskei came to birth, might be thought to be a bit much. And the suggestion that Bophuthatswana should be thought of as akin to a state made up of a group of islands does not carry much conviction, as land is a much more potent divisive factor than sea. But none the less there is no reason in principle why a state should not consist of any number of territorial units, even ones divided by land. And if that had been Bophuthatswana's and Ciskei's only unusual feature it is perhaps unlikely that it would have been treated as a ground for refusing to take official note of the new states. But they and the others did have another unusual characteristic, in that their delivery was by a route which was deemed to be highly objectionable.

One rather obvious way of dealing, analytically, with the situation which has arisen regarding the independent homelands would be to draw on the distinction which has already been suggested between the existence of a sovereign state and its participation in international relations. The mere existence of a territorial entity which is also constitutionally independent is one thing – and is generally a straightforward matter of fact. The extent to which it participates in international life is another matter altogether, and again is a matter of fact. It depends on the number of other states which are wanting or willing to enter into relations with the state concerned, and a prerequisite for such relations is the formal act of recognition. The fact that the homelands have been recognized only by each other and South Africa says nothing about their existence as distinct governmental units or about their sovereignty. What it does say is that the world at large wants nothing to do with them, which is a perfectly respectable position. No state is obliged to have dealings with any other, or even to take formal note of another's existence. But it does not follow that that existence is somehow conjured away if an entity is ignored, not even if it is ignored universally. An outcast or hermit state is in no way a contradiction in terms. Thus in respect of the independent homelands it could be said that they exist as sovereign states in the same sense in which other such states exist. Recognition presupposes a state's existence; it does not create it.

This approach to the problem finds support in the prevailing contemporary view regarding the legal doctrine of recognition. It has sometimes been argued that recognition has a constitutive effect, meaning that a territorial entity only becomes a sovereign international person, and therefore subject to rights and duties of international law, through its recognition as such by existing sovereign states. However, the weightier opinion nowadays is that this is not so, and that recognition is of a declaratory nature – a mere declaration by the state concerned that it takes official note of someone's existence. And, whereas the constitutive doctrine can be and occasionally is associated with the argument that sovereign states have a legal duty to recognize any entities which have fulfilled the appropriate requirements, the declaratory doctrine accords well with the abundantly evident fact that most states regard recognition as a political act. Thus they will refuse to recognize entities of whose existence or policies they strongly disapprove.

However, in this particular instance, states are not at all anxious to avail themselves of the distinction between a sovereign state's existence and its participation in international life. For this is an issue on which they would much prefer a blurred picture to a clear one. They can hardly deny that recognition is now a political matter, and therefore that the non-recognition of the independent homelands has no bearing on their existence as sovereign states. But they also want to do all they can to cast doubts on the legitimacy of these entities and, if possible, on their very existence as sovereign units. Accordingly, in this case, they would like to avail themselves of the benefits of the constitutive view of recognition, and they certainly want to bring the least possible comfort to South Africa and her racial offspring. The results range from righteous indignation to studied vagueness, from the Organization of African Unity's reference to Transkei's 'fraudulent pseudo-independence' and the United Nations General Assembly's view that it is a 'sham'[14] to the somewhat barrel-scraping process by which a legal case for such opinions might be provided. One writer,[15] trying hard to find a satisfactory ground for state practice regarding Transkei, has referred to the illegality regarding the nationality law which accompanied its creation, to its failure to reflect the principle of self-determination, to its dependence on South Africa and to it being an integral part of a policy which violates the principle of racial equality and non-discrimination, this now being said to be a part of general international law. On these bases he comes to the view that there is a case for saying that Transkei is not independent for the purposes of statehood in international law, but he also has to allow that this is a tentative and precarious judgement.

The student of international relations, while taking full account of the fact that the world at large regards the homelands as illegitimate and refuses to have any dealing with them, need not lose his clarity of sight on the issues of their existence and their sovereignty. Although states may not like it, certain defined territory has recently changed hands, and is now under the formal control of regimes which are constitutionally separate from that of South Africa. The latter state may still wield huge influence on the future of the new states in question. But, in as much as sovereignty is a formal matter, the answer to questions about their sovereignty must rest on evidence of a formal kind, as it does in all other cases. It may be that what is going to happen here is the appearance of a category of states which, in terms of post-1945 history is new: that of outcasts, or even outlaws. But, arguably, it would be a category of sovereign states, and not states whose unpopularity had in some way resulted in their having lost their sovereignty.

The usefulness of distinguishing between the existence of a sovereign state and its participation in international relations is also demonstrated in respect of those states which, on account of their allegedly very improper creation, are ostracized by some – but not by others. Clearly, if some states have regular dealings with another, it can hardly be maintained that that state does not exist, or even that it does not exist in a sovereign condition. The most that could be said in this vein is that some states choose to proceed on the assumption that it does not exist, there being no pretence that this is an accurate description of physical and diplomatic reality. However, this is an awkward way of making a fairly straightforward point. An alternative way of expressing it is to rely on the distinction between the state's existence and its legitimacy. It could simply be said that some states have decided to take no official notice of another's existence. This does not deny the evident fact that the state concerned exists in the same sense as do other sovereign states, but it cannot be taken as an acceptance of its right to exist. More particularly, it does not allow that the state has a right to occupy the land which is its territorial basis. And it follows that the states which deny its legitimacy will do no official business with it.

This approach is a particularly suitable way of dealing with the problem arising from the different attitudes which have been taken towards the state of Israel. It was created on land which had long been generally accepted, albeit in a somewhat vague sense, as part of the Arab world. It may have been ruled for centuries by the Ottoman Turks and then, briefly, by Britain. But its inhabitants were recognizably members of what was becoming known as the Arab nation, which in the second quarter of the present century found expression in a number of sovereign states. However, on a longer historical perspective the Jews also had a claim to what Britain governed as Palestine, and in 1917 Britain had acknowledged that it was desirable to establish there a national home for the Jewish people. This scheme began to go ahead in the interwar years, but was increasingly difficult to implement in accordance with the expressed intention of not prejudicing the rights of the existing occupants – the Arabs. After the Second World War things came to a head, and, amicable partition evidently being impossible, the Jews decided to establish themselves by force of arms. On Britain's withdrawal in 1948 they took over most of Palestine, proclaiming it to be the new state of Israel, and occupied the rest in 1967, although in respect of these latter gains it was allowed that, with the exception of East Jerusalem, their future had not been finally settled.

Not surprisingly, the existing and subsequently created Arab states took strong objection to the expropriation of what they regarded as their people's land. In consequence, for many years all of them resolutely refused to take formal note of Israel's existence. In their view she was an illegitimate entity, with whom they could have no dealings. However, other states have been under no such constraints, and Israel has been widely accepted as a sovereign state. And, clearly, there can be no doubt regarding her existence or her sovereignty. She has demarcated territory, people, a government, and is not part of any wider constitutional structure. Implicitly, too, the surrounding Arab states have shown that they are very aware of her existence. One or more of them have, after all, fought wars against her on no less than six occasions during the past thirty-six years. More recently, Egypt has had official contacts with her of a peaceful nature, starting with President Sadat's visit to Jerusalem in November 1977 and followed by the peace treaty of 1979. In 1983 Lebanon reached an agreement with Israel regarding the withdrawal of the latter's troops (albeit one which Lebanon purported to abrogate in the following year). There is much to be said, therefore, for the view that the most accurate and helpful way of summarizing this situation is to speak of it as one where Israel is unable to have regular diplomatic relations with a number of nearby states on account of their rejection of her legitimacy, this stemming from the way in which she established herself. This form of words casts no doubt upon Israel's existence as a sovereign state, and therefore does no violence to present reality – although it may be contrary to the aspirations of some.

Racist States

The fifth and final category of states which others may be averse to accepting as sovereign are those which give offence on account of a central aspect of their mode of being. A key element in the political philosophy or set-up which underlies and is reflected in their behaviour is deemed to be so obnoxious as to keep them beyond the international pale. It may be that they were also created for the very purpose of implementing the body of ideas or safeguarding the power structure to which outsiders now take objection. But, unlike the previous category, the complaint which is made about these states relates chiefly to the way in which they conduct themselves rather than simply to the reasons which may have led to their establishment. It is their actual day-to-day behaviour or the assumptions on which that behaviour is based that causes others to say that they want to have nothing to do with them and to deny that they possess sovereignty.

There are a number of reasons which cause some states to take a low view of others. The political basis of a state may arouse abhorrence – republicanism in a monarchical age for example, or communism where economies are almost universally run on capitalist lines. Alternatively, a state's harsh and aggressive foreign policy may produce the same effect. As might its internal policy, if, for example, it involves the wholesale violation of what are widely regarded as fundamental human rights. However, in the normal way such matters would not result in the state concerned being regarded as having lost its sovereignty. Governments which are both unpopular and have come to power by an unorthodox route may be denied recognition, or diplomatic relations with badly behaved states may be abrogated. In either event the effect would be the shunning of the regular company of the damned, and very possibly additional measures would be taken with a view to making their life less comfortable. But there would be no question about the continued sovereignty of such states – not, that is, unless specific steps were taken to attempt its deprivation. Steps of this kind would presumably take the form of an announcement by a large number of states that they would no longer take official cognizance of the existence of a certain sovereign state, in which case one of two sets of consequences would be intended to follow.

First, such an announcement might just be meant to effect a withdrawal of recognition as a sovereign state, so that the state would become a territorial entity existing in an unrecognized and, by implication, non-sovereign condition. In other words, this procedure would invoke, however inconsistently with practice elsewhere, the operation, in reverse, of the constitutive theory of recognition. In these circumstances such an entity would not be considered as henceforth exempt from the rights and duties of general international law, as lack of recognition is not regarded as having this effect. This would mean, however, that the state concerned would not be put in a very different position from that which would exist if it was subject to a widespread breaking off of diplomatic relations. Some foreign courts might refuse to take note of its official acts and questions might arise regarding the continued operation of treaties which the offending regime had signed. But otherwise its situation would probably be much the same. On the other hand, the withdrawal of recognition might entail a number of problems and disadvantages for the states taking this step. For example the awkwardness which might arise regarding existing treaty relations could cut both ways. Then, too, a concerted step of this nature might help to throw domestic opinion in the accused state behind the government. A widespread withdrawal of recognition might also be difficult to organize on account of reservations not just about its practical utility but also as to the desirability of setting what might prove to be an embarrassing precedent. In short, this particular ploy might seem to be not worth the effort involved, and even counterproductive, suggesting that reliance on existing methods of expressing disapproval would be much more satisfactory.

But, secondly, such an announcement might be intended to go a good deal further, placing the state concerned outside the protection of international law. A considerable company of states might declare that in their view a former sovereign state no longer enjoyed any legitimacy at all, so that its territory was there for the taking by any internal opposition group or any external power. The state in question would thus be in the position of an outlaw. This, too, might make little immediate difference of a material kind to the situation which the state would be in if it was subject to a diplomatic boycott. Its government could hardly be expected to lay down its claim to authority and quietly disperse just because of an internationally organized anathema. Quite the contrary. But none the less such a step would be a very grave theoretical move. It would represent both a high degree of outrage and an invitation to considerable disorder. However, no matter how great their sense of outrage, states might well, for a variety of reasons, baulk at the possibility of disorder and the admission that the situation was beyond the reach of a less drastic approach. They might have interests which would be jeopardized by such an unfriendly act, and which might be even more drastically endangered if disorder ensued. They might well be concerned about the precedent-setting effect of such a move. They might find, too, that it was exceedingly difficult to convince their publics of its necessity or even desirability. Moreover, any attempt to give teeth to such a declaration would require that the most important outsiders keep in step, which could not be guaranteed. And should the teeth prove ineffective the whole affair might prove inglorious.

It might be added that any such consequences, whether of the more limited or the more far-reaching kind, depend on the assumption that sovereignty is something of which a state can be deprived by way of an international declaration. This is very problematical. For if, as state practice suggests, sovereignty is a factual matter, the relevant facts having to do with a territorial entity's constitutional situation, it cannot, once obtained, be affected by anything which is said by out-siders. It does not require a continuing imprimatur from the inter-national world but is solely a reflection of a particular constitutional condition. It would be a considerable innovation for the international community, in the shape, say, of the General Assembly of the United Nations, to declare that, exceptionally, sovereignty could be with-drawn by international fiat. It would imply that the criteria for the maintenance of sovereignty consist not only of a territorial entity's continued constitutional independence but also of the absence of severe external disapprobation – a position which states have certainly not accepted thus far.

It is, therefore, not hard to see why states are reluctant to attempt a deprivation of sovereignty, even in the more limited fashion, no matter how unpopular a state might be. This no doubt is why no such effort has been made in relation to South Africa, which over the past twenty-five years has been subject to a degree of vilification which could not be greatly exceeded were the rest of the world at total war with her. However, such considerations do not apply in the case of new states, for here it is a question not of the removal of sovereignty but of its acquisition. Which means, in turn, that in the case of a very unpopular entity it would be possible to impose an extra condition which the entity was unable to meet. It might also be thought to be desirable, as sovereignty has a certain psychological, almost a mystical, significance. The attempt to take it away from a state which has been accepted as sovereign may be difficult and attended by some danger. But the attempt to keep it from a state which indisputably was but re-cently in a non-sovereign condition is likely to be not only much easier but also more worthwhile, in the sense that it may cause some genuine irritation in the entity concerned. It may have little practical signifi-cance, as if a state can be prevented from participating in international life – which it clearly can – it does not make any difference on this score whether it is designated as sovereign or not. But it remains that states like to be spoken of as sovereign once they are constitutionally inde-pendent, and withholding of this term may cause annoyance on the one hand and be seen as something of a moral victory on the other.

A case in point is Rhodesia (or Southern Rhodesia) from its uni-lateral declaration of independence in 1965 up to its temporary re-admission to the non-sovereign fold at the end of 1979, this being prior to its agreed independence in April 1980 under the name of Zimbabwe. Land-locked in southern Africa, it was settled by a British company and, having rejected an opportunity to join South Africa, became a self governing colony in 1923. Beginning in 1953 it was for ten years part of a colonial federation, but reverted to its former status upon the federation's collapse. The other two components of this abortive federal enterprise, Northern Rhodesia and Nyasaland, were then firmly set on the road to sovereignty, and soon achieved it as Zambia and Malawi respectively. In Southern Rhodesia, however, the situation was complicated by the fact that there was what amounted to a relatively large white minority – about a quarter of a million as compared with 4 million Africans – and that this minority had for a fairly long time been accustomed to governing the country with a virtually free internal hand. Understandably enough, it was reluctant to embrace the principle of majority rule, at least with anything more than very deliberate speed. But in these circumstances Britain felt herself unable to grant independence, as by this time minority rule, by a white minority, had become widely unacceptable in the world at large and was also repudiated by an increasing number of Britons. A generation earlier it had seemed the most natural thing in the world, and honourable too. But in this as in some other respects the years following the Second World War had seen a remarkable change in attitudes and values. Power in a territory could, now, as a practical matter, only be handed over by its colonial superior to those whose skin was of the same colour as the majority of its inhabitants. By this standard Rhodesia's white government was quite unacceptable, and negotiations between it and Britain made it very clear that agreement over a transfer of power was impossible. Accordingly, on 11 November 1965 – Armistice Day – the Rhodesian government made a unilateral declaration of independence, trying to give the event even greater resonance by using a terminology which was familiar to those many who had nothing but regard for the similar announcement made by the American colonies two centuries earlier.

It might seem that Rhodesia fulfilled all the requirements for sovereignty. It was a distinct territory, possessed a government which undoubtedly ruled over subjects, and now did so on a basis of asserted constitutional independence. Moreover, the state from which it had separated itself made it clear that it did not intend to challenge Rhodesia's move by force of arms. Verbal and economic challenges there might be, and not only from Britain. But, despite the optimism of the British Prime Minister, there seemed little chance of these measures doing much to undermine the authority and control of the Rhodesian government. In any event, Britain had certainly lost ultimate control over Rhodesia for the time being. Her constitutional claims on Rhodesia had been repudiated and were without local effect. In their place a new, and separate, constitutional basis for the territory had been adopted, and manifestly was in working order. Britain, however, stoutly denied that there had been any change in the formal position. From her point of view the unilateral declaration of independence was without legal effect and Rhodesia was still part of the British constitutional scheme. Those actually in control of Rhodesia were regarded simply as rebels. Here, therefore, were two mutually contradictory assertions about Rhodesia's constitutional situation, for each of which validity was loudly claimed by its proponents. In the absence of any constitutional court superior to both there was no way of resolving the matter at the level of law.

In circumstances of this sort, which were by no means new to the international scene, the customary approach of third parties was to take official note of the assertion which had the backing of effectiveness. This did not necessarily carry any approval of what had been done. It just signified that where two governments claimed authority over a particular territory it made sense to pay heed to the one which actually exercised it. At a deeper level it reflected the view that legitimacy in governed societies is finally based on nothing more – but nothing less – than a significant congruence between the decisions of those who purport to rule and the actual behaviour of their alleged subjects. Viewed in this light there could be little doubt that a new sovereign state had emerged bearing the name of Rhodesia. In the presence of a dispute at the constitutional level, it met the crucial test of effectiveness. As one writer put it, 'it is difficult to say by what traditional criteria Rhodesia fell short of being, after 11 November 1965, an independent State. It had the traditional qualifications of an established community and a defined territory and, in particular, an effective government. Its capacity to enter into relations with sovereign States was limited only by the residual responsibilities of the United Kingdom in its external affairs; but it was this responsibility, hitherto constitutionally accepted, which the declaration of independence repudiated. Could the assertion of United Kingdom authority over Rhodesia still prevent its being an independent State? Earlier practice suggests that it could not.'[16]

And yet, on all sides states refused to accept the conclusion to which earlier, and subsequent, practice pointed. On the very same day that Rhodesia announced her birth, the event was condemned by an overwhelming vote in the General Assembly of the United Nations, Portugal and South Africa being the only dissentients. On the following day the UN Security Council followed suit, and soon added for good measure that the action of the 'racist settler minority' had produced an 'extremely grave' situation, the continuance of which constituted a 'threat to international peace and security'.[17] Despite the fact that Rhodesia maintained itself as a constitutionally independent territorial entity for fourteen years not a single state recognized it as such. Moreover, this was not just a refusal to recognize a territorial entity because the states concerned disliked it and chose not to have dealings with it. That would be quite in accordance with previous practice. But in this particular case what states were in effect saying was that Rhodesia was not even eligible for recognition, on account of its lack of sovereignty. It was, as it were, the case of a woman applying for admission to a club which is based on the principle of masculinity. This aspect of the matter was put very clearly by the lawyers. 'It may ... be the case that Southern Rhodesia is not a State,'[18] said one. 'Rhodesia is ... not a sovereign State,'[19] said another. A third concluded that its declaration of independence 'was without international effect'.[20] And two others declared roundly that the argument that Rhodesia was a new state was 'contrary to fact'.[21]

It was, of course, not hard to find reasons of some sort for this proposition. If the constitutive view of recognition received any kind of support it would be possible simply to argue that Rhodesia was not a sovereign state because it was not recognised by anyone. But this does not accord with the currently preferred practice on recognition and therefore, although it fits the desired conclusion in this particular case, can hardly be advanced. However, there were a number of other possibilities. All the grounds which have so far been discussed as possibly putting states in a quandary when it comes to acknowledging the existence of another sovereign state could have been relevantly advanced. There was, for example, no doubt that Rhodesia was created in an illegal manner. The only lawful route along which a dependent territory can obtain sovereignty is by way of grant from its constitutional superior. As, however, this was not forthcoming Rhodesia acted unilaterally, and quite unlawfully. Then, too, it can be argued with entire conviction, from one point of view, that Rhodesia's continuing existence as an allegedly independent state was also illegal, in that Britain always claimed that the territory was still rightfully within her domain. In the words of her parliament immediately after the unilateral declaration of independence, 'It is hereby declared that Southern Rhodesia continues to be part of Her Majesty's dominions, and that the Government and Parliament of the United Kingdom have responsibility and jurisdiction as heretofore for and in respect of it.'[22] In accordance with this view the Judicial Committee of the Privy Council subsequently ruled that the Rhodesian regime and all its works were illegal. Rhodesia's highest court, it is true, made the 'agonizing decision' that the Smith regime was the only legal government and the Rhodesian constitution of 1965 the territory's only valid constitution, this decision being taken with a view to protecting 'the fabric of society and to maintain law and order'.[23] But from Britain's perspective, and also that of all other states, this decision was a nullity. In their estimation it was the judgement of the Privy Council that expressed the situation correctly. In consequence, although Britian was not in control of Rhodesia, in law she could be considered as its ultimate ruler, and as having international responsibility for the territory.

It was also asserted that Rhodesia was a puppet state of South Africa, albeit a 'rather wilful'[24] one, which could provide another ground for shying away from accepting it as a sovereign state. And it could be argued, as with Transkei, that Rhodesia was established as a separate entity for an immoral purpose, in this case that of perpetuating the rule of the white minority. This, too, could provide a basis for the claim that it lacked sovereignty. As the earlier discussion of all these positions has indicated, none of them carries much weight. But as it happens none of them was much relied upon in this case. Instead, a fifth argument was advanced in support of the assertion that Rhodesia was in a non-sovereign condition. It reflected the emphasis since the end of the Second World War on the importance of human rights and, more particularly, on the argument that one of the international fruits of this development bears on so fundamental a matter as the admission of new entities to the international society. For it was contended that Rhodesia had failed to meet a new requirement for sovereignty, that which says that all adults should have a voice in the creation of their country, and perhaps also in its running. As one writer expressed it, 'a new rule has come into existence, prohibiting entities from claiming statehood if their creation is in violation of an applicable right to self-determination'.[25] Or, as it has been put rather more widely, 'to the traditional criteria for the recognition of a regime as a new State must now be added the requirement that it shall not be based upon a systematic denial in its territory of certain civil and political rights, including in particular the right of every citizen to participate in the government of his country, directly or through representatives elected by regular, equal and secret suffrage'.[26]

It cannot be denied that on this kind of basis Rhodesia failed to measure up to what was said to be the required standard or at least it failed to do so until its last-gasp election of April 1979. From which it indeed follows that states and commentators were right to refuse to speak of Rhodesia as a sovereign state. And those who equate sovereignty with statehood could not even refer to it as a state, but had to use some such terminology as 'effective international entity'. For it cannot be denied that Rhodesia was effective. 'The fact is that Rhodesia is independent,'[27] observed a leading newspaper. And the British Foreign Secretary himself said in the House of Commons, in reply to a question regarding developments in Rhodesia, that 'The Government consider the new executive council to be illegal, as was the previous regime, but we have to take account of the fact that it exists, as we have done with Mr. Smith's regime. When it is appro-

priate either officials from my department or myself will be prepared
to discuss matters with this illegal regime.'[28] In these circumstances
one wonders whether it would not have been more satisfactory to rely
on the traditional standards for sovereignty, and to have said that
Rhodesia was a sovereign state but one which could not participate in
international life on the usual basis because the rest of the world, in
response to its internal policy, declined to have normal dealings with
it. This would have had the great merit of dealing with the facts in a
straightforward and unemotional way and in accordance with well
established and easily understood criteria.

However, this would not have been an easy position for the United
Kingdom to adopt, for it would have involved relinquishing her
claim to ultimate authority of Rhodesia, which would have been a
considerable blow to her pride. And if she refused to take this line she
could probably, in this particular case, persuade a lot of others to do
likewise. For no state nowadays, apart from South Africa, is willing to
countenance the rule of a white minority over a black majority. Other
forms of minority rule appear to give little trouble to foreign con-
sciences, but not this one. Indeed, it is pretty certain that even if
Britain had come to terms with the rebel regime at any time prior to
the developments of the late 1970s many other states in Africa and
Asia would have refused to follow her lead. What such states were
interested in was nothing less than outright black rule, and, it seems,
black rule only by those groups which had taken the most hostile line
towards the white regime. This helps to explain why the extended
concept of sovereignty advanced in response to the Rhodesian situation found such easy acceptance. The denial of the designation
'sovereign' was an extra psychological weapon in a conflict where
feelings ran extremely high but where those who were most exercised
were least able to do much about the situation they abhorred. The
maintenance of white rule in Rhodesia for fourteen years, and against
the fulminations of almost all other states, was frustrating to a quite
exceptional degree.

Moreover, the content which is given to the principle of
sovereignty is entirely within the province of states – when, that is,
the term is used to refer to that which makes a territorial entity
eligible to participate in international relations. Philosophers and
others may use the term as they wish, historians of thought may take
account of how it has been used, and students of the contemporary
domestic and international scenes may draw attention to the various
political ploys which involve its use. But it is only existing sovereign
states which can decide on how, if at all, the requirements for
eligibility to participate in international life should be amended. If
they wish to add a requirement, that is wholly up to them, and there

are, in principle, no restrictions on the sort of additional conditions which they may impose. If, therefore, they wish to say that new applicants must show that they have gone through a proper process of self-determination, or that they must give the appearance of conducting their internal affairs on democratic principles, that is their prerogative. It is then the duty of the student of international relations to take note of the new arrangement.

Comment, however, remains free. And it may be remarked, in passing, that the new requirement for sovereignty, although couched in general terms, was rather obviously directed towards a specific case, which does not give the best impression. Much international attention has been directed since 1945 to the questions of self-determination and of civil and political rights, but not, hitherto, in the context of the possible denial of sovereignty to an effective international entity. The Rhodesian affair, however, facilitated the speedy transfer of the idea of self-determination from a means of undermining colonial rule to a means of denying legitimacy to a colonial territory which got away (for a while) under the wrong sort of auspices. The new doctrine thus provided an easy justification for the aversion which states felt to accepting Rhodesia as a sovereign state, as did the universal lip service which is now paid to civil and political rights. But it was highly unlikely that other new entities which appeared on the scene supplicating for acceptance as international persons would be subject to rigorous scrutiny on these scores. If they were constitutionally independent, that would in all probability be enough. And so it proved.

It can be said, of course, that new territorial entities are highly unlikely to have the sort of political set-up to which objection was taken in the case of Rhodesia. Which is true. But it also draws attention to another point. It would not always be reasonable to require of those entities which attained a certain status under an old set of rules that they never change the rules unless they already satisfy the amendments in every particular. But it might be thought that they should not effect a very far-reaching extension of the rules if they themselves manifestly fall short of the new standard and have no realistic expectation of meeting it, or perhaps even of trying to do so. Something of this kind, however, took place over Rhodesia. Almost all sovereign states could probably satisfy the test of self-determination if it was very narrowly interpreted, to mean nothing more than that the people of an established unit are ruled over by those of their own racial kind. But if it were interpreted more broadly, to encompass the idea of a people having a genuine choice as to their rulers, very many states would be found wanting. And if it was extended further to include the basic political rights which are common in Western democracies still others would have to be added to the list of defaulters. Yet in the case of Rhodesia the objections to her acceptance as a sovereign state were put in precisely these terms. It might have done states more credit if their aversion to the white minority regime could have been expressed on grounds on which they themselves were less vulnerable.

Rhodesia provides another instance of a tendency which has been noted before in this chapter. It is the viewing of sovereignty not just as the concomitant of certain facts but also as a kind of moral accolade, which must therefore be refused to those who fall short. States which are a product of the system of apartheid, like new states which embody white racism, must be cast as far as possible into outer darkness, a process which has included the denial of their sovereignty. There is no need for this if the purpose is simply to stop them participating on a full and regular basis or, indeed, at all in international life. A refusal to take official note of a state is quite compatible with its existence as a sovereign entity. But evidently states have felt the need to go beyond the mere non-participation level and to signal their distaste for certain entities by declaring that they are without sovereignty. Students of international relations have therefore to be aware that it is no longer sufficient to say that a new territorial entity is sovereign, and hence eligible for inter-state activity, if it is constitutionally independent. To this there must now be added the further requirement that it must not have been created in violation of the principle of self-determination, and perhaps also that it must not be based on the denial to its people of certain civil and political rights.

However, the student of the international world will also appreciate that the situations which will attract the application of this further test are likely to be minimal. To all intents and purposes, sovereignty can still be said simply to amount to constitutional independence. Moreover, the circumstances in which states are likely to find themselves in a quandary on account of an aversion to describing a particular territorial entity as a sovereign state are very few. Straightforward illegality of origin gives rise to no difficulty, and the problem of divided states has now almost disappeared. Puppet states are unlikely to be widely perceived, as all forms of dependence are nowadays played down. Only in respect of the present and future tribal homelands carved out of South Africa might embarrassment arise; for states are averse to calling them sovereign states even though they appear to satisfy all the requirements. But here the small size of the problem on the one hand and the great dislike of South Africa and all her doings on the other are likely to mean that, practically, speaking, no embarrassment will ensue. Anything connected with apartheid can safely be condemned without worrying overmuch about consistency.

Generally speaking, therefore, just as it is easy to deal with such doubts as arise over whether the facts point to the existence of a sovereign state, so it is the case that states but rarely find themselves in a difficulty on account of an aversion to drawing the conclusion to which the facts obviously point. Sovereignty, or constitutional independence, is a criterion which is not at all hard to apply, and in the overwhelming majority of cases it is applied as it stands, with no further questions asked or requirements imposed. Territorially based entities only have to show that they are not a part of any wider constitutional scheme for them to be accepted as eligible to partici- pate fully on the international scene, and in the normal way nothing arises in this regard to put states in any sort of quandary. The matter could hardly be simpler. However, analysts and commentators often find some ground for quarrelling with the designation of a constitutionally independent state as sovereign, and states them- selves are sometimes found to be saying the same thing. It is to a consideration of these matters that attention will be turned in Part Three.

Notes: Chapter 6

1   James Crawford, 'The criteria for statehood in international law', *British Yearbook of International Law, Vol. 48, 1976–1977* (Oxford: Oxford University Press, 1978), p. 92.
2   On dependent states, see below, Chapter 7, pp. 171–7.
3   James Morris, *Farewell the Trumpets* (London: Faber, 1979), p. 260.
4   ibid., pp. 261 and 260.
5   F. C. Jones, *Manchuria since 1931* (London: Oxford University Press, 1949), pp. iv and 28.
6   See, for example, *U.N. Chronicle*, vol. 20, no. 11 (December 1983), pp. 29–30.
7   See *The Times*, 30 May 1980, in a report based on information compiled by the United States.
8   See *The Times*, 4 February 1984.
9   Crawford, 'The criteria for statehood', p. 129.
10   *The Times*, 26 October 1976.
11   Christopher Coker, 'Bophuthatswana and the South African homelands', *The World Today*, vol. 39, no. 6 (June 1983), p. 235.
12   Keesing's *Contemporary Archives*, 1976, p. 28063.
13   *The Times*, 7 December 1977.
14   Both quoted in Crawford, 'The criteria for statehood', at p. 179.
15   loc. cit.
16   J. E. S. Fawcett, 'Security Council resolutions on Rhodesia', *British Yearbook of International Law, Vol. 41, 1965–66* (London: Oxford University Press, 1968), pp. 110–11.
17   Security Council Resolution 217 of 20 November 1965.

18   Crawford, 'The criteria for statehood', p. 163.
19   Rosalyn Higgins, 'International law, Rhodesia, and the U.N.', *The World Today*, vol. 23, no. 3 (March 1967), p. 98.
20   Fawcett, 'Security Council resolutions', p. 113.
21   Myres S. McDougal and W. Michael Reisman, 'Rhodesia and the United Nations: the lawfulness of international concern', *American Journal of International Law*, vol. 62, no. 1 (January 1968), p. 11, n. 44.
22   Southern Rhodesia Act 1965.
23   Quoted in the *New York Times*, 19 September 1968.
24   Leader in *The Times*, 27 February 1970.
25   Crawford, 'The criteria for statehood', p. 164.
26   Fawcett, 'Security Council resolutions', p. 112.
27   Leader in *The Times*, 3 March 1970.
28   *The Times*, 23 March 1978.

Part Three

Quarrels

7

Political

Whether sovereignty should be thought of as constitutional independence has often been doubted – usually in an implicit way as it is very rare for any explicit consideration to be given to the possibility of it having anything to do with constitutional law. Instead it is common for sovereignty to be presented as essentially political in nature, as being constituted by political independence. The suggestion here is that, by contrast with the idea of sovereignty as something which is associated with international law – the other popular approach – it should be conceived in more down-to-earth, man-of-the-world terms. The sovereign state, it is argued, is one which can look after itself, which can chart and follow its own course upon the turbulent waters of international life. Further, it is implied that it can do so with some success, reaching many of the goals which it has set itself. Politically speaking, it is a free or independent entity. This, it is said, is the approach which should be adopted if one wishes to know about the reality of sovereignty, as distinct from what theorists may think about it. One needs to address oneself to the day-to-day goings on at the international level and see how states actually fare in the hurly-burly, how the sovereign men distinguish themselves from the only dubiously sovereign boys.

The great appeal of this argument is that it fits in so easily with preconceptions about what sovereignty means. In the fields of both religion and politics the adjective 'sovereign' is most readily associated with the idea of supremacy. God, the King and Parliament are all spoken of as sovereign when, in one way or another, the intention is to convey the idea that the person or entity concerned is all-powerful. And in the sphere of international relations the ascription of power, unless it is in a specifically legal context, usually carries with it the idea that the state in question is in a reasonably good position to get its way. Of course, in the context of a multiplicity of states, political independence is necessarily a relative concept. No one state, however powerful, is in a position to get all of its way all of the time, and even the most successful of states has to recognize that on a number of issues even its moderately formulated aims are unlikely to be completely realized.

Nevertheless, the grip of the idea that absolute supremacy makes up the core of sovereignty is so great that definitions meant to be of international relevance are sometimes encountered in just these terms. The sovereignty of the state, says one theorist, is 'the claim to unchecked and unlimited power in foreign affairs'.[1] And, even where it is recognized that as a practical matter any such conception is quite ridiculous, obeisance may nevertheless be paid to the idea that, 'in theory', sovereignty amounts to complete political independence. As another writer has put it, 'external sovereignty . . . means freedom to conduct foreign relations', by which it is evident that he means freedom to conduct an entirely successful foreign policy. For he goes on: 'Theoretically this freedom is absolute but an international system consisting of fully sovereign states is as unthinkable as an anarchist society consisting of fully free individuals.'[2] One cannot help wondering what is the point of a concept which, being meant to summarize an important aspect of reality, is in fact largely out of touch with it. Far better to recognize that 'sovereign states, so far from being legally and practically free to do as they like, face innumerable limitations on their freedom to do even those things they are legally entitled to do [so that] sovereignty . . . even in theory, does not mean absolute freedom to act as one likes'.[3]

If, therefore, sovereignty is sensibly advanced as meaning political independence, it must mean a political independence which is not complete or total but one which has to be calculated in terms of more or less. It is a quantitative and not a qualitative conception, leading to such judgements as that one state is more sovereign than another, that a third is less so than either, and so on. And undoubtedly there is great merit in speaking of states in terms of their varying political independence. To do so identifies and relies upon an aspect of their life which is of very great importance. Moreover, it accords both with the everyday manner in which the international world is discussed and with the terminology which lies near or at the centre of the academic discipline of international relations. Great powers and small powers, super-states and mini-states, these and other such terms testify not just to the physical size of the entities concerned but also to the importance of their political weight. This kind of language does have its limitations, both on account of its lack of precision and because it can provide a faulty guide to what happens when a state in one category clashes with one in another. Not always is it the case that the state from the upper league comes out on top. But by and large it does give a roughly accurate picture of the dynamics of life at the international level. What is more, questionable, however, is whether it is helpful to speak of political independence in terms of sovereignty. There is no reason why this terminology should not be adopted, for people may use words as they like. But it may prove to have less utility and to introduce more confusion than might be immediately apparent. This will be considered later in the chapter – until which point sovereignty will be used to mean quantitative political independence.

Attention will first be paid to the perceived link between political independence and sovereignty. One way in which this could be done would be to focus upon how a change in the situation of a particular state, whether in general terms or in response to a specific event, is said to have a corresponding effect on its sovereignty. Of the concluding military and diplomatic skirmishes of the October 1973 war in the Middle East, for example, it has been said that 'Egypt emerged more independent and sovereign than she had been for some twenty years previously'.[4] The same train of thought was expressed by a high-ranking Israeli when he asserted, albeit tendentiously, that 'those countries that allow themselves to be bullied into submission by the Arab League Boycott Committee are in a sense renouncing their national sovereignty'.[5] And, keeping to the same part of the world, it has been observed that 'Independence has always been a qualified notion for the states of the Middle East, except perhaps for a brief period at Nasser's zenith when he conceived of an Arab world truly free from great-power tutelage . . . [N]ational sovereignty must accept its limitations under the shadow of an external power'.[6]

Another way of looking at the alleged link between political independence and sovereignty, however, is to examine certain twentieth-century developments of a general kind. This is not only a more interesting approach but also one which concentrates upon issues which, besides being important in themselves, are of considerable significance from the point of view of a conception of sovereignty which rests upon quantitative political independence. For it is arguable that, severally and jointly, these developments have tended to diminish the sovereignty of most states, relegating, as it were, the whole range of states by several notches. Thus, while the position of one state relative to another might not have changed, the amount of sovereignty which each has at its command is said to be less than hitherto. There are four separate but not unconnected processes which all point in the same direction, although it is also the case that in respect of each of them the argument is often taken too far. The first relies on the assertion that states are no longer impermeable. At one time they could be pictured as effectively protected by a hard shell, which both kept out potential malefactors and prevented them from subverting the local population. This territorial intactness, it is said, constituted the heart of sovereignty, providing political independence of a negative kind. Now, however, technological developments in the sphere of both weaponry and communications have resulted in states being open to outside force and influence to a degree which was quite unknown in times past. They have been penetrated, or at least are susceptible to penetration. Or, putting it in slightly different words, they have become permeable – and as such are much less sovereign than before.

The second development is less universal in effect but is none the less wide-ranging. It relates to the fact that the breakdown of empires and the process of decolonization have produced, most notably during the third quarter of the century, a large number of new and on the whole relatively weak states. On account of their weakness they are particularly susceptible to the pressures of their larger fellows, and some of them habitually follow lines laid down beyond their borders or are always careful not to offend certain outsiders. Thus the number of states apparently at the lower end of the sovereign range has been considerably enhanced, not only making it, as it were, bottom-heavy but also reducing the amount of political independence enjoyed by the average state. In consequence it is arguable that the overall configuration of the collectivity of states has been noticeably changed. A connected argument here is that some states have become dependent not so much on others but on large multi-national corporations which operate within their frontiers. The third development is of wider import in that it rests on the claim that political independence, or sovereignty, is diminished not just by the general dependence of an inferior on a superior but also by any significant degree of interdependence. In as much, therefore, as the world's political and commercial system brings virtually all states into fairly intimate contact with each other and entwines the fortune and maybe even the fate of each state with those of a multitude of others, the conclusion is that all states are nowadays less sovereign than before.

Fourth, and last, it is argued that the same process is at work through the greatly increased amount of international co-operation which now takes place on a quasi-permanent basis, usually through the working of an international institution. Quite apart from the question of whether states may be bound in law by institutional decisions to which they were opposed or on which they had no voice,[7] their mere participation in an institution may well result in their feeling less free to take a line contrary to that which is being urged by the majority of members. This may be due to the straightforward discomfort which would come in respect of that particular issue, to an apprehension about the possible consequences within or beyond the institution when other matters are discussed, or to the existence of a specific and unwelcome sanction hanging over their head to encourage compliance. In any event, institutional co-operation may diminish a state's political independence, and hence its sovereignty.

Permeability

The idea that impermeability is the essence of the traditional sovereign state and that it has been undermined by mid-twentieth-century developments is particularly associated with the name of Professor John H. Herz. He has argued that what accounts, ultimately, for the special nature of the modern nation state, permitting it to be characterized as independent or sovereign, is its 'physical, corporeal nature. It is an expanse of territory, encircled for its identification and defence by tangible, military expressions of statehood, like fortifications and fortresses'.[8] In this, says Herz, lies its impermeability, its impenetrability, or simply its territoriality, terms which 'are meant to indicate the peculiar nature of the modern territorial state as it was surrounded with what may be called its "hard shell" which protected it from foreign penetration'.[9] However, of late it has become possible for adversaries 'to overleap or by-pass the traditional hard-shell defense of states',[10] the factors which have led to this being the possibility of economic blockade, ideological-political penetration, air war and atomic war. As a result concepts such as sovereignty 'no longer retain the full meaning peculiar to them under the classical system of territoriality'.[11]

This line of argument has been echoed by a number of writers. One has said that 'the militarily sovereign nation-state is an anachronism',[12] from which he concluded that the 'classic nation-state has perhaps lost its principal *raison d'être*'.[13] Another has observed that 'military, political, and economic power overwhelms and undermines the fragile barriers of national sovereignty',[14] and a third has commented that 'if sovereignty is more than a sterile legalism, if it means the real power of a nation to assure by itself the security and welfare of its citizens, then it is obvious that no nation is any longer truly sovereign'.[15] Some would not include the nuclear powers in this list, or at least the two major nuclear powers, but in the absence, as yet, of a secure defence against nuclear attack there would seem to be no good ground for excluding them. The nuclear capacity of the superpowers underlines the permeability of the rest of the world, but this does not mean that they are themselves immune from the effects of the technological developments which, from one perspective, make them pre-eminent.

It is true, however, that in less than extreme situations the super-powers are, in military terms, in a relatively safe situation – much safer, in fact, than great powers have ever been before. For on the one hand even the great could hardly be said to have been completely impermeable prior to the nuclear age. Those unprotected by the sea were always exposed to the possibility of invasion by their larger enemies. And, on the other hand, nuclear weapons and other aspects of modern technology have rendered those possessing them physically secure – outside a nuclear confrontation – to a degree almost unknown hitherto. It might be said of such states, therefore, that they have become more and not less impermeable. It is also possible to construct a fairly compelling argument of the same sort in respect of lesser powers. For again it is not the case that permeability is for them something new. As a reviewer of Herz's book observed, 'In every age the majority of Powers have been Small Powers, and for them territorial impermeability . . . has been largely a fiction'.[16] But their physical vulnerability does not mean that they are incapable of surviving in the contemporary world. In fact all the evidence points in the opposite direction. For since 1945 one of the most notable features of international life has been the emergence of a large number of weak states and the survival, intact, of virtually all of them.

It has been said that this is because, in situations short of nuclear war, the state not only continues to fulfil its protective functions, 'but for the most part . . . fulfils them more effectively than in the past'.[17] There are, however, factors contributing to this result beyond those which flow from the physical and organizational capacities of each individual state. One matter which needs to be taken into account is the overall structure of the international system, the bipolarity of which has deterred the major powers from making physical advances in the uncommitted part of the world. Another, and more important, consideration is to be found in the ideas about proper behaviour which have been prevalent since the end of the Second World War. For prominent among these has been the belief that annexation is now out of court, not only beyond one's sphere of influence but also within it. Thus even if one state goes so far as to send its troops into another with aggressive intent – itself a fairly rare thing – it is assumed on all sides that the object is just to obtain a new, and more favourable, indigenous regime, and that assumption is hardly ever confuted.

It is, therefore, possible to assert that in a political sense states are nowadays less and not more permeable. And, further, that in times past they were, both militarily and politically, very far from being impermeable. The whole argument about the former impermeability of states has, in fact, very much of an Anglo-Saxon ring. From the point of view of Britain and the United States it may sound convincing, but to France or Poland much less so. Be that as it may, it has to be allowed that in a broader context recent developments have greatly increased the theoretical permeability of all states. Propaganda can be transmitted and received much more easily than before, and any state could be bombarded with nuclear-headed missiles – to the point, in most cases, of the virtually complete destruction of organizational life. If, therefore, sovereignty rests on the absence of such possibilities, it is indeed the case that there are no longer any states in the world that can claim to be fully possessed of this condition.

Dependence

The habitual subservience of one state to another in respect of an important area of policy indicates, to many eyes, that it is gravely lacking in sovereignty. In this connection, and following the Czechoslovakian crisis of 1968, the phrase 'limited sovereignty' is often used. Czechoslovakia had shown signs during the early part of that year of wanting to follow a more independent path within the Eastern bloc, 'to exercise genuine sovereignty . . . perhaps playing a role more like Rumania's'.[18] However, this was unacceptable to the Soviet Union, and in August the errant state was brought to heel by an invading force drawn chiefly from the bloc leader but also including contingents from some other members of the Warsaw Pact. In a comment typical of many made in the West, this action was said to be a 'brutal assault against an ally's sovereignty and political independence'.[19] Not surprisingly, however, the Soviet Union presented a rather different explanation.

On 26 September 1968 an article in the newspaper of the Soviet Communist Party, *Pravda*, discussed the question of 'Sovereignty and the International Duties of Socialist Countries'. It referred to criticism of the invasion as contrary to the principle of sovereignty and said[20] that the 'groundlessness of such reasoning consists primarily in that it is based on an abstract, non-class approach to the question of sovereignty'. It went on: 'The sovereignty of each socialist country cannot be opposed to the interests of the world of socialism . . . Communists would not allow the socialist states to be inactive in the name of an abstractly understood sovereignty when they saw that the country stood in peril of antisocialist degeneration . . . the actions of the five allied socialist countries [were] directed to the defence of the vital interests of the socialist community, and the sovereignty of socialist Czechoslovakia first and foremost.' Commenting on this, an

American spokesman said that 'sovereignty has thus been collectivized',[21] but the more popular term which was quickly applied in the West to what was also called the Brezhnev Doctrine was 'limited sovereignty'.

Evidently this terminology struck a sore spot in the Soviet Union, and at a session of the Supreme Soviet in July 1969 the Foreign Minister, Gromyko, claimed that the 'allegations that socialist countries favour a somewhat curtailed and not full sovereignty for states should be firmly rejected. This is nothing but slander. Nothing can impart fuller meaning to the concept of sovereignty than the right of people to defend to the end the road they have chosen against any encroachments.'[22] However, in the light of the record he had to add that while 'no one can deprive such a people of the right to rely for support on its friends' it was also the Soviet position that 'its friends cannot be deprived of the right to give assistance to this people'.[23] In other words, if it judged it necessary a larger friend could insist on helping someone who was seen as straying from the straight and narrow path, no matter how much that help might be resented by its supposed beneficiary.

This, of course, was not a new idea in international relations. Rather, it was a fresh expression of the traditional determination of great powers to keep states within their spheres of influence from engaging in embarrassing behaviour, or from being interfered with by a rival great power. It was an American President, Monroe, who in 1823 had responded to the possibility of European support for Spain's desire to retrieve her former colonies in South America with the announcement, or doctrine, that any such acts would be regarded as a threat to the peace and safety of the United States. At the end of the nineteenth century this doctrine was invoked against Britain in connection with her border dispute with Venezuela and in support of a solution by way of arbitration. It led to the assertion by the American Secretary of State that his country was 'practically sovereign in this continent, and its fiat is law upon subjects to which it confines its interposition'[24] – although as it happened events did not entirely bear out this claim. It was echoed half a century or so later when the Organization of American States was persuaded by its largest member to declare that 'The domination or control of the political institutions of any American state by the international Communist movement ... would constitute a threat to the sovereignty and independence of the American states'.[25] All of which suggests that dependence, or, as some would put it, limited sovereignty, is not peculiar to one part of the political globe.

In thinking about this matter it is helpful to distinguish between various types of dependence. In the first place there are those cases where the weaker state keeps closely in step with the stronger on a number of significant issues. They march together, but there is no doubt as to who decides both the destination and the route. This kind of positive dependence has been most noticeable since 1945 in Eastern Europe. During the Stalinist years it was not so much a matter of marching shoulder to shoulder as, almost, of the Soviet Union frog-marching the rest. Soviet troops were prominently stationed in the area, economic links were carefully constructed for Soviet benefit, the Soviet Union was able to intimidate individuals throughout the bloc, and on international issues all bloc members followed an identical, Soviet, line. After Stalin's death in 1953 there were a number of changes. Albania, following the Yugoslavian precedent, slipped away, Rumania began to take a relatively independent line, and an atmosphere of modest liberalization gradually developed. Thus by 1976 Moscow was having to make a number of concessions to her East European allies, and at a conference of European communist parties the final declaration spoke of 'equality and sovereign independence of each party, non-interference in national affairs and respect for their free choice of different roads for the struggle for social change and socialism'.[26] But during the same period the Soviet Union had not only invaded Czechoslovakia in 1968 but had done the same to Hungary in 1956 when it had begun to show signs of going its own way. And throughout, Soviet dominance, both military and economic, and its interest in maintaining a dominant position were omnipresent. Thus, while the early, Stalinist, pattern has certainly been modified, and smooth words are often used, the overall picture of dependence has not been changed, and it may still be fairly described as positive dependence.

A rather different form of dependence exists where the emphasis is not on the lesser state always having to toe a particular line but on it just avoiding certain specific kinds of undesirable behaviour. This might be referred to as negative dependence. To a large extent the dependent state may be left to its own devices, but on some very important matters, such as the ideological nature of its regime or its international affiliations, it is expected to avoid troubling a large and powerful neighbour. And if it does step out of line it may expect a great deal of trouble in return. This kind of situation has occurred most notably since 1945 in the Caribbean and, latterly, in Central America, where the United States has left no doubt about its determination to hold general sway. Thus in 1954 it engineered the overthrow of a left-wing government in Guatemala. In 1961 it was unsuccessful in an attempt to depose the Cuban regime led by Fidel Castro, but in the following year succeeded in preventing Cuba and the Soviet Union from co-operating militarily in a manner of their own choosing. Three years later there was a very large armed descent by the United States on the Dominican Republic to head off the possibility of that state moving to the left – a move which was dignified, if that is the word, by being wrapped up in the clothing of the Organization of American States and soon presented as the doctrine of the American President, Lyndon Johnson. The likeness of these aspects of the operation to what the Soviet Union did in Czechoslovakia in 1968 is worth noting, although there was no equivalence between the brutality of the incursions by the two super-powers into their respective back yards. In 1983 the United States in effect deposed a regime which had moved far to the left in the tiny Caribbean state of Grenada. And at the same time it was bolstering up the right-wing government of El Salvador and trying to upset the left-wing government of Nicaragua, not least because of the considerable support the latter was getting from Cuba.

A third form of dependence is more general in kind, existing where a weak country has close connections with a larger one and perhaps over a fairly wide range of key issues. The French-speaking countries of Africa, for example, have often attracted comment on account of the extent of the economic, financial, educational and cultural aid which they receive from France. In the particular case of the Ivory Coast it has been said that 'Eighteen years after independence, France remains [its] main supplier and customer, and French companies still control forty per cent of its industry and fifty per cent of its commerce'.[27] In turn, President Houphouët-Boigny of the Ivory Coast has such prestige among the political elite of Gabon that he has been said to be a 'sort of super-president of Gabon',[28] with all that that implies about the receptiveness of Gabon to suggestions made by the Ivorian government. The important copper industry in Zaire, although nationalized, is in effect run by a Belgian company which employs relatively few Zairian technical personnel. In Asia India's influence in Nepal and Bhutan is widely recognized. Lebanon relies heavily on Syria for such authority as it possesses. The United States has been said to pay for 42 per cent of the Israeli defence budget.[29] In the early postwar years Greece was heavily dependent on the United States. And for her part Greece has tried to ensure that Cyprus takes no important decisions without her prior consent.

Dependence which flows from weakness, therefore, in one form or another, and to this degree or that, is a fairly common phenomenon at the international level. As has been noted, it is often spoken of, implicitly if not explicitly, in terms which suggest that it involves a curtailment of the sovereignty of the dependent state. One writer has referred to the situation in Eastern Europe and also that in Latin America (on account of the economic dependence of many of its states) as clear instances of 'semi-colonial status'.[30] Another has said that the states of Eastern Europe, Central America and the Caribbean 'cannot be said to be independent in the normal sense'.[31] A former permanent under secretary at Britain's Foreign and Commonwealth Office has written – after his retirement – that such states as Czechoslovakia and Finland 'lack the sense of minimum security – and therefore the political self-confidence – which is necessary for the exercise of real as distinct from nominal sovereignty'.[32] And Guatemala and Cuba have been discussed in a chapter headed, 'Limited Sovereignty and the Inter-American System'.[33] The situation of the Ivory Coast has been spoken of as 'a classic neocolonialist one',[34] and it has been said of new states that 'sovereignty as the sum of attributes of a successful modern society seems beyond the reach of many'.[35]

Such quotations and the situations to which they refer should not be allowed to obscure the fact that dependent states are not wholly and at all times having to act in a manner which reflects dependence. Even the most subordinate of states will have a certain amount of leeway, and some will have considerably more. Further, it will sometimes be possible for such states to take an independent line in relation to the states on which they are perceived as being, in general terms, dependent. It is also the case that states which are usually seen as being in this condition will sometimes reject suggestions to this effect, and may do so with considerable vigour. Hot on the heels of the Czechoslovakian crises of 1968, for example, both Yugoslavia and Rumania made it very clear that they did not accept the doctrine of limited sovereignty which had been enunciated in *Pravda*. Of course, they had good political reasons for doing so, especially Rumania, which was most anxious both to maintain such distance between itself and the Soviet Union as it had already established and to make it as hard as possible for the Soviet Union to contemplate in respect of the Bucharest government the kind of action which had been taken against the one in Prague.

But just as words cannot on their own create a situation of dependence nor can they remove it. And given the existence in international relations of many varieties and degrees of dependence it follows that the states concerned are not completely sovereign, if sovereignty amounts to political independence of a quantitative kind. One Soviet scholar has been quoted as defining sovereignty as 'the independence of the state of any other state . . . the right to decide freely and according to its own judgment all its domestic and foreign affairs without interference on the part of other states',[36] which is the sort of definition assumed by many of those quoted in this section. In which case, if sovereignty is also taken to be something which is possessed in greater or lesser degree, a state's sovereignty is curtailed or limited in accordance with the extent of its dependence, although how that could possibly be calculated is something of a mystery. In any event, the conclusion to which this argument points is that there are many states operating at the international level which lack a full measure of sovereignty.

A rather similar conclusion is reached from an examination of the role in relatively weak sovereign states of multinational corporations, although here it is perhaps even easier to underestimate the freedom of action of such states than it is when considering their relations with larger states. The apparent strength of multinationals in relation to many of the smaller member states of international society is often depicted by comparing the former's gross annual sales with the latter's gross national product. One such table, for example, using 1970 figures, shows that out of a total of one hundred and twenty listed states, more than half had a gross national product of less than the gross annual sales of any of the forty listed multinational corporations.[37] From this kind of picture some observers found themselves jumping very easily to the conclusion that 'nation states are becoming entities without substance'[38] or, as an economist put it, the 'nation state is just about through as an economic unit'.[39] Nor was it only the smaller states who were being referred to. An unnamed British Cabinet minister has been quoted as saying in 1968 that national governments, including his own, 'will be reduced to the status of a parish council in dealing with the large international companies which span the world'.[40] As a quip had it, Standard Oil would buy Ruritania – if Gulf Oil would sell.

However, it was before long realized that these alarmist reactions went much too far. One observer commented that the increased attention being paid to multinational corporations came just at a time when they were 'withdrawing from their traditional more or less overt political role in world affairs'[41] to a 'more flexible'[42] relationship with their hosts. Others underlined this point, noting that the corporations (which were not a united group) needed to get on well with their hosts, just as the hosts needed to establish a good relationship with them. Thus the most profitable approach for both of them was the mode of co-operation, not battle. Moreover, it was increasingly observed that in this process it was often the host who called the tune, through its ability to mould the law to which the multinational was locally subject. One commentator went so far as to suggest that far from having 'the nation-state by the throat' the multinational corporation, assailed by its home government as well as its host, might well wonder 'whether the contrary is more accurate'.[43]

Wherever the exact balance is struck, it seems clear that some credence must be given to the argument that the multinational corporations, while they may be economic assets to their hosts, also place some limits on their freedom of action, and not necessarily in the economic field alone. As one student has put it, while the 'number of cases of clear and major threat to national control seem relatively small', the multinationals have sometimes 'intervened in important ways in political processes in host states'.[44] Accordingly, if sovereignty is taken to mean political independence, here is another ground for saying that many states do not enjoy it in full.

Interdependence

Over the last decade or two much has been heard about the interdependence of states. Just as the new student of economics used to be instructed about the ramifications of the world economy by way of a discourse upon the diverse origins of the various items which might that day have appeared upon his breakfast table, so now the student of international relations is frequently abjured to take due note of the interconnections of things political, as evidenced, maybe, by the matters reported in his morning newspaper. They will illustrate, it is said, the point that when one country sneezes another might well catch cold, and a third may be in for a nasty bout of influenza – and that the first may then be in further trouble on account of the complaints of the other two, and so on. Infection is, as it were, in the international air. But, while its ubiquity is not in doubt, its exact nature is hard to pin down and it is even harder to provide a detailed account of its effects.

One analyst has it that interdependence refers to 'the extent to which events occurring in any given part or within any given component unit of a world system affect (either physically or perceptually) events taking place in each of the other parts or component units of the system'.[45] Elsewhere it is defined as 'the direct and positive linkage of the interests of states where a change in the position of one state affects the others and in the same direction'.[46] It can thus be seen that the core of the interdependence argument has to do with the erosion of 'the old barriers between foreign and domestic policy'.[47] In the area of security and, pre-eminently, in the economic sphere it is held that states are no longer able to control their own destinies. Whether they like it or not they are subject to many important influences from abroad. As one commentator has put it in respect of the Western industrial nations, they are 'now so intermeshed with one another at so many different levels that it grows increasingly difficult for a single national government on its own to exercise effective power over many of the actions of its citizens'.[48] In consequence, during the 1960s, these states found themselves 'engaged in continuous negotiations over a widening range of topics. They were allies who needed each other's active assent to a number of decisions on which their national security, as well as their economic welfare and convenience, were felt to depend'.[49] From which the same author concludes that 'We live with more international constraints on our freedom of political action than many politicians care to recognize publicly'.[50]

It ought not to be supposed, however, that it is only recently that analysts and politicians have stumbled on the idea of inter-dependence. The term has been referred to as 'a catchword of the Second World War era'.[51] In 1933 a book was published which included the word 'interdependent' in its title, and opened by saying that 'It has become a platitude to say that the whole world is now interdependent'.[52] Even earlier, in 1919, the Secretary-General of the League of Nations was reported as being much aware of 'the fast developing interdependence of the world as an economic unit', from which he concluded that 'the sheer necessities of the situation will force the growth of some kind of world organization, even if we were to muff this particular attempt'.[53] And a well-known historian has referred to the late nineteenth century and early twentieth century as 'the *belle époque* of interdependence',[54] by which he means economic interdependence. Nor ought it to be thought that interdependence has necessarily been on the increase throughout the century. It has been suggested that, on the contrary, 'It is very questionable whether the interdependence of states has grown over-all since the period prior to World War I. In a number of important respects inter-dependence appears to have diminished rather than increased'.[55] A less impressionistic attempt to assess fluctuations in inter-dependence, by examining the interactions of six industrialized states during the period 1890–1975, bears this out. For the authors conclude that whereas interdependence was fairly insignificant before the First World War it declined during the interwar period and that, while it increased in the years following the Second World War, 'since 1958 the measures appear much more mixed'.[56] Moreover, whatever the relative incidence of interdependence at different times during the century, it is also arguable that the general significance of the phenomenon is often overestimated. One writer, indeed, has gone so far as to say that it is 'the great illusion of our times ... that economic and technological interdependence among the various factions of humanity has definitely devalued the fact of ... the existence of distinct states'.[57]

Be that as it may, there is no doubt that in various ways and degrees states are closely involved with each other, so that it makes sense to talk, in general terms, of their interdependence. The question for the present study, however, concerns the impact of this phenomenon on state sovereignty, and, on the assumption that sovereignty stands in direct relation to a state's political independence, there can be no doubt that interdependence makes the states concerned less sovereign than if they were not in that condition. That this is so is very clear to a number of commentators, although they often express this belief in words which are notably lacking in precision, and sometimes also in arguments which appear to be somewhat lacking in logical rigour. One analyst has suggested that 'taking place before our eyes is a revision of the very concept of national sovereignty. The dogma of absolute and inalienable independence, which is still defended by some, and taken for granted by the very large countries, is being replaced by the idea of interdependence.'[58] This raises several questions, but the gist of what is being said seems clear: that the circumstances giving rise to interdependence are bringing about a change in the content which has hitherto been given to the term 'sovereignty'. Or, as it has been put elsewhere, 'The traditional principle of sovereignty which plays a central role in the foreign policies of all states is now increasingly counteracted by the growing facts of interdependence which are being gradually shaped into a new, opposed principle'.[59] Another way in which essentially the same point is often expressed is to say that on account of inter-dependence what remains of sovereignty is 'more the shadow . . . than the substance'.[60]

The picture, therefore, is of a world in which states are in the process of losing, or maybe have already lost, a good part of their sovereignty. This is an argument which makes a lot of sense, provided that sovereignty is taken to mean the ability to take one's decisions on the basis solely of internal calculations and desires. For the day of completely autonomous decision-making does seem, for most states on many issues, to be past. Interests and economies are now so interwoven that it is unrealistic for states to try to detach themselves from all external strands. Security and prosperity are much influenced by what goes on, from day to day, beyond a country's borders. This is not to say that states are without any freedom of action, or even any effective freedom of action. They are still sometimes able to make a success of going their own individual ways, quite apart from occasionally being able to affect the nature of the international configuration in which they find themselves. But none the less it carries conviction to say of contemporary states, and maybe it was also true of the not-so-contemporary, that their life is significantly influenced by their interdependence.

Institutional Co-operation

A notable feature of the present century has been the growth of international institutions. From small beginnings in the second half of the nineteenth century, when certain so-called 'technical' matters were first dealt with on a regular international basis, institutions extended their range during the period between the two world wars, and since 1945 have greatly increased. Thus there are now about two hundred and fifty intergovernmental organizations, and Britain, to take one lively example, is a member of about half. They deal with everything from the issue of peace and security on a worldwide or regional basis, through a host of economic matters, down to what seem to be relatively mundane questions which are of concern only to a few states. In consequence, anyone trying to present an overall picture of the inter-state scene must now pay considerable attention to the extent to which diplomatic business has been institutionalized, and the student of international co-operation finds himself with a veritable mass of institutional data on his hands.

From one point of view these institutions may be seen as the expressions of the national purposes of their member states. They were established because the founder members judged that their individual interests would be advanced by such a move, and those states which joined or were admitted later will have done so under the same conviction. Of course, not all the members will be satisfied all the time by every aspect of the institution's activity. In the nature of things international, or of politics in any context, any two or three or more who are gathered together in one place are most unlikely to find that they are of a common mind about the exact nature of any proposed joint action. But it remains that any action which an institution takes, whether physical or verbal, must have been supported by at least a simple majority of those who were sufficiently interested or empowered to come to a clear view on the matter. It therefore makes good sense to analyse the working of any international institution by way of a question as to which group or faction is generally in control or which set of states had the predominant say on any particular move. In this way the work of an institution can be directly related to the policies and aspirations of its member states.

It is not, however, the case that an institution is a straightforward, passive channel for the expression of the majority's will. Just as the membership as a whole is not going to find itself in full agreement on this problem or that, so the majority on any particular matter will not have come to it sharing precisely the same point of view. Rather, that point of view will have been hammered out in a bargaining process which may have been very long and involved, and in which much ground, on many sides, may have been given in the interests of agreement. Thus, in consequence of membership in an institution, a state may find itself espousing a position which may be different in a not unimportant way from that which it would have adopted had the institution not existed. Moreover, in so far as the more general institutions are concerned, it is also the case that a state may find itself lining up on one side or other of a dispute which, but for its membership in the institution, it might very well have been able to ignore. It may do this out of a feeling for its responsibilities as a member. But it is also possible that such a move may be part of a process whereby its support of a certain formula has been traded for the support of other states on another matter before the institution on which it has a more immediate interest and hence a stronger view.

There are numerous permutations along these lines but the general theme is clear: that membership in any institution may bring about a modification of a state's perceived interests or the way in which those interests are expressed, and may also result in a state having to limit the range of its options in respect of a matter on which it would otherwise have had a free hand. Putting it differently, it can be said that institutional co-operation may be expected to place some restrictions upon a state's political independence, to curtail the extent of its political freedom. And this will happen not just in consequence of the work of those institutions which are able to take binding decisions by majority vote or which possess executive powers in the fields of security or economics – enabling them, for example, to establish peace-keeping forces or make loans. For the reciprocal pressures which occur within an institution are no less potent where the institution can act only on the basis of unanimity or where its typical form of decision is the recommendation, whether general or particular. The possession of a veto does not mean that it can be used without adverse political repercussions. Nor is it the case that states are unconcerned about the expression of an institution's opinion. Words may break no bones, but states are usually very keen to do what they can to ensure that the ones which are spoken are not critical of their cause and, if at all possible, advance it.

Even, therefore, in respect of so loose and informal an arrangement as the Congress system which followed the Napoleonic Wars, and which found expression in four meetings of the Great Powers during the years 1815–22, it has been said that, for the sort of reasons just discussed, it 'had a fundamental impact on the structure of international relations. National and state interests now had to be formulated in accordance with international formulae. Methods of action now had to include the international conference. Whatever a state did, it had to be prepared, ultimately, to face a conference and to defend its actions before an international assemblage. Policies calculated in terms of historic interest had to be considered in the light of institutional precepts.' From which the author concluded that 'though institutions are at their inception the result of antecedent forces, they soon come to have a measure of independent impact upon the course of events'.[61] One hundred years later, after the First World War, the League of Nations was set up and both its Council – a kind of executive committee, on which the major victorious powers were permanently represented – and its Assembly – where all states had a seat and which immediately took to meeting each year – were empowered to consider 'any matter within the sphere of action of the League or affecting the peace of the world'.[62] During the next twenty years a very large number of matters were discussed at meetings of the League in Geneva and often led to modifications in the positions of the member states.

However, it was not until after the Second World War that institutions made their most startling impact on the international scene. The body which achieved the greatest prominence was, of course, the United Nations, in the General Assembly of which (the successor to the League's Assembly) debate has each year ranged far and wide. Quite apart from any limitations on the effective freedom of speech or action of particular states which may have occurred in respect of specific issues as a result of discussions at New York, it is arguable that the UN has also had a more general and quite far-reaching influence on international relations. For its debates have played a big part in altering the balance of opinion on certain large issues of the day, and thus have placed some not inconsiderable obstacles in the way of states which might in other circumstances have been tempted to act in a manner which has proved unfashionable. One such issue concerns the use of armed force for national ends. The UN Charter itself outlaws the threat or use of force against the territorial integrity or political independence of any state, and the organization's history has heavily underlined the prevalent condemnation of the employment of arms for what might be called traditional international purposes. That is not to say that they have never been so used since 1945. But states have known that in addition to such physical opposition as they will meet on the ground they are also very likely to face a battery of diplomatic condemnation, the magnitude of which may seem all the greater on account of its emanation in concentrated form from the resonant halls of the UN's headquarters. And it is a matter of fact that the usual consequence, in times past, of the successful use of force – annexation of territory – has been virtually non-existent. As a counterbalance to these remarks it should be added that on some issues – the overthrow of colonial or racist regimes – the UN, far from condemning the use of force, has gone some way to encourage it. But that has to be seen in the context of the overriding commitment which the organization has developed to the majority's conception of international justice.

Besides helping to place some limitations on resort to force, the UN has also had a significant impact on the development of opinion regarding three other important questions of the postwar period. Two of them have just been mentioned, the linked issues of colonialism and racialism. The historical tide had already turned against the colonial powers of Western Europe by 1945 but this was not fully appreciated at the time. Fifteen years later, however, almost all of them were in full retreat, and it may be that steady UN pressure towards this end over the previous decade had had some effect. Certainly from then on the UN was in full cry against the remnants of colonialism, and except in one case, Portugal, the principle of colonial withdrawal was uncontested by those against whom it was directed. Indeed, they seemed to be almost falling over themselves in their eagerness to display their compliance with the prevailing mood. The position is very similar regarding racialism. For many years no one at the UN has had a good word to say for South Africa, and on account of its racial complexion the rebel regime in Rhodesia received a consistently icy shoulder. It is unlikely that some states would have acted in exactly this way had it not been for the existence of the UN and the embarrassment they would have suffered there, and elsewhere, had they expressed an unorthodox view.

The other major issue on which the UN has effectively limited the freedom of states is that of economic development. During the last twenty years the North-South divide has figured with increasing prominence on the international agenda, which has largely meant the agenda of the UN and its associated agencies. Not too much has happened in consequence of the barrage of verbal attention which it has received, but no state now denies, in principle, that the existence of large economic disparities between states is a scandal about which something should be done, and some action has followed from this position. Had the UN not existed, it is at least possible that official expressions of a contrary view would not have been under such a complete prohibition, or at least that a closer look would have been taken at the argument that the moral obligation of states to each other in this matter is exactly analogous to that of individuals within the same governed society.

The same kind of process which has been at work in the UN has also operated in other international institutions. In some of the UN's specialized agencies – associated with the UN but independent of it – the procedure of standard-setting appears to have had some informal impact on the freedom of action of the member states. This has been so, for example, in the International Labour Organization and the UN Educational, Scientific, and Cultural Organization. In the field of security, membership in such organizations as NATO and the Warsaw Pact inevitably carries with it considerable restrictive implications. For if industrialized states are to co-ordinate their defence in an effective manner they have to be willing to work together very closely, with all that that implies for the business of compromise. Likewise in the economic sphere, co-operation in trade, through such arrangements as the General Agreement on Tariffs and Trade, involves far-reaching limitations on the autonomous action which would otherwise be open to the participating states. Economic co-ordination of a more general kind, as has been organized by the Benelux countries (Belgium, the Netherlands and Luxembourg), the Nordic Union countries (Denmark, Finland, Iceland, Norway and Sweden) and the members of the European Free Trade Area, requires corresponding restrictions on their economic freedom – and hence, using the term in its wider sense, on their political freedom. Co-operation in the field of energy by the members of the International Energy Agency means that effectively they are no longer able to go their own independent ways in this increasingly important area. And in the European Economic Community, too, although the members have the formal power to obstruct moves to which they are opposed, they are in practice caught up in a variety of co-operative enterprises with which, in general terms, they usually feel politically obliged to go along.

Co-operation, in short, tends to generate its own momentum. And even where, as in the more general organizations, there is a lack of specific common purposes to create this kind of impetus, none the less the conduct of private discussion and public debate can often, as in the UN, produce the sort of diplomatic accommodations which will, in effect, limit the political independence of the members. In an institution such as the Organization of American States, for example, all the members, not excluding the largest, are susceptible to the pressures of their fellows. The same is true of a body such as the Commonwealth, although here, no doubt largely on account of the historical circumstances out of which it emerged, most of the pressures seem to go in one direction – towards Britain. The fact that the Organization of African Unity is somewhat less notable as a co-operative body is due to the rigidity of the divisions which exist between the members on a number of issues. The institutional channel has got, as it were, silted up at a number of points, or has never been properly cleared. The same can be said of the Arab League. But it also needs to be noted that, even though the members may currently be unable to compromise over a wide range of topics, the mere fact of the continued existence of the institution means that there is an immediately available framework for co-operative activity should an appropriate issue emerge or the times become, in a general way, more auspicious for this activity. At the height of the cold war, for example, the UN was frozen into immobility in many areas. As the ground gradually, and fitfully, thawed, ensuing developments could very conveniently be accommodated, in part, within the existing institution, and the existence of the institution may even have provided them with some marginal encouragement. Certainly it would have been enormously difficult for any new body to have been set up from scratch.

The whole process of co-operation through an institution is very often spoken of as a prime instance of internationalism, and it is frequently said to be directly opposed to the principle of sovereignty. One author, for example, although hedging on sovereignty by saying that it would need to be 'defined in its extreme forms', argues that sovereignty makes 'effective international organization impracticable'.[63] It has in fact been credited, if that is the word, with the failure of the Congress system in the early nineteenth century, from which the analyst in question went on to conclude, in 1914, that 'any attempt at international organization would come up against the difficulty that . . . the authority of the international institution would clash with the sovereignty of its constituent states'.[64] And it has been said that for the first two years of the First World War the reason why the question of an Allied transport pool could not be tackled head on was that it was 'too big a problem: it threatened to raise questions of sovereignty that no one was ready to answer'.[65] As it turned out, it was possible to solve the transport problem on a co-operative basis, and in the latter years of the war about twenty Allied bodies were set up by Britain, France, Italy and the United States to deal not only with shipping but also with food and materials. They consisted of the relevant parts of the national administrations integrated into separate agencies which allotted the resources and commodities in question on the basis of agreement. Their disbandment after the conclusion of hostilities, however, led to the comment that the countries concerned were 'once more sovereign'.[66]

Anxieties about sovereignty did not prevent the establishment of the League of Nations. However, the root of the difficulties which lay in the way of its development of new methods of co-operation has been said to be 'national sovereignty'.[67] And in a very familiar type of statement, a secretary-general of its successor organization has said that 'The history of the United Nations . . . has essentially been the story of the search for a working balance between national sovereignty and national interests on the one hand and international order and the long-term interests of the world community on the other'.[68] The very establishment of the UN and of other international agencies has been said to be an act by which 'governments agree to sacrifice their sovereignty'.[69] In respect of one such body, UNESCO, the same point has been made in a more modest way by the statement that in joining 'Member States have in a sense voluntarily surrendered a small part of their sovereignty', although it was given even greater modesty by the additional comment that 'hardly one of them is willing to recognize this except very rarely and slowly'.[70] And, to take just one other and rather more typical instance, it has been asserted that the states which established the International Energy Agency 'in effect surrender[ed] much of . . . their so-called "sovereignty" '.[71]

These remarks point very clearly to the fact that there is a good deal of uncertainty about the exact content which should be given to the principle of sovereignty, and some unease about how, in theory, it can be reconciled with participation in an international organization. States themselves do not always help on this point as sometimes, for the advancement of their own national purposes, they themselves assert that courses over which in other contexts they do not bat an eyelid must be rigorously eschewed on account of the threat which they would present to their sovereignty. Thus, for example, the Soviet Union and its East European allies refused to join in the American Marshall Plan for the economic recovery of Europe after 1945 on exactly this ground. However, this is just a reminder not only that sovereignty is a term which can be used in a variety of ways but also that so far as references to general principles are concerned states are not greatly worried by the problem of consistency. Sovereignty, like democracy or justice, is, on account of its high emotive content, often used by states as nothing more than a handy semantic weapon, to be thrown into an argument as an additional reason for supporting this or opposing that.

But at a very general level it is possible to discern a common thread running through all the statements about sovereignty that have just been referred to. It is that this condition has something to do with freedom of action, or political independence. Given this terminology, it certainly follows that institutions may be spoken of as expressing an idea which is contrary to that of sovereignty. For, quite apart from the possibility that they may provide for the taking of binding decisions by majority vote, the whole object of setting them up is to encourage co-operative action. In as much, therefore, as the successful working of an institution almost inevitably places some restriction on the effective freedom of action of its member states, this process may be referred to as a cutting down of their sovereignty. On this matter, however, two points need to be made.

The first is that membership in an international institution generally involves not just giving but also taking. In other words, states benefit from their participation, the channel to which an institution may be likened enabling political traffic to be carried in both directions for all members. Thus, while membership may lead to concessions and compromises on a number of issues on which the states concerned would in other circumstances have had a free choice, it also has a countervailing effect. For on many questions, on account of their membership, states will have a better chance of realizing, if not their precise goals, at least something which bears a close approximation to them. It was, after all, with this sort of aim in view that they will have joined in the first place and not out of any abstract commitment to the cause of international organization. Accordingly, from time to time individual members will unite with others of like mind to mobilize a particular institution in their favour, and in this way may well be able to move further in a preferred direction than their own several strengths would have been able to take them.

Thus, when the impact of the UN on opinion and action regarding certain broad issues was discussed, the matter could have been presented as instances of large numbers of states using the organization to promote their policies. As it was, emphasis was placed on the need for mutual accommodation and hence on the restrictions on the individual members' freedom, but it would have been equally valid to concentrate on the overall advance towards certain goals. Of course, not everyone will have an equal degree of success in this kind of enterprise. But any state which feels that the costs of membership far outweigh its gains is always able to leave, for it is still clearly the case that, at bottom, institutions are subordinate to their members. States are the free constituents and not the captive clients of the bodies to which they belong. It is for this reason that one should be cautious about describing the world's institutional arrangements as an instance of internationalism, with all the implications which that word carries about the moral worth and deserved political weight of what is deemed to be the expression of the common will. For this terminology tends to obscure the fact that institutions are very much rooted in the international political scene. Their operation may place restrictions on the effective extent of their members' independence, but this is part of the process whereby those members endeavour to use the institutions to advance their national purposes.

On this basis it may be said that political independence, in the sense of being able to get one's way, is enhanced by institutions as well as diminished. From which it follows that many of the remarks which are made about institutions reducing sovereignty present too one-sided a picture. Some states might even feel their sovereignty to have been increased as a result of their membership in one or more such bodies. Certainly the claim that the increased role of international institutions has necessarily had a severely adverse effect on state sovereignty is hardly convincing. This, however, leads to the second point, which concerns the use of the term 'sovereignty' to mean political independence, and not just in respect of the establishment and working of institutions but in a more general way. As has been shown, it is so employed in a number of wide-ranging contexts, but it is arguable that this is an unhelpful and even a confusing image. It is to this issue that attention will now be turned.

Critique

There are five reasons why the use of 'sovereignty' to mean political independence may attract criticism. The first relates to a difficulty which lies at the very heart of the idea of political independence, in as much as its content seems to consist of an uneasy amalgam of both freedom and success, with many observers requiring a considerable measure of each. For example, it is quite possible to conceive of a state which has considerable freedom in international relations yet which would not be generally regarded as possessing an equivalent amount of political independence. Such a state might be one which lived an uncontroversial and largely self-sufficient life, enabling it to decide on its foreign policy unhampered by many outside pressures. Its policies might make little impression on the rest of the world, in the sense either that little notice was taken of them or that they were lacking in success. But freedom, of a sort, such a state would certainly have. Contrariwise, it is equally possible to imagine a state which enjoys international success, in the sense that it achieves many of its goals, but which does not have much freedom, on account of its close and dependent links with another and larger state. Here, too, there might be a widespread reluctance to speak of the state as having an equivalent measure of political independence.

Political independence is, therefore, a rather fuzzy concept. Like a number of other things, it is more easily recognized than defined, but most analysts and commentators appear to assume that it is made up of some quantity of both freedom and success. It is not necessarily any the worse for being rather vague, but this *is* a disadvantage if it is to be equated with sovereignty. For sovereignty is, after all, usually said to be a key or basic concept in international relations, and it might therefore reasonably be expected to be something which possesses a fair measure of clarity – even if those referring to its importance are often themselves unable to present it in this way.

The second doubt about the wisdom of defining sovereignty as political independence concerns the difficulty which attaches to any attempted calculation of the extent to which a particular state enjoys this condition. For, even assuming that one knows what one is looking for, it is enormously hard to reach any firm overall finding. It might be possible to come to a fairly assured conclusion about the amount of political independence which a state has on a specific issue, but once one moves to wider areas serious problems are encountered. Even in respect of one sector of a state's life, such as its security or financial situation, there are difficulties, and they become greater when one tries to make a judgement about the political independence of one state in relation to another. When, therefore, the effort is made to combine all these strands into a convincing and reasonably precise general statement regarding a state, one is faced with a task which is virtually impossible. Instead one is reduced to remarks of very considerable generality. Again, there is nothing necessarily wrong in this, but it does seem a bit odd to end up in this way if one is also talking about a concept which is said to be of fundamental importance at the international level. For it amounts to saying that of this concept one can go no further than remarks of the vaguest kind. And, while in respect of political independence it might be possible to conclude that there is not much point in speaking of it in general terms and that it is more profitable to relate it to particular aspects of a state's life, it is hardly open to one fully to follow suit in respect of sovereignty. One *could* speak of a state's sovereignty in this or that area, but it is clearly established that sovereignty is something which, more usually and more importantly, refers to the condition of a state when viewed as a whole.

The next objection to the equation of political independence with sovereignty has to do with the fact that the exercise which has been discussed in the previous paragraph is very familiar to students of international relations under another name – the attempt to calculate a state's power. For if by power one means not just a state's strength on paper but its ability to get its way in international relations – and this is a common and reasonable use of the term – one meets exactly the same problems as those just considered, and for that very reason efforts are rarely made to estimate a state's overall power in anything approaching precise terms. Thus the accepted terminology of great, medium and small powers, and so on, is recognized as being little more than a useful form of very general shorthand, and often a very unreliable guide to the way in which a clash between two states will be resolved. There is no reason why sovereignty should not be treated as a synonym for power – it has, indeed, been called 'a fancy phrase for power'[72] – but it does seem a superfluous use, for power is a very well accepted term and the idea it conveys is fairly clear. Moreover, in the literature sovereignty is often regarded as something which is distinct from power. To define it in a similar way might therefore lead to confusion between two important but separate aspects of reality.

The fourth reason for thinking that sovereignty is best kept separate from political independence is that the latter idea is not one which applies exclusively to states. Difficult though it might be to assess it exactly, none the less one can speak of the political independence of entities other than those which engage regularly in international relations. The constituent elements of a federal state, for example, may be weighed in this manner, as may lesser territorial entities or bodies which have no territorial base at all, such as an industrial firm, a trade union, or even an individual. And this exercise relies on the same idea as that which is used when one discusses the political independence of states. Thus if sovereignty is used synonymously with political independence, it does not tell one anything which is distinctive about the states to which it is applied. There is no reason why it should not be so used, whether of states or of bodies other than states – and one does come across references to the sovereignty of non-state entities where the term is being used synonymously with political independence. But it is also the case that in at least one of the usages of sovereignty reference is being made to a factor or element which is peculiar to those territorial entities which participate in international relations. There must, after all, be such a factor – for otherwise there would be no way of determining which entities were eligible to act at the international level – and if it is called sovereignty it is not just unnecessary but also confusing to give the term an additional content, such as political independence.

The fifth and final argument against the use of sovereignty to mean political independence is that it does not accord with the way in which states speak of themselves and their fellows. In this they are not always consistent, but when they refer to their international status, especially their own, they do not seem to have in mind something which is assessed in terms of more or less, such as political independence. Instead they appear to be speaking of a characteristic which, when its existence is inquired about, attracts the answer yes or no – something which is either present or absent and cannot be possessed in degree. And sometimes this characteristic is specifically distinguished from independence, or the concessions which co-operation requires. France's Minister of the Interior, for example, has said in answer to the question whether his country must remain independent that 'A main aim of this government is the idea of sovereignty. Note that I do not say "independence" '.[73] He then went on to speak of the way in which all countries were growing more involved with each other and how some problems required a world-wide approach, but distinguished these from 'a nation's own sovereignty'. Likewise, a President of the United States, when he was referred to the world's growing economic interdependence and asked 'How much sovereignty is the United States willing to give up in the decision-making process?', answered, 'None.' To which the interviewer, apparently taken aback, said, 'None?', and the President replied: 'Not to give up sovereignty. I think, though, within the bounds of sovereignty to be maintained by all the nations, that co-operation is very important.'[74]

This points to a clear conclusion about political independence and sovereignty. It is that there is a real and substantial distinction between sovereignty as meaning that which makes a territorial entity eligible to participate in international relations – that is, constitutional independence – and political independence. It is entirely in order for sovereignty to be used synonymously with political independence, but in that event it must be remembered that there is another, quite different and arguably more important usage of the term – one which does apply distinctively to the states making regular appearances on the international stage, and can convincingly be said to be the concept which is at the very basis of international relations. From which it might be concluded that it is unhelpful and possibly confusing to speak of sovereignty as meaning political independence.

What is *not* to be concluded from these remarks, however, is that questions relating to political independence are of no consequence. Vague though this idea is, and hard to pin down, none the less it is a very important one for both student and practitioner. Anyone wishing to understand the dynamics of international life needs to know a lot about the extent to which the territorial actors are free and successful, and also to appreciate the subtlety of the issue. But what is being considered under this heading is the political independence of sovereign states – sovereign, that is, in the sense of constitutionally independent. The whole question of permeability, for example, concerns the extent to which sovereign states have become subject to new and far-reaching influences, but these influences have no bearing at all upon their constitutional separateness, and, in consequence, none upon their sovereignty. A permeable state is by that token no less constitutionally independent than it was in its less permeable days, for the matter of permeability has everything to do with its political independence but nothing to do with its constitutional situation.

The same line of argument applies to dependent states. Dependence has no bearing on sovereignty, when that term means constitutional independence, for the two are quite separate matters. One has to do with a state's formal position in constitutional law, and the other with its political situation in the vicissitudes of international relations. One can have sovereign states which are dependent, very dependent, and even paralytically dependent – and on account of their dependence they may be quite unimportant. But dependence has no more bearing on a state's sovereignty than does a man's health upon his citizenship. Interdependence attracts the same response. No matter how far this process has gone, it cannot by itself have any influence upon a state's constitutional independence, or sovereignty. It may be of vast significance for a state's political life and future, in that the state may be much more restricted than hitherto – although it may also on account of the same process be much better off. But interdependence cannot infiltrate, as it were, a state's sovereignty – unless sovereignty is defined in terms of political independence. Defined in terms of constitutional independence, sovereignty and interdependence are ideas which exist on quite different levels, connected, no doubt, but entirely distinguishable. It is a situation which may be likened to the bonds existing between the members of a family, in that no matter how closely knit the family the members retain their separate identities.

The position is the same regarding institutional co-operation. International institutions are created by sovereign states and only those which are sovereign, meaning constitutionally independent, are normally eligible to join. Such an act may be regarded as a form of confirmation of a new state's sovereignty, 'a palpable sign that their status is recognized in the eyes of the world . . . Sovereignty is thus epitomized and personified in a rite of independent national maturity and individual political manhood'.[75] But this must not obscure the fact that membership in an international organization in no way bestows sovereignty on a state. It is because it is sovereign that it is eligible to join. Once inside, it may find itself subject to all sorts of pressures (as well as privy to all sorts of opportunities). These may be regarded as restricting its freedom or independence, but they have no impact on the state's constitutional situation and none, therefore, upon its sovereignty. The members of an institution may have congregated closely together, but it is still a matter, as it has been graphically put by President de Gaulle, of 'everyone drinking from his own glass'.[76]

Thus, nothing that has appeared in this chapter diminishes the force of what has been said earlier in the book regarding the use of 'sovereignty' in its most fundamental sense, to mean constitutional independence. What has been noted here is the fact that another and very popular use of the term is to make it synonymous with political independence. The individual points which may be advanced in that connection are important, but the employment of the term 'sovereignty' to characterize them is unnecessary and confusing. For sovereignty has another meaning which is both distinctive and of great importance, an importance which relates not to the process of international relations but to their basic structure. However, the use of 'sovereignty' in this latter way, to mean constitutional independence, also receives a challenge on the legal front, one which asserts that sovereignty has to do with independence in relation not to constitutional but to international law. This is the matter which will be considered in the next chapter.

Notes: Chapter 7

1 Hannah Arendt, *Crises of the Republic* (Harmondsworth: Penguin, 1973), p. 85.
2 Joseph Frankel, *International Politics: Conflict and Harmony* (Harmondsworth: Allen Lane/Penguin Press, 1969), p. 38.
3 F. S. Northedge and M. J. Grieve, *A Hundred Years of International Relations* (London: Duckworth, 1971), p. 344.
4 Shlomo Slonim, 'American-Egyptian rapprochement', *The World Today*, vol. 31, no. 2 (February 1975), p. 55.
5 Yigal Allon, 'The Arab-Israeli conflict', *International Affairs*, vol. 40, no. 2 (April 1964), p. 217.
6 Patrick Seale, 'The Egypt–Israel treaty and its implications', *The World Today*, vol. 35, no. 5 (May 1979), p. 191.
7 On which see further below, Chapter 8, pp. 210–21.
8 John H. Herz, *International Politics in the Atomic Age* (New York: Columbia University Press, 1959), p. 40.
9 ibid.
10 ibid., p. 97.
11 ibid., p. 143.
12 K. Knorr, *On the Uses of Military Power in the Nuclear Age* (New York: Columbia University Press, 1966), p. 174.
13 ibid., p. 84.
14 J. L. S. Girling, ' "Kissingerism": the enduring problems', *International Affairs*, vol. 51, no. 3 (July 1975), p. 340.
15 R. N. Gardner, *In Pursuit of World Order* (New York: Praeger, 1964), p. 4.
16 Martin Wight, in a review of John H. Herz, *International Politics in the Atomic Age* (note 8, above), *American Political Science Review*, vol. 54, no. 4 (December 1960), p. 1057.
17 R. E. Osgood and R. W. Tucker, *Force, Order, and Justice* (Baltimore, Md: Johns Hopkins University Press, 1967), p. 325.
18 Editorial in *New York Times*, 11 April 1968.
19 *New York Times*, 18 November 1968.

20   As quoted in New York Times, 27 September 1968.
21   Harlan Cleveland, quoted in NATO Letter, vol. 17, no. 2 (February 1969).
22   The Times, 11 July 1969.
23   ibid.
24   Quoted in W. Strang, Britain in World Affairs (London: Faber/André Deutsch, 1961), p. 229.
25   Quoted in Ronald Steel, Pax Americana (New York: Viking Press, 1968), p. 202.
26   Quoted in Aurel Braun, 'New dimensions and directions in the Warsaw Pact', Millennium, vol. 6, no. 3 (Winter 1977/8), p. 240.
27   Leader in The Times, 11 January 1978.
28   Suzanne Cronje, The World and Nigeria (London: Sidgwick & Jackson, 1972), p. 300, quoted in John J. Stremlau, The International Politics of the Nigerian Civil War, 1967–1970 (Princeton, NJ: Princeton University Press, 1977), p. 137.
29   K. Kyle, 'The Palestinian Arab state: collision course or solution?', The World Today, vol. 33, no. 9 (September 1977), p. 352.
30   H. Seton Watson, 'Nationalism and imperialism', in V. Degras (ed.), The Impact of the Russian Revolution, 1917–1967 (London: Oxford University Press, 1967), p. 140.
31   Hedley Bull, The Anarchical Society (London: Macmillan, 1977), p. 116.
32   Denis Greenhill, 'The future of security in Western Europe', International Affairs, vol. 50, no. 1 (January 1974), p. 2.
33   T. M. Franck and E. Weisband, Word Politics (New York: Oxford University Press, 1971), ch. 4.
34   Leader in The Times, 11 January 1978.
35   Charles Burton Marshall, The Exercise of Sovereignty (Baltimore, Md: Johns Hopkins University Press, 1965), p. 207.
36   Quoted in R. J. Erickson, International Law and the Revolutionary State (Dobbs Ferry, NY: Oceana, 1972), p. 50.
37   See Marshall R. Singer, 'The foreign policies of small developing states', in James M. Rosenau, Kenneth W. Thompson and Gavin Boyd, World Politics (New York: The Free Press and London: Collier-Macmillan, 1976), pp. 265–9.
38   R. Murray, in New Left Review (May–June 1971), p. 87. Quoted in Guy Caire, 'Dependence, independence and interdependence in economic relations', in H. W. Morris-Jones and Georges Fischer (eds), Decolonisation and After: The British and French Experience (London: Cass, 1980), p. 148.
39   C. P. Kindleberger, American Business Abroad (New Haven, Conn.: Yale University Press, 1969), p. 207, quoted in Robert O. Keohane and Van Doorn Ooms, 'The multinational enterprise and world political economy', International Organization, vol. 26, no. 1 (Winter 1972), p. 115.
40   In G. McDermott, The New Diplomacy and its Apparatus (London: Plume Press, 1973), p. 17.
41   Louis Turner, 'Multinational companies and the Third World', The World Today, vol. 30, no. 9 (September 1974), p. 394.
42   ibid., p. 401.
43   Seymour J. Rubin, 'Developments in the law and institutions of international economic relations: the multinational enterprise at bay', American Journal of International Law, vol. 68, no. 3 (July 1974), p. 486.
44   Joan Edelman Spero, The Politics of International Economic Relations (London: Allen & Unwin, 1977), pp. 103 and 199.
45   Oran Young, 'Interdependencies in world politics', International Journal, vol. 24 (Autumn 1969), p. 726, quoted in R. O. Keohane and J. S. Nye, 'Introduction: the complex politics of Canadian–American interdependence', International Organization, vol. 28, no. 4 (Autumn 1974), p. 599.
46   R. Rosecrance et al., 'Whither interdependence?', International Organization, vol. 31, no. 3 (Summer 1977), p. 425.

47 William Wallace, *The Foreign Policy Process in Britain* (London: Allen & Unwin for the Royal Institute of International Affairs, 1976), pp. 268–9.
48 A. Schonfield, *Europe: Journey to an Unknown Destination* (Harmondsworth: Penguin, 1973), p. 14.
49 A. Schonfield, 'Overall view', in his (ed.) *International Economic Relations of the Western World, 1959–1971, Vol. 1, Politics and Trade* (London: Oxford University Press, 1976), p. 124.
50 Schonfield, *Europe*, p. 22.
51 Wm Roger Louis, *Imperialism at Bay, 1941–1945* (Oxford: Clarendon, 1977), p. 110.
52 R. Muir, *The Interdependent World and its Problems* (Boston, Mass.: Houghton Mifflin, 1933), p. 1, quoted in Andrew M. Scott, 'The logic of international interaction', *International Studies Quarterly*, vol. 21, no. 3 (September 1977), p. 429.
53 Jean Monnet, *Memoirs* (London: Collins, 1978), p. 81.
54 Asa Briggs, quoted in Kenneth N. Waltz, *Theory of International Politics* (Reading, Mass.: Addison-Wesley, 1979), p. 140.
55 Osgood and Tucker, *Force, Order, and Justice*, p. 325.
56 Rosecrance *et al.*, 'Whither interdependence?', p. 425.
57 R. Aron, *Peace and War* (New York: Praeger, 1967), p. 748.
58 J.-B. Duroselle, 'Changes in diplomacy since Versailles', in B. Porter (ed.), *The Aberystwyth Papers* (London: Oxford University Press, 1972), p. 127.
59 J. Frankel, *National Interest* (London: Pall Mall, 1970), p. 150.
60 Wallace, *Foreign Policy Process*, p. 269.
61 R. N. Rosecrance, *Action and Reaction in International Politics* (Boston, Mass.: Little, Brown, 1963), p. 56.
62 Arts III and IV of the Covenant of the League of Nations.
63 Alan Watt, *The United Nations: Confrontation or Consensus* (Canberra: Australian Institute of International Affairs, 1974), p. 10.
64 Carsten Holbraad, *The Concert of Europe* (London: Longman, 1970), p. 194, referring to W. Alison Phillips's *The Confederation of Europe: A Study in the European Alliance, 1813–1823, as an Experiment in the International Organization of Peace* (London: Longman, 1914), pp. 293–8.
65 Monnet, *Memoirs*, p. 57.
66 ibid., p. 75.
67 ibid., p. 96.
68 *Report of the Secretary-General on the Work of the Organization, 1976–1977*, UN Document A/32/1, 1 September 1977, p. 3.
69 Evan Luard, *International Agencies* (London: Macmillan for the Royal Institute of International Affairs, 1977), p. 304.
70 Richard Hoggart, *An Idea and its Servants. UNESCO from Within* (London: Chatto & Windus, 1978), p. 55.
71 Richard B. Lillick, 'Economic coercion and the international legal order', *International Affairs*, vol. 51, no. 3 (July 1975), p. 359.
72 Benn W. Levy in a letter to *The Times*, 31 December 1969.
73 Prince Michael Poniatowski, *Newsweek*, 4 November 1974.
74 President Carter, *The Times*, 'Europa' supplement, 3 May 1977.
75 James P. Sewell, 'UNESCO: pluralism rampant', in R. W. Cox and H. K. Jacobson, *The Anatomy of Influence* (New Haven, Conn.: Yale University Press, 1973), pp. 149–50.
76 Quoted in Monnet, *Memoirs*, p. 485.

8

Legal

It has been argued earlier in this work that sovereignty is legal in nature, and this is in fact quite widely accepted. What is not widely accepted, however, is that the law with which it has to do is constitutional in character. Instead, it is very often thought to be related in some way to international law, expressing the independence of the state in terms of that body of rules. It may therefore, on this basis, be summed up as legal independence, it being understood that it is international law to which reference is being made.

The idea of legal independence is not one which has attracted a single interpretation. In the literature about international relations it is possible to discern a number of meanings which have been given to it, all of which are intended to convey the suggestion that the sovereign state is one which has a special relationship with international law. They may, for convenience, be divided into two broad categories. One concentrates on what it conceives to be the internal immunity of the state from the claims of international law, asserting that sovereignty consists of the legal right of a state to conduct itself within its own borders entirely as it wishes. It will be considered in the next chapter. The other focuses on three different ways in which the state in its international aspect is related to international law. In the first place, it is said that a state of this nature is, in essence, a construct of international law and should be conceived in terms of the basic rights and privileges which it derives from this source. Sovereignty amounts to sovereign rights, without which the state would have no international standing. An approach which is in one respect similar to this is that which emphasizes not the basic rights which are bestowed upon a state by international law but the freedom which a state retains after all its international legal obligations are taken into account. Sovereignty, in other words, consists of legal freedom, and is restricted by the various legal duties incumbent upon a state in its international capacity. In consequence, a state's sovereignty will vary from time to time in accordance with the extent to which its freedom of action has been limited by international law. The third approach to the idea of sovereignty as legal independence is that which sees its core to lie in the right to determine the extent of one's own legal obligations, and also to interpret them oneself. Sovereignty is thus, on this view, intimately connected with consent, in that a sovereign state is one which need be bound in law by nothing to which it has not agreed. Non-sovereign territorial entities, like individuals within the state, often find that they have legal obligations which flow directly from the fiat of a superior body. Internationally, by contrast, there is no such body, and sovereign states are in control of their own legal destinies. In this sense they have, in their international relations, a free hand so far as the assumption of obligations is concerned.

The ideas which underlie these conceptions of sovereignty are not mutually exclusive. There is, however, a further approach to sovereignty as legal independence which follows a quite different path. Those mentioned so far all base themselves on the assumption that sovereignty is compatible with international law. This other approach, however, speaks of sovereignty as something which is contrary to the idea of law, contrary, that is, to bindingness. It suggests that the sovereign state is legally independent in the sense that it is independent of international law, and therefore in no way bound by it. If this line of argument is valid, the other approaches which have been mentioned all fall to the ground as possible descriptions of what, essentially, it means to be a sovereign state, or, indeed, as descriptions of certain attributes of sovereign statehood. In that event it would have to be asked how it comes about that they continue to be mentioned in the literature and by practitioners. This last approach will therefore be considered first.

Above the Law

The argument that a sovereign state is above international law in the sense of not being bound by it appears to reflect the feeling that there is something in the very idea of sovereignty which necessitates this conclusion. Sovereignty, it is implied, connotes a lack of restraint, total freedom, the absence of any fetters whatsoever. By definition, the holder of sovereignty is entirely free to do what he likes. It follows that if the territorial entities participating in international relations are sovereign, which they all claim to be, they cannot be subject to international law. From which it follows either that states are not sovereign or that international law is a sham. Not everyone starting out from the above premiss goes the whole hog to this conclusion. But it is certainly implicit, logically speaking, in the starting point of the argument. And a number of writers who accept both the starting point and the claim of states to sovereignty find themselves being drawn ineluctably towards the conclusion that such states cannot be regarded as bound by international law.

One student of the international scene puts it this way: 'The very concepts of sovereign individual states and of an international legal system are fundamentally opposed: if the states are truly sovereign, the legal rules cannot be binding; if the legal rules are binding, the states cannot be truly sovereign.'[1] In this he echoes the statement of a historian that 'the claim to sovereignty is tantamount to the denial of the existence of any higher authority or law'.[2] Nor have the lawyers always felt able to guide their readers away from this conclusion. A British authority on international law who later rose to the bench of the International Court of Justice has said that 'the truth of the matter is that sovereignty and international law are ultimately opposed notions',[3] and an American who did likewise has observed that some states still cling to the idea of 'absolute sovereignty above the law'.[4] An academic-cum-practitioner has also made a comment in a very similar vein, saying that the growing acceptance by governments of rules to govern their behaviour slowly encourages the belief that 'national sovereignty is not overriding'.[5] There is, as it has been put by two others, a 'battle for the supremacy of international law over national sovereignty'[6] – though it is far from clear what sort of world is envisaged as emerging should this battle be won by the law. For if states are not supreme there would presumably be an authority to govern them, and in that event the law of such an authority could hardly be 'international'.

One way in which it would be possible for states to be placed above international law would be through the existence of a system of law superior to it which made such a provision. This would establish the lawfulness of this position, and it is the only way of making it lawful. But a system of law of this kind does not exist. One therefore has to ask whether, as a matter of practice, states habitually treat international law as of no consequence, and of no relevance to their concerns and activities. The answer is an unequivocal no. Indeed, one of the most obvious, and also one of the most basic, facts about international relations is the existence of a system of law to which sovereign states are subject. All states are bound by the customary law of the international society, and any two or more of them may, among themselves, amend and extend that law by way of treaties. There is, in principle, no question about this, nor has there ever been throughout the existence over five centuries of the modern states system. As the first Chief Justice of the United States said in the eighteenth century, 'The United States, by taking a place among the nations of the earth, [became] amenable to the law of nations'.[7] Of course, states may not like particular provisions of that law – and will therefore seek to change them. There may also be dispute about what the law requires, or its proper interpretation. But as a matter of theory the position is wholly clear: states are bound by international law – and, moreover, are so by virtue of their sovereignty. International law is, after all, as Vattel said long ago, a law for sovereigns – or, as would now be said, for sovereign states.

In view of this it is exceedingly surprising that respected commentators can commit themselves to the view that there is a fundamental incompatibility or a diametrical conflict between sovereignty and international law, for manifestly, in both the theory and the practice of the international society, there is nothing of the kind. It might be possible to come to this view through the belief that international law is not true or proper law, for this belief might in turn reflect the thesis that the nature of law is such that it cannot exist in a society of sovereign states. Another route to the same position could involve a confusion between bindingness and observance. For if it is assumed that international law is very largely disregarded, and then assumed that this means that it is to all intents and purposes without binding effect, it could be concluded that the law's lack of bindingness is a necessary consequence of its attempt to exist in the midst of a collectivity of sovereign bodies. Once again, law and sovereignty would appear as totally opposed. In fact it can be shown that both the assumptions of this second argument are false. And so far as the first argument is concerned it can be said in reply that, quite apart from the speech and practice of states, there are respectable jurisprudential arguments in support of the proposition that law can exist perfectly well at the international level.

It is unlikely, however, that the presumed incompatability between international law and sovereignty flows from assumptions about the nature of law. It is much more probable that it is a consequence of the sort of *a priori* assumptions about the nature of sovereignty which were mentioned at the beginning of this section. In turn, these reflect the fallacy that a word can have only one proper meaning. But in fact a word such as 'sovereignty' can be given many meanings, or usages, and no one of them is more right or wrong than any other. Rather, it is a question of asking in relation to any one context, which is the orthodox or appropriate meaning. And there is no doubt that at the international level 'sovereignty' does not carry a meaning which makes it incompatible with law, at least not when it is used by states to denote that which makes them eligible to participate in international relations on a regular basis, nor, indeed, when they use it to describe any part of their condition. This is not to say that in some other context – in some political philosophizing for example – 'sovereignty' may not be given a meaning which places it in opposition to law. But there is no ground at all for carrying such a usage over to another sphere, especially if in that other sphere the word has a settled meaning of a different kind. Which, in respect of international relations, 'sovereignty' has. The idea that at this level 'sovereignty' means independent of international law may therefore be firmly rejected.

Sovereign Rights

This approach is very different from the one just discussed. Far from asserting an incompatibility between sovereignty and international law, it claims that sovereignty consists of certain legal rights which are bestowed upon a state by international law. These sovereign rights are of fundamental importance in two connected ways. In the first place they deal with matters which are central to the existence and activity of the state in the international context. And, second, they provide a legal basis for this activity, enabling states to go about their business in a legitimate way. In this usage, therefore, sovereignty amounts to legal independence in the sense that it comprises the legal powers which are necessary for a state to act independently on the international stage.

The most basic of these powers is the right of the state to exercise jurisdiction within its borders and to take its own decisions regarding its internal and external affairs. Indeed, this is quite often referred to as the right of sovereignty. However, the idea of sovereign rights generally includes other rights of an elemental kind, such as the right of self-defence. The state also benefits from correlative rules which prohibit other states from intervening in its domain and from mounting an act of aggression against it. Two further rights which are essential if the state is to participate in international life are those enabling it to establish embassies in foreign capitals and to make treaties with other states – although a state has no right to insist that another state receives an ambassador from it or signs a treaty with it.

Sometimes the idea of sovereign rights is extended to all a state's legal capacities. No doubt it is in this sense that the constitutions of some West European states – the Netherlands and West Germany for example – provide for the possible renunciation of the states' sovereign powers in favour of international organizations. Another expression of this point of view is the observation that 'the sovereignty of the State consists of its competence as defined and limited by international law'.[8] But more usually the phrase 'sovereign rights' refers only to those elements in a state's legal make-up which, from the external angle, are of its essence in that they provide the necessary juridical basis for the state's international activity. These key areas have been referred to judicially as the state's 'organic powers',[9] and collectively they are often spoken of as constituting the sovereignty of the state. In the view of an international judge, for example, sovereignty is 'a quality conferred by international law',[10] and an academic lawyer has said that states are sovereign 'only in virtue of international law'.[11] From which it is but a short step, if indeed it is any step at all, to seeing the state itself as an international entity which exists only in consequence of international law.

In this approach to sovereignty there is a good deal of merit. There can be no doubt, for example, about the importance of sovereign rights. If inter-state activity is not to be chaotic it must take place within the framework of a system of rules which awards rights and assigns duties. This is the primary function of international law. Within this system some of the rights which attach to states will have a very basic character, in the sense that they delineate the bare legal bones of the state in its international capacity. On them much else may be built. But for its building a foundation is needed, and internationally it is supplied by the group of sovereign rights which is enjoyed by each internationally active state. These rights make it clear, in general terms, what each state may do and, therefore, what other states may not object to it doing. In some areas states will be under a specific duty to respect the rights of others, of which the duty of non-intervention in the domestic affairs of others is an instance. Then, too, sovereign rights establish a means of doing business internationally – of communicating with other states through diplomats and of amending and extending one's rights and duties on a bilateral or multilateral basis through the making of treaties. And, quite apart from more specific sanctions, the principle of reciprocity goes some way to ensuring that a state's sovereign rights are by and large respected. If a state does not interfere with another's enjoyment of its sovereign rights, that second state will have no encouragement to disregard the rights of the first state.

In this way the sovereign rights possessed by each state, multiplied one hundred and seventy or so times, establish the sort of normative framework which is essential for order in any human group. It sets out at a basic level what may and may not be done, and establishes a procedure for the creation of further and more specific rights and duties. But for this framework it is impossible to see how international relations could be conducted in an orderly manner. This is not to say that order is thereby ensured internationally. There are several other requirements, besides fundamental legal rules, that are necessary for the achievement of this condition. But it is to say that if states were not provided with sovereign rights there could be no possibility, even, of an orderly international scene. It is in this sense, therefore, that sovereign rights may be said to provide the foundation for all that goes on between states and to be an essential constituent of international order.[12]

There is also merit in the claim that sovereign rights may be envisaged as a collective whole, which is often implicit in the argument that they constitute a state's sovereignty. For when states and commentators speak of sovereign rights they usually seem to conceive of them as a collective bundle of basic rights which comes, as it were, ready packed and attaches equally to all states. So viewed, a state's sovereign rights are not diminished in any way by their exercise. What a state does when it makes a treaty is to cut down its legal freedom (in all probability) but not its sovereignty. For, as the Permanent Court of International Justice observed in a famous case in the 1920s, treaty-making is an attribute of state sovereignty. It follows that this approach does not give rise to any problems about the calculation of sovereignty. It is simply something – a collection of special rights – which either one has or one does not. In consequence, this approach appears to have the additional benefit of relatively easy application. To see which territorial entities are eligible to participate in international relations on a regular basis one simply makes inquiries about which of them are endowed with sovereign rights. For sovereignty as sovereign rights is pictured as a kind of birthright of the internationally active state.

It should be added, however, that it is also possible to conceive of sovereign rights as comprising sovereignty in a quantitative sense, as something which exists in terms of more or less. This is likely to be associated with a fairly wide concept of sovereign rights, one which takes into account many if not all of a state's international legal powers. On this basis states will be deemed to vary in the extent of their sovereignty, as it will fluctuate in accordance with the changing extent of their legal rights and duties. If the latter grow in proportion to the former, the sovereignty of the state in question will be said to have diminished; but this may subsequently be made good by an increase in the state's rights as compared with its duties – although how any calculation of a state's overall position along these lines could possibly be made is very hard to see.

One further point in favour of the 'sovereignty as sovereign rights' approach is that it provides a satisfactory explanation of the international legal personality of the state. It says, in effect, that legal personality is a concomitant of the attribution of sovereign rights to the state by international law. In this way the state is equipped to act as an international legal person, drawing its authority so to do from the body of law which is specific to the international context. But for this, its international position would have no legal basis. States may therefore be seen, from an international viewpoint, as having a legitimate claim to existence, for they have been lawfully erected as sovereign entities. As such they are constructs of international law. It needs to be remembered, however, that the state appears to rest on international law only when seen from an international vantage point. This is not the only position from which its legal nature can be appraised, nor the only one from which its claim to legitimacy may flow. It can also be examined from within, whence, arguably, a more fundamental picture of its lineaments may be obtained.

This last point draws indirect attention to the very considerable shortcoming of the approach to sovereignty as sovereign rights. For the key question which it leaves unanswered is the basis on which sovereign rights are attributed to territorial entities. Clearly, it is not the case that all territorial entities are so endowed – international law does not, for example, give them to the states making up a federation or to colonial territories. Nor is it the case that any territorially demarcated area can have sovereign rights for the asking. A criterion has to be satisfied. And it is quite insufficient to say that the criterion is that of regular international activity. For the whole point about this activity is that it takes place on the basis of sovereign rights. Logically speaking, these rights are prior to the activity. One cannot therefore argue that the rights are attributed to any territorial body which makes a full and regular appearance on the international stage. Moreover, if one did the question would then arise as to the criterion which enabled some territories and not others to play an international role.

The question therefore remains: on what criterion are sovereign rights attributed to territorial entities? The answer, practice shows, is that sovereign rights are enjoyed by entities which are in a certain internal condition, the condition of having constitutions which are independent of other constitutions. In other words, sovereign rights are ascribed to sovereign entities – those which are sovereign in the sense of being constitutionally independent. It is the position of a state in terms of its own constitutional law, therefore, which determines whether or not it is to be given sovereign rights, for this is the determinant of sovereignty in its most basic sense. There is no reason why sovereign rights should not also be spoken of, collectively, as sovereignty, for there is no right or wrong in the matter of usage. But if they are so referred to there is the possibility of confusion, and not only in terms of semantics. For it can also very easily lead to the impression that the sovereignty which distinguishes international territorial actors from other entities is based directly on sovereign rights, whereas it is in fact the case that sovereign rights are enjoyed by those whose claim to sovereignty is based on other and prior grounds. It would therefore be a contribution to clarity in thought and understanding if sovereign rights were always referred to as such, and distinguished from sovereignty in the sense of constitutional independence.

It should be added that nothing which has been said here diminishes the force of most of the remarks which were made earlier about the merits of the sovereign rights approach to sovereignty. For almost all those merits related not to the use of the term 'sovereignty' but to the importance of sovereign rights. It is on account of the application of the concept of sovereign rights that order is possible between states; it is the idea of sovereign rights that enables one to distinguish between the maintenance, unimpaired, of the basic legal attributes of a sovereign state and the restriction of its legal freedom; and it is on account of sovereign rights that the sovereign state can be described as in the lawful enjoyment of international personality. But there is no need to rely on sovereign rights as a means of identifying sovereign states, and it is in fact undesirable to go about it in this way. For certain states are not sovereign because they enjoy sovereign rights. On the contrary, they enjoy sovereign rights because they are sovereign.

Legal Freedom

The approach to sovereignty as legal freedom is rather similar to the one just discussed in that it focuses on the opportunities for lawful action of a non-obligatory kind that are provided for states by international law. But, whereas the sovereign rights approach usually deals only with the basic legal rights which attach equally to all sovereign states by virtue of their sovereignty, the legal freedom approach has a much wider ambit. For it encompasses the whole range of lawful action which is open to states. Thus the greater the legal freedom which a state has, the greater is its sovereignty; and any addition to a state's legal duties has the effect of diminishing its sovereignty. It is a very popular approach indeed, no doubt on account of the feeling which many people have that sovereignty is both something to do with law and something to do with freedom of action.

A British lawyer, and former International Court judge, for example, has said that sovereignty is 'the residuum of what is left to the State outside its engagements and the rules of international law'[13] and a leading American international lawyer has pronounced it to be 'that competence which remains to States after due account is taken of their obligations under international law'.[14] From a work of political science has come the observation that the 'sovereignty of all states is affected when they sign a treaty, insofar as they surrender their freedom of action for the purposes and duration of the treaty'.[15] A former Foreign Minister and Prime Minister of Canada has referred to the 'limitation of national sovereignty through the acceptance of international commitments'.[16] Membership of international organizations is also widely perceived as cutting down sovereignty, on account of the legal obligations which participation involves. Both the League of Nations and the United Nations have been spoken of as diminishing the sovereignty of members, sometimes approvingly, sometimes disapprovingly, and sometimes neutrally, depending on the predilections of the speaker and his assessment of his audience. The latter can, of course, be misjudged. When a British government minister once observed in the House of Lords in a matter-of-fact way that membership in the United Nations automatically involved the derogation of 'a certain amount of sovereignty to it' he created such a furore that he had later to say that his remark had been 'philosophical'.[17] The reason for this was that he had been questioned about the Falkland Islands, and it was supposed by his auditors that he was suggesting that the views of the islanders were less important than those of the United Nations. This was a conjunction of issues and suggestions which not surprisingly raised some blood pressures in the Upper House of the British Parliament. A decade and a half later the Falkland Islands were no less able to evoke strong feelings in Britain.

The use of 'sovereignty' to mean legal freedom is in fact admirably suited for the making of debating or other points of a similar nature. If one state is raising difficulties about something on the ground that it would infringe sovereignty, then it can be pointed out that treaties have exactly this effect. Further, because on this view sovereignty is, as it were, something that comes and goes in bits, some renunciation of it in the service of a higher cause may safely be urged by those who are disposed, whether individually or professionally, towards this kind of advocacy. Not too much is being ventured by such an appeal, but it can sound very impressive. On one occasion, for example, the Convocation of Canterbury (of the Church of England) called unanimously, in the interests of establishing the rule of law in international relations, on 'the Government and people of Great Britain, in common with all nations, to make such sacrifices of independence and sovereignty as may be right and necessary'.[18] More recently, however, instead of legal undertakings being seen as involving a limitation or sacrifice of sovereignty, they have been presented, by those in their favour, as involving nothing more than a sharing or pooling of sovereignty. This was a line of argument much plied by those in favour of Britain entering the European Communities. As a former foreign and prime minister took pains to explain to a domestic audience, 'Sovereignty in a partnership is not lost. It is shared for certain common ends which all the partners judge to be to their advantage'.[19]

Some of these quotations are capable of bearing the interpretation that all states are equally sovereign, no matter how far their legal freedom has been restricted. For, on this view, sovereignty consists of the area within which a state remains legally free. It is like a cake of varying diameter, which shrinks or expands in accordance with a state's legal commitments, but which continues to exist for as long as some legal freedom, or sovereignty, is left. And as long as some sovereignty is left the state remains sovereign, no less so than a state whose sovereignty extends over a wider area. Just as some monarchs ruled over states which were larger or more powerful than those of other monarchs, and some head teachers are in charge of schools which are bigger than those looked after by other head teachers, so also is it the case that some sovereign states have more legal freedom than others. But they are none the less equally sovereign states, enjoying a like status – that conferred by sovereignty, just as in point of status all monarchs, and head teachers, coexist on a level of equality. They may differ in importance or wealth, but they are the same kind of animal.

This is the view of sovereignty as a state's reserved domain, to use a phrase which used to be favoured by lawyers. A sovereign state is one which has an area over which it is sovereign in the sense that it is, in law, able to do as it wishes. It follows that there is no problem about the calculation of a state's sovereignty, for states are either in possession of a reserved domain or they are not. The extent of that domain may vary, but sovereignty over it is something which is non-quantifiable. It is a qualitative matter, which is either enjoyed or not. However, this interpretation of the approach to sovereignty as legal freedom is probably uncommon. Statesmen and analysts rarely spell out what exactly it is that they have in mind when they speak and write in these terms. But the drift of their remarks suggests that usually they are thinking of sovereignty in quantitative terms, and all the remarks quoted above are capable of bearing this interpretation if, indeed, they do not point to it.

The quantitative approach to sovereignty as legal freedom envisages it as something which may be curtailed or eroded. Thus, in, as it were, an international state of nature, where there is no legal system, the state will be one hundred per cent sovereign, although then its freedom could not, strictly speaking, be referred to as legal freedom because it would not exist in terms of a system of law. But with the emergence of international law the state will acquire certain basic duties towards others which will diminish its legal freedom, or sovereignty, by a number of percentage points. And as it makes treaties with other states its legal freedom, or sovereignty, will be restricted still more. To pursue the tea-table image, sovereignty is like a cake which starts off at the same size for all states, but which is cut into by different amounts and at different times in accordance with the acceptance of legal obligations – a slice here and a sliver there. It follows that sovereignty is something that must be conceived not in the absolute terms of yes or no but in the relative terms of more or less – although, as was observed in connection with the sovereign rights approach, how one goes about trying to assess a state's sovereignty is anybody's guess. Clearly, a new legal obligation can be said to diminish a state's sovereignty, but from what and to what figure is always left in complete obscurity, and understandably so.

There are a couple of oddities about this approach. The first is its apparent concentration upon the legal obligations which a state incurs towards others, to the total disregard, it seems, of the rights which a state often receives in exchange for an obligation. This does, it is true, accord with the emphasis of the approach on legal freedom. But, although a legal claim which a state has on another does not enhance its freedom, it does improve its overall legal position. It would, therefore, not have been surprising if this had been at least mentioned by some commentators as evidence of a kind of counter-balance to the diminution of legal freedom which is the effect of many treaties. But it is a point which appears always to be ignored. The second oddity is associated with the first. It is that the extent of a state's sovereignty, given that it is to be conceived in relative terms, might be thought to be some kind of indication as to the state's importance. Sovereignty is, after all, usually taken to be a matter of some significance, and therefore the two might have been expected to march hand in hand: the more powerful and prestigious the state, the greater its sovereignty. Yet on this approach the correlation will probably be almost exactly the opposite. Power and importance do not necessarily lead to an increased involvement in international relations, but they are very likely to do so. And one aspect of such an increased involvement will be the making of more treaties, promising assistance here and there, and making arrangements with another for substantial commerce. All of which will have the effect of reducing the state's legal freedom – and hence, on this approach, its sovereignty. By contrast, a state which is small and unambitious, and hopes for a quiet international life, will enter into relatively few international undertakings, especially if it is strategically insignificant and does not possess any scarce economic resources. But the consequence of this will be that it will have appreciably more legal freedom, and thus sovereignty, than the larger and more important state. Which does not accord with the usual conception of things.

However, the real problem with the approach to sovereignty as quantitative legal freedom lies in the fact that it does not draw attention to anything which is exclusive to sovereign states. Every person, human or notional, who lives under a legal system will have some legal freedom, an area which is not covered by mandatory or prohibitive law and in which therefore they are, by law, entitled to do as they like – provided they do not infringe anyone else's rights. Accordingly, while it is undoubtedly true that sovereign states enjoy legal freedom, which will vary in extent and over time, this points to nothing distinctive about them. It is in no sense a consequence of or otherwise related to their sovereignty, but is simply a reflection of the fact that at the international level their activities take place in a context to which a body of law applies. Thus it is not possible to identify sovereign states by operating the test of legal freedom. What this test reveals, in so far as it can reveal anything in detail, is the amount of legal freedom left to sovereign states. But their sovereignty, in the sense of that which makes them eligible to participate in a full and regular way in international relations, must be and is based on quite different grounds.

The same criticism has to be made of the reserved domain approach to sovereignty, which sees the mark of a sovereign state to lie in the fact that it has an area, limited by law, within which its sovereignty, or legal freedom, continues unlimited. For all persons subject to law possess such an area, and there is no reason why it should not be spoken of as their reserved domain. Thus the fact that sovereign states have a reserved domain says nothing about that which distinguishes them as a special type of entity – their sovereignty. It simply says that under the applicable law they have a measure of freedom, and that this is conceptualized in a way which enables one to speak of that freedom, whatever its extent, in an absolute way. This area of legal freedom happens also, by some, to be termed 'sovereignty'. But it is not the case that certain territorial entities are regarded as sovereign on account of their having a reserved domain. The position is that a number of states, designated as sovereign on some quite separate ground, and hence deemed eligible for international life, are also seen to have an area of legal freedom. This area is sometimes referred to as their sovereignty, but it is an instance of the use of the term in a quite different way from that which seeks to identify what it is which is distinctive about the territorial entities which are internationally active.

It would, however, be possible to add to the definition of reserved domain in such a way as to try to limit its applicability to states which operate at the international level. It might, for example, be suggested that the concept should connote not just an area of legal freedom but also one which cannot be limited without the express permission of the state concerned. Individuals and organizations within the state, like non-sovereign territorial bodies outside it, are liable to find that their legal obligations are amended without their having been consulted, or, in the event of their having been asked, against their will. With sovereign states it is arguable that this is not so, and their immunity from this type of intrusion could be regarded as an integral part of the concept of reserved domain as it applies to them. This still leaves open the large question of what it is that provides such an immunity. But for the moment it is simply necessary to note that the idea of sovereignty as something which involves entire responsibility for the nature and extent of one's own legal obligations is one which is separate from that of sovereignty as legal freedom. It will therefore receive separate examination in the next section.

Consent

A third approach to sovereignty in terms of international law is that which says that a sovereign state is one which can determine the extent of its own legal obligations. It can only be bound by international law through the process of consent. It is not subject to a superior body nor can it be overruled in this matter by a majority of its peers. It is therefore in a position which is fundamentally different from that of groups and individuals within a sovereign state. It may be said to be legally independent in the sense that the extent to which it is bound in law at the international level is entirely a matter of its own volition.

It is arguable that this concept of sovereignty finds reflection in the well established principle that no state can be bound by a treaty to which it has not put its signature. Until fairly recently this did not mean that pressure could not be brought against a state to elicit its formal consent. It was not permissible for the individual representatives of the state concerned to be subject to coercion in order to persuade them to sign, but it was quite legitimate for the state itself to be subject to all sorts of carrots and sticks, including the most drastic. Many peace treaties exemplified this principle, as they were very far from being the product of gentlemanly discussion between equals.

Quite the contrary, for they often represented the terms which were more or less dictated to the vanquished by the victor. Of this the Treaty of Versailles of 1919 which terminated the First World War is an excellent example. The victorious Allies had considerable difficulty in their negotiations amongst themselves. But once they had reached agreement the terms were simply presented to Germany and her acquiescence demanded. She was in no position to demur, and her representatives made but a brief and chilly appearance at the signing ceremony in the Hall of Mirrors at Versailles. Likewise in 1938, the four major powers of West Europe having decided at Munich that Czechoslovakia should make substantial territorial concessions to Germany, the outcome of their deliberations was just passed on to the state most concerned for her formal agreement. However, the central point about these types of situation is that the formal consent of the state under pressure was necessary for the proposed arrangements to have legal effect. In practical terms, a defeated or threatened state may have had, as it is put colloquially, no option. But in theoretical terms it could always have refused – and taken the consequences. For states, the suicidal alternative has even less appeal than it has to individuals in a tight corner. But formally speaking it is an alternative, and the distinction between the process by which consent is elicited and the actual giving of consent is, in logic, perfectly legitimate. It is therefore the basis on which a dictated treaty may be seen as wholly compatible with the consensual theory of sovereignty.

Nowadays it is held in a number of quarters that at least in some respects this situation has changed. For since the Second World War there has been great antipathy towards the threat or use of force for the traditional purposes of national aggrandisement. This has produced the view that treaties of the Versailles and Munich type are no longer permissible. Consent, it is said, has to be real as well as formal. This is inscribed in the 1961 Vienna Convention on the Law of Treaties, which, in Article 52, has it that a 'treaty is void if its conclusion has been procured by the threat or use of force in violation of the principles of international law embodied in the Charter of the United Nations'. The treaty came into force in the 1980s and is also widely regarded as expressing the contemporary law on the matter. It raises a number of questions, such as the exact position of the line between legitimate and illegitimate pressure, and of that between the proper and improper purposes to which force may be put – for the use of force in the interests of generally accepted notions of justice is seen by many as constituting an exception to the new rule. It also leaves open the issue of the practical impact which the rule can have on a treaty between two states which does reflect one's fear of the other.

But these problems may all be left on one side here, as may the recent development in international law regarding the employment of force. For what it does is to set out some additional requirements which must be met if a state is to be regarded as having given its consent to a treaty. It does nothing to undermine the principle that a state can only be bound with its own consent. Indeed, many would say that it gives greater reality to that notion.

A corollary of this principle is that which asserts that in international conferences or organizations states cannot be bound against their will. In other words, the decision of such bodies must be based on the rule of unanimity. As one writer has expressed this point, 'the nature of the international community, resting as it does upon the independence or sovereignty of its component parts, makes acceptance of any other rule impossible'.[20] Another said that the unanimity rule is 'a necessary logical corollary of the doctrine of sovereignty'.[21] Or, as a statesman put it, 'all international decisions must by the nature of things be unanimous'.[22] Critics of this principle may see it as reflecting an 'ancient nationalistic'[23] approach to sovereignty, but none the less it has been and remains influential. It extends, moreover, to the interpretation of international engagements, in the sense that by virtue of its sovereignty each individual state has been seen as the sole judge of what is entailed by its obligations as a member of an international organization.

This was the position in the League of Nations, which was established immediately after the First World War. For, as a leading member put it in its official commentary on the League's Covenant, 'sovereign States will not consent to be bound by legislation voted by a majority, even an overwhelming majority, of their fellows'.[24] As it happened, in the League Assembly, where all members were represented, and each had one vote, the practice grew up of distinguishing between decisions, for which unanimity was required, and recommendations, which carried no legal weight and for which a majority vote sufficed. This arrangement was extended and formalized in the General Assembly of the United Nations, where all decisions are made by majority, sometimes simple, sometimes two-thirds, depending on the issue. But except on internal matters relating to the running of the organization, such decisions do not have binding force and are therefore in the nature of recommendations. In this way the Assembly is said to respect the sovereignty of the member state. In organizations where decisions are of greater moment, the unanimity rule is preserved – the North Atlantic Treaty Organization, for example. As its official handbook puts it, 'NATO, being an organization of sovereign states equal in status, all decisions are expressions of the *collective will of member governments*, taken not by majority vote but by common consent'[25] (italics in original). The Council of the Organization for Economic Co-operation and Development, one of the leading economic organizations in the West, also conducts itself on the unanimity principle. The position is the same in the Eastern bloc. The Warsaw Pact organization operates on the unanimity rule, as does its economic counterpart, Comecon, the charter of which emphasizes in this connection that 'the member countries are not required to surrender any of their sovereignty'.[26] Soviet attempts to change this arrangement in favour of majority voting were condemned by Rumania on the ground that they would turn sovereignty into 'a notion without any content',[27] a view which finds support in the recent statement of a theorist that 'To say that a state is sovereign means that it decides for itself how it will cope with its internal and external problems'.[28]

This approach to sovereignty also finds expression in attitudes which are sometimes taken by states to recourse to third-party arbitration and international tribunals. For this involves allowing a body external to the state to determine the precise nature of its legal obligations in a particular matter. As such it is a procedure which can be resisted in the cause of maintaining one's sovereignty. The Soviet Union and other Eastern bloc states, for example, have always taken this line, and a representative of the United States has said, in a general vein, that the unwillingness of states to use the International Court of Justice is a reflection of their refusal 'to surrender part of their sovereignty'.[29] But the issue which arouses the greatest concern in this connection is that of compulsory jurisdiction, that is to say, the acceptance in advance by a state of the jurisdiction of a court. Such an acceptance may be made without any qualifications, but it may also be limited to a specific range of matters and situations. In either event, it is a move which has often been said to undermine a state's sovereignty. As one jurist put it, 'the acceptance of the obligatory jurisdiction of an international tribunal means that within that field the country imposes upon itself an authority to which we all must bow. It means the voluntary renunciation by the State of that non-subordination to any other authority which is the distinguishing feature of sovereignty.'[30] China, too, has made the same point, her representative saying that 'if a sovereign state were asked to accept unconditionally the compulsory jurisdiction of an international judicial organ, that would amount to placing that organ above the sovereign state, which was contrary to the principle of State sovereignty'.[31] While, therefore, states may if they wish accept the compulsory jurisdiction of the International Court of Justice (which is an independent organ of the United Nations), this is not automatically entailed in a state becoming a party to the Statute of the court, or joining the court, as it is often put. As with its interwar predecessor, the Permanent Court of International Justice, recourse to the court is voluntary, indicating, it has been said, the need to respect 'the sacred principle of national sovereignty',[32] or, alternatively, the hindrances to a better world which are presented by 'the old and new nationalistic conceptions of sovereignty'.[33]

On this approach, therefore, a sovereign state is one which is legally independent in that it is in total control of the extent of its obligations under international law. But, despite what has been said along these lines, even a cursory inspection of the legal position of states reveals that none of them is wholly independent in this sense. In the first place, there is the problem which is presented to this argument by international customary law. This is the general law of the international society, and applies to all sovereign states, equipping them with certain rights and duties by virtue of their sovereign statehood. It is, as it were, the basic legal clothing with which states are endowed. They are not asked whether they like what they receive, nor may they pick and choose from these customary rules. Being bound by this body of law is an attribute of statehood at the international level. States may amend customary law among themselves by way of treaty. And a state which dislikes some part of it may try to evade its claims, whether openly or covertly. But at the legal level mere dislike is no ground for ignoring the law, no more than it is in contexts other than the international, and fellow states are unlikely to take kindly to such an idiosyncratic and cavalier approach. Of course, if there is considerable pressure for a change in some of the international customs which have hitherto been accepted as law, it is likely that such a change, following changed practice, will be widely deemed to have occurred. But this is a different situation from that of an individual state or two resenting certain aspects of existing customary law. Such states have, in one way or another, to make the best of the situation. Thus the existence of international customary law means either that states are not sovereign in an absolute sense of the term, or that they are not fully sovereign, or that sovereignty is something other than being able to determine the full extent of one's legal obligations.

Then, secondly, account has to be taken of the fact that it is now generally accepted that some part of international customary law has the status of *ius cogens* – obligatory law, which may not be amended through the making of a treaty between two or more states. There are a number of difficulties associated with this concept of international public policy, as it is also called, not least of which is that there is little agreement on its content. And where there is broad agreement, as on the principle that force is prohibited in inter-state relations, the terms of the agreement are also so broad and subject to such qualifications as to reduce their value considerably. This is, of course, quite separate from the huge problems of adjudicating on any alleged breaches of *ius cogens*, and then preventing the state concerned from enjoying the fruits of its wrongdoing. All of which suggests to one or two observers that the international scene is as yet insufficiently cohesive to support a meaningful public policy. Be that as it may, the fact is that international lawyers and the states they advise are now more or less unanimous in saying that *ius cogens* exists internationally. In the face of this agreement the student of sovereignty can only conclude that here, at least in theory, is another ground for saying that states do not have a free hand in deciding on their obligations in law. For there is no question of consent to *ius cogens*. Like the customary law of which it forms a part, it applies automatically to sovereign states. Accordingly, if sovereignty is to be equated with consent to restrictions upon a state's legal freedom, it may be concluded that *ius cogens* constitutes 'a limitation on the sovereignty of states',[34] such a limitation being 'inherent in the concept of an international public policy'.[35] But two other possibilities are that states are not sovereign or that they are, and completely so, but in terms of some other conception of sovereignty.

A further consideration pertaining to the validity of the consensual theory of sovereignty has to do with the undoubted fact that there is a certain amount of judicial activity at the international level. The nineteenth century saw a good deal of it, relatively speaking, and the present century has seen attempts to encourage it through the establishment of international courts. The Permanent Court of Arbitration, set up in 1899, was, as has often been said, neither permanent nor a court; it was, however, a means of facilitating *ad hoc* arbitration. The Permanent Court of International Justice, instituted after the end of the First World War, was a court properly so called, and during the interwar period considered several cases, on average, each year. Its successor, the International Court of Justice, has been less busy, but has hardly ever been without work. It is true that such work as it, or any *ad hoc* arbitral tribunal, receives is based on the voluntary principle, in the sense that states cannot be forced to go to independent adjudication if they choose not to do so. It is also true that the court or any *ad hoc* tribunal is non-political in character. Individual jurists sit in judgement and give their decisions on the basis of their perception of the law and not of their political preferences. When, therefore, states do resort to this means of settling disputes, they are not giving other states the right to deal with their affairs. But none the less it remains that any submission to such a body does mean that on that particular matter the states concerned are giving a third party the right to decide authoritatively on their legal duties. They are consenting to the issue being decided in this manner, but it is not a process which is based on consent in the way in which the term is being used in this section. For the parties are, on the specific question, relinquishing their control over the nature and extent of their legal obligations. Any instance of international judicial activity, therefore, is one which runs counter to or diminishes the sovereignty of the states involved, if their sovereignty is thought to consist of unqualified control over their legal affairs.

In principle the position is no different when a case comes to be heard as a result of the parties having accepted the compulsory jurisdiction of the International Court. The Statute of the Permanent Court of International Justice provided for this possibility, as does that of its successor, and a number of states have made use of it. Indeed, during the interwar period the proportion of adherents to the Statute of the Court that did so was, in retrospect, surprisingly high. For in December 1938, out of the forty-eight states which were parties to the Statute, thirty-nine had accepted the compulsory jurisdiction of the Permanent Court. These acceptances were often hedged about with reservations. But even so it meant that there was some chance of disputes coming to the court on the initiative of only one of the disputants, as this was possible if both states concerned had accepted the court's compulsory jurisdiction and the issue between them was not excluded by the reservations of either. Since 1945 the proportion of states accepting the compulsory jurisdiction of the International Court of Justice has fallen considerably. Less than one-third of its one hundred and sixty or so adherents have done so, and reservations during this period have generally been both more numerous and more far-reaching than hitherto. But what any measure of compulsory jurisdiction signifies is a willingness, in certain circumstances, to go to court at the behest of another state. It therefore leaves the way open to some loss of control by the state concerned over the extent of its legal obligations. A few more of them are likely to be determined by a process other than the state's specific consent than if it had not accepted a court's compulsory jurisdiction. This, too, means that if sovereignty amounts to control over one's legal duties, compulsory jurisdiction is more likely to result in its extinction or diminution than if recourse to a court is entirely voluntary. But on another concept of sovereignty compulsory jurisdiction may have no impact at all.

The final matter which has to be considered in this section is the claim that sovereignty, conceived as consent to all legal obligations, requires that international gatherings operate on the basis of the unanimity rule. One qualification which can immediately be made to this proposition is that the principle of unanimity need only be operative if the decision to which a debate may give rise is binding on all members or, in the case of *ad hoc* meetings, all participants. Recommendations do not carry legal force and therefore may emanate from a majority vote. But, where a state is bound in law by the decision of an international body, majority rule would clearly infringe the principle that states must remain in control of the extent of their legal duties. However, international practice clearly shows that states, asserting themselves to be sovereign, have often agreed to be bound by the majority vote of an international institution. The Zollverein, the commercial union of Prussia and most of the other independent German states which was in being for most of the second quarter of the nineteenth century, took its decisions on a majority basis. The Universal Postal Union, established in 1874, was able to amend its constitution by majority vote and as a practical matter these votes bound all members: those not ratifying the amendments by the due date were, in theory, obliged to leave, but in practice all members applied the revised provisions irrespective of whether they had ratified them. The constitution of the International Labour Organization of 1919 could also be amended without the consent of all states, and the International Commission for Air Navigation set up a few years later had the power to alter the existing obligation of members by majority. Other bodies which deviated from the majority principle were the Committee of Experts concerned with the transport of goods by rail, the Permanent Central Opium Board, the International Sugar Council, and various commissions established to regulate navigation and other uses of rivers of international concern. At international conferences in the nineteenth and early twentieth century, too, procedural and secondary matters were disposed of by majority vote.

It may, of course, be objected that all these matters were of secondary importance. 'Technical' is the term which is often used to describe them, the implication being that they are of so little significance as contrasted with weightier 'political' questions that states can afford to lose some control of the extent of their obligations. The supposed unimportance of these matters is in fact arguable, but whether that is accepted or not it remains that on them states breached a principle which, on one view, could only be absolute. Moreover, there were other circumstances in the earlier part of the twentieth century which might generally be thought to have some political consequence and on which states could be bound by a majority vote. For example, in eight or nine places the Covenant of the League of Nations provided, contrary to its general rule of unanimity, for decisions by a majority. These related to questions which, from one angle, were of an internal, organizational nature. But not only were they of importance for the running of the League; they could also affect the rights and obligations of states, and on issues of very considerable weight. For it was provided that in the procedure for the settlement of disputes reports were to be made on a majority basis. It was also the case that a state's expulsion from the League did not require its consent – obviously a desirable provision but none the less one which meant that a state could be deprived of a whole range of rights against its will. Additionally, the peace treaties which followed the First World War provided for the League Council to exercise a number of important functions by majority vote – the overall administration of the Saar, for example, and the modification of minorities treaties. A number of other treaties also conferred on the League Council or Assembly the power to act on a majority basis.

It was, however, after 1945 that the most far-reaching modifications of the unanimity rule have occurred. It has already been noted that in the UN General Assembly all decisions are taken by majority vote, and that on internal questions these are binding on the whole membership. They include even such an important matter as the budget of the organization. But it is in the Security Council that the most drastic developments have taken place. For this body, which is in the nature of the organization's executive committee, is charged with primary responsibility for the maintenance of international peace and security, and in so behaving it acts on behalf of all UN members. Further, it is laid down in the UN Charter, in Article 25, that 'The Members of the United Nations agree to accept and carry out the decisions of the Security Council'. To take a decision none of the five permanent members of the Council – Britain, China, France, the Soviet Union and the United States – must vote against the proposition, and if they do in circumstances in which it would otherwise have been passed they are said to have cast a veto. But if the required majority is obtained – seven out of eleven until the end of 1965 and nine out of fifteen thereafter – and there is no veto the Council may bind all members of the organization to take or refrain from certain action on an issue which the Council deems to be a threat to the peace, a breach of the peace, or an act of aggression.

In practice the effect of this arrangement has been vastly less than might be imagined from this sketch of the Council's powers. For one thing, the Council has no authority to call on member states to use armed force to maintain or restore peace except to the extent to which they have agreed to do so in a special agreement negotiated with the Council. In fact, no such agreements have been reached. Then, too, the veto means that the Council cannot require any of five large and powerful permanent members to do anything to which it is opposed.

Additionally, the facts of life indicate that power on paper is not always the same as effective power, especially at the decentralized and competitive international level, where it can be very difficult to make even a small state take or refrain from action against its will. Thus the UN Security Council is very far from being a legislature, where a majority vote can have very large consequences. Instead it is more like a body in which strong interests are represented and in which argument and bargaining, inducements and pressures are necessarily the order of the day. Certainly states will sometimes give way to the representations of others, but if an issue arises on which one or two have reason to be recalcitrant it could well be that the majority deems it wise to accept at least a temporary defeat. It also must be borne in mind that the Council's powers relate to action on specific issues, and are not of a general legislative type.

But it remains that these powers are very considerable indeed and mark a sharp change with previous practice. In consequence, if sovereignty is seen as consisting of consent to legal obligations, and, further, as something which can be cut down bit by bit, the position of most members of the UN can very easily be expressed in terms of a loss of sovereignty. One writer has spoken of Article 25 of the Charter as the 'most remarkable' of the 'serious inroads into the concept of state sovereignty' which were made by the UN Charter, and 'perhaps the most significant renunciation of sovereign power in our era'.[36] Another has said that it involved 'a limitation of sovereignty for all Members except the permanent members of the Security Council' and was 'a historic act and may turn out to be the modest nucleus from which some system of world government gradually develops'.[37] A third has spoken of it as a 'revolutionary relinquishment of sovereignty'.[38]

It is not, however, just the United Nations that has seen the continuation and expansion of the practice of taking binding decisions by majority vote. The period since 1945 has seen a very considerable growth in the number and range of international institutions, and the majority principle finds expression in a number of them. It is, for example, not at all uncommon regarding the internal law of institutions – the law which regulates decisions about their day-to-day functioning. Then, too, the constitutions of some organizations provide that after amendments to them have been ratified by a required majority they become binding on all members. This is so in the case of the UN and also, for example, the Arab League, the World Health Organization, and the International Atomic Energy Agency. Some bodies go further, in a psychological sense, and provide for the amendment of their constitutions by majority vote without the need for ratification. The UN Educational,

Scientific, and Cultural Organization and the Council of Europe are cases in point. In all these cases it is possible that member states will find themselves subject to legal rules to which they have not agreed. It is also the position that in some bodies regulations may be made by majority vote which dissentients may reject or accept subject to reservations – which presents no threat to the principle of consent. But in some of these cases a state is, as a matter of practice, less free than the formal position suggests, in that it would be subject to considerable disadvantages if it did contract out of a decision taken by the majority.

The position regarding international organizations, therefore, is that a number of them take binding decisions of one sort or another on the basis not of unanimity but of majority voting. If sovereignty is thought to connote the ability to control the extent of one's legal obligations it follows that the members of these organizations are either not sovereign or not fully sovereign. This is also the conclusion which was drawn from a consideration of other aspects of the relation between consent and the creation of duties under international law. Sovereign states are bound by international customary law whether they like it or not. They are also bound by some peremptory rules, which may not be amended by treaty, although the exact identity and scope of these rules is noticeably vague. And the occasional practice of submitting disputes to arbitration or judicial decision, whether voluntarily or in consequence of having accepted the International Court's compulsory jurisdiction, also shows that there is another area in which states sometimes leave the determination of their obligations to an external body.

Accordingly, it cannot be said that *any* state is sovereign in the sense of being in total control of the extent of its legal obligations. For, even if a state keeps out of all institutions which may take binding decisions by majority vote and never goes to arbitration or an international court, it will still be subject to international customary law, including that part of it which is *ius cogens*. And it might be added that while a state may not find it difficult to avoid arbitration or judicial settlement it would be rather surprising if, in the complex international world of today, it found it practical to join only those institutions which were unsullied by the majority principle. For the occasional conduct of business on this footing is a reflection of the fact that when a large number of states come together closely and regularly in an institution, absolute adherence to the unanimity rule gives rise to a number of difficulties, some of which are likely to be widely perceived as unnecessary. Even if these expressions of the idea of majority rule are limited to the institution's internal affairs, they may, as has been pointed out, have an impact on the rights and duties of states. And sometimes the majority principle is used in relation to decisions regarding the external conduct of the institution.

Too much, however, must not be made of all this. It remains the position that on most issues, including virtually all those which are thought to be of considerable importance, states are in control of the extent of their legal obligations. This is underlined by the large number of treaties which are now concluded each year, so that while international customary law remains at the juridical base of the international legal system its importance in practical terms has declined. In consequence, a state wishing to find out what its legal duties are on any matter will probably find the answer in a treaty which it has itself signed. In a very real sense, therefore, the principle of consent is still of central and fundamental significance in any attempt to depict the way in which states acquire obligations in law. This is only to be expected in a context which displays little loyalty to the concept of the whole but a fierce regard by each of the individual parts – the states – for its own well-being. Thus, any meeting of such entities, whether *ad hoc* or in the setting of an institution, is in the nature of a coming together of competing interests. The size and strength of these interests will vary greatly, but none can be regarded as insignificant, as they are all territorially based and have some physical resources, and also because of the principles on which their interaction is based. These principles are hallowed by custom and generally respected in practice, and very prominent among them is the one which has it that there should be respect for the individuality of each state. In this milieu the idea of majority rule has been unable to make much headway, except at the outermost margin, and, in the absence of a much stronger sense of community feeling and a consequential willingness to think in terms of the primacy of the whole rather than the parts, it is unlikely to do so. Even within many states the principle receives little more than lip service on account of there being an inadequate societal base for its effective operation, and supposed majority rule is in practice the rule of an entrenched group. In England, Parliament worked for several centuries more as a conference which decided by consensus than as a legislature resting on the majority principle; it was not until the second half of the sixteenth century that majority decision appears to have become well established, and even then it was not routinely used. It is not surprising, therefore, that where national self-interest is to the fore, majority rule has made little headway. This does not mean that self-interest is never what is usually called 'enlightened', nor that co-operation is excluded. Quite the contrary. But it does mean that there is prime emphasis on the principle that the state is, at least in form, largely in control of its own affairs, including its legal affairs.

But the fact remains that its control over its legal obligations is not complete. Consent may be a fundamental principle in the matter, but it does not have the field to itself. In a number of respects states find themselves bound in law as the result of a process or situation which is not specifically related to the exercise of their own will. It follows that the most which can be said about the nature of sovereignty when defined in terms of consent is that it is a relative and not an absolute concept. No state is in these terms one hundred per cent sovereign, on account of the obligations which attach to all states by virtue of their statehood. The further deductions from one hundred per cent which have to be made will vary somewhat from state to state in accordance with the extent to which the state has subjected itself to a majority in international institutions and to the decisions of international courts and tribunals. This immediately gives rise to two problems. The first is the by now familiar one of the calculation of sovereignty: it is a virtually impossible task. All one can say of a particular state is that it has limited its sovereignty somewhat and that a specific instance of the withdrawal of consent limits it still more. This may or may not be regarded as desirable, depending on the view taken by the observer of the individual limitation of consent which he has in view. More generally, such limitations are often regarded as a good thing, as in the statement that 'progress in international law, the maintenance of international peace and, with it, of independent national states, are in the long run conditioned by a practical surrender of their sovereignty'.[39] Or, as it has been put the other way round, 'the unanimity rule is the bane of international organisations, the cause of their substantial ineffectiveness'.[40] This is not, however, the only view which may be taken of the matter.

The second problem to which this concept of sovereignty gives rise is that it does not provide a basis for distinguishing those territorial entities which participate regularly in international relations from other bodies and individuals. For everyone has some control over the extent of his legal obligations – and therefore, on this definition, could be said to have some sovereignty. Individuals and firms within a state, as well as subordinate territorial groups, are indeed subject to the requirements of its law-making bodies. But they may also make use of their legal freedom to add to their legal rights and duties by way of contract and the acquisition of property. They will still be vastly less in command of their overall legal position than states, but in principle there is no way, on this basis, of distinguishing states from other individuals and entities. From one point of view there is no reason to look for such a distinction. It could simply be noted that the idea of consent, while relevant to everyone's legal position, applies much more to states than to non-states. But there must be some characteristic which sets apart those territorial entities that are eligible to participate in international relations from those that are not. And this characteristic is often thought to be sovereignty. It is evident, however, that it cannot be sovereignty in the sense of a measure of control, not even a very large measure, over the extent of one's legal obligations.

One final point must be made in this connection. It is that even if internationally active states were absolutely in control of their legal duties this would not provide an adequate basis for a distinction between them and other bodies. For the question would arise as to why some territorial entities were in this privileged position and others not. It would presumably not be attributable to mere chance or assertion, but to some characteristic which the privileged enjoyed. There would, in other words, have to be a prior and more fundamental distinguishing feature. In fact there is a feature which accounts for some territorial bodies – those which participate regularly on the international stage – being able to control most, but not all, of the external law by which they are bound. It is constitutional independence, and those that enjoy it are, by that token, not subject to a superior territorial authority. They also, and for the same reason, have a great deal of legal freedom, and possess sovereign rights. Each of these legal qualities is an international consequence of their constitutional independence, or, on one definition, their sovereignty, but it is not synonymous with it. Sovereignty, therefore, in the sense of that which makes some territorial entities eligible for full international actorhood, cannot be defined in any of these terms. Sovereign rights, legal freedom and consent may each be said to connote the exercise of sovereignty, but it cannot be the sort of sovereignty which is the most fundamental – which distinguishes the territorial entities which play a full and active international part from those which do not. There is, however, a school of thought which has it that the essence of sovereignty consists of domestic inviolability, of the internal imperviousness of the states which fall into this class to legal claims which have an external origin. This is the argument which will be considered in the next chapter.

Notes: Chapter 8

1   Joseph Frankel, *International Politics: Conflict and Harmony* (Harmondsworth: Allen Lane/Penguin Press, 1969), p. 189.
2   René Albrecht-Carrié, *The Meaning of the First World War* (Englewood Cliffs, NJ: Prentice-Hall, 1965), p. 23.

3   R. Y. Jennings, *The Progress of International Law* (Cambridge: Cambridge University Press, 1960), p. 2.
4   P. C. Jessup, *The Use of International Law* (Ann Arbor, Mich.: University of Michigan Law School, 1959), p. 152.
5   Evan Luard, *The United Nations. How it Works and What it Does* (London: Macmillan, 1979), p. 88.
6   Wolfgang Friedmann and Lawrence A. Collins, 'The Suez Canal crisis of 1956', in Lawrence Scheinman and David Wilkinson (eds), *International Law and Political Crisis* (Boston, Mass.: Little, Brown, 1968), p. 125.
7   Quoted in Louis Henkin, *Foreign Affairs and the Constitution* (Mineola, NY: Foundation Press, 1972), 127.
8   C. W. Jenks, *A New World of Law?* (London: Longman, 1969), p. 132.
9   Judge Anzilotti in his Separate Opinion in the Austro-German Customs Union case (Permanent Court of International Justice, 1931), quoted by J. E. S. Fawcett, 'General course on public international law', in Académie de Droit International, *Recueil des cours 1971*, Vol. 1 (Leyden: Sijthoff, 1971), p. 385.
10 Sir Hersch Lauterpacht, quoted by Sir Gerald Fitzmaurice, 'The future of public international law and the international legal system in the circumstances of today', *International Relations*, vol. 5, no. 1 (May 1975), p. 756.
11 Leo Gross, 'Some observations on the International Court of Justice', *American Journal of International Law*, vol. 56, no. 1 (January 1962), p. 61.
12 For an elaboration of this argument, see the present writer's 'Law and order in international society', in Alan James (ed.), *The Bases of International Order* (London: Oxford University Press, 1973), pp. 65–72. See also his 'International society', *British Journal of International Studies*, vol. 4, no. 2 (July 1978), pp. 100–2.
13 Sir Gerald Fitzmaurice, 'The future of public international law and the international legal system in the circumstances of today', *International Relations*, vol. 5, no. 1 (May 1975), p. 770.
14 Myres S. McDougal, quoted in R. J. Vincent, *Nonintervention and International Order* (Princeton, NJ: Princeton University Press, 1968), p. 38.
15 Cyril E. Black *et al.*, *Neutralization and World Politics* (Princeton, NJ: Princeton University Press, 1968), p. 297.
16 Lester B. Pearson, *Memoirs 1897–1948. Through Diplomacy to Politics* (London: Gollancz, 1973), p. 92.
17 Lord Chalfont, quoted in J. C. J. Metford, 'Falklands or Malvinas? The background to the dispute', *International Affairs*, vol. 44, no. 3 (July 1968), p. 465.
18 *The Times*, 12 May 1960.
19 *The Times*, 17 April 1971.
20 C. A. Riches, *Majority Rule in International Organization* (Baltimore, Md: Johns Hopkins University Press, 1940), p. 8.
21 William E. Rappard, *Collective Security in Swiss Experience* (London: Allen & Unwin, 1948), p. 17.
22 Lord Robert Cecil, quoted in ibid., p. 11.
23 Lord Gladwyn, in a letter to *The Times*, 5 June 1972.
24 United Kingdom, in Cmd 151, 1919, p. 15.
25 *NATO Handbook* (Brussels: NATO, 1977), p. 35.
26 A. Korbonski, 'Comecon' *International Conciliation*, no. 549 (September 1964), p. 13.
27 *The Times*, 23 May 1964.
28 Kenneth N. Waltz, *Theory of International Politics* (Reading, Mass.: Addison-Wesley, 1979), p. 96.
29 Ambassador Goldberg at the 69th annual meeting of the American Society of International Law, *Proceedings* (Washington, DC, 1976), p. 127.

30 Sir Cecil Hurst, in his introduction to J. W. Wheeler-Bennett and Maurice Fanshawe, *Information on the World Court: 1918–1928* (London: Allen & Unwin, 1929), p. 5.

31 Samuel S. Kim, *China, the United Nations, and World Order* (Princeton, NJ: Princeton University Press, 1979), p. 456.

32 F. S. Northedge and M. Grieve, *One Hundred Years of International Relations* (London: Duckworth, 1971), p. 146.

33 Mr Terje Wold, Chief Justice of Norway, quoted in *The Times*, 9 September 1969.

34 Erik Suy, 'The concept of *jus cogens* in public international law', in Carnegie Endowment for International Peace, *The Concept of Jus Cogens in International Law* (New York: CEIP, 1967), p. 60.

35 Ralph Zacklin, 'Challenge of Rhodesia', *International Conciliation*, no. 575 (November 1969), p. 9.

36 F. O. Wilcox, 'International confederation in the United Nations and state sovereignty', in E. Plischke (ed.), *Systems of Integrating the International Community* (Princeton, NJ: Van Nostrand, 1964), pp. 31–2.

37 Richard Hiscocks, *The Security Council* (London: Longman, 1974), p. 56.

38 Evan Luard, *A History of the United Nations*, Vol. 1 (London: Macmillan, 1982), p. 50.

39 L. Oppenheim, *International Law, Vol. 1, Peace*, ed. H. Lauterpacht, 8th edn (London: Longman, 1955), p. 123.

40 P.-H. Spaak, quoted by Richard McAllister, 'The E.E.C. dimension: intended and unintended consequences', in James Cornford (ed.), *The Failure of the State; On the Distribution of Political and Economic Power in Europe* (London: Croom Helm, 1975), p. 182.

9

Jurisdictional

The assertion that sovereignty amounts to constitutional independence may be quarrelled with on the ground that it is unnecessarily general. There is no call, it may be argued, to go right to the roots of a state's internal arrangements to identify what distinguishes a sovereign from a non-sovereign entity. A sovereign state may indeed have a constitution which is unconnected with any other constitution, but the essential manifestations of its sovereignty are much closer to the surface than that, and much nearer the demands and refusals of international relations. On this argument, sovereignty is to be seen in a state's exclusive right to conduct itself within its borders exactly as it wishes. It alone has jurisdiction over everything that goes on inside its frontiers. So far as its territory and the people who occupy it are concerned, the state legislature is the only law-making body; the state executive never has to give way to one which is foreign-based; and the state judiciary is the final court of appeal. In a phrase, and a familiar one, a sovereign state is master in its own house.

Two points about this approach require immediate emphasis. The first is that it is legal in character. It asserts that a sovereign state is in sole and complete control of its internal affairs – in law. No other state or external authority has the *right* to be heard about what happens within a state, or to act in any part of its territory. In practice, of course, a state may deem it wise to hearken very attentively to the views of an influential friend or neighbour about desirable domestic behaviour. Thus there may be important political restrictions on its internal freedom of action. Or a state may be subject to unlawful incursions from outside. But as long as it remains in being and its freedom is not compromised by any legal undertakings the state concerned maintains its jurisdictional independence, and hence its sovereignty. In the theory of the matter – and here the theory is crucial – it has a free and unfettered legal hand.

The second point is that this jurisdictional concept of sovereignty is not associated with or qualified by the principle of consent. It is *not* being suggested that if the host state has agreed to it an exercise of jurisdiction by an outsider leaves sovereignty unimpaired. Permission does not, as it were, carry absolution, as this criterion for sovereignty is, quite simply, the *fact* of jurisdictional independence. A non-sovereign entity is one in respect of which an externally based legislature, executive, or judiciary is entitled to make claims. Sovereignty, by contrast, has to do with not being subject to outside authorities. Consent does not enter into it, as the key issue is not the manner in which superior legal rights have been granted but whether or not they exist.

There is little doubt that this conception of sovereignty has considerable appeal. It brings together the popular ideas that sovereignty has something to do with law and something with supremacy, and it links both these characteristics with the most obvious ingredient of statehood – territory. It satisfies the picture of the sovereign as king of his castle, of someone who allows his fellow sovereigns no legal standing inside his ramparts. More specifically, it is possible to identify four ways in which sovereignty is often spoken of in these jurisdictional terms. They are overlapping and connected through their common focus on the idea that a sovereign state has exclusive legal control over its internal affairs, but they are distinguishable from each other. If it is to be allowed that sovereignty is most helpfully defined in terms of jurisdictional rather than constitutional independence, it must be possible to show that those entities which manifestly enjoy full international status meet the requirements of at least one of the various ways in which the phrase 'jurisdictional independence' is used.

The first of these usages has it that sovereignty consists of the absence of any legal obligations to outsiders regarding one's internal conduct. Behind one's front door – to revert from the grander metaphor of the castle to that of the house – one is entitled to get on with things as one likes. Other states and intergovernmental bodies may well look in through the window and may even make adverse comments about what they see. But they have no legal grounds for complaint and, concomitantly, the state is under no legal obligation to listen to them. How the state behaves at home is, in law, its own and no one else's business.

The next usage has it that the essence of sovereignty lies in the actual exercise of jurisdiction over every inch of one's soil. There must be no pockets of foreign jurisdiction within the state, no letting off of rooms or even corners to other states or international organizations. Foreigners may, of course, be admitted, but not with the right to substitute their own governmental arrangements for any of those of the host state. The writ of the host must run in all parts of its domain – if, that is, its sovereignty is to be preserved. For this it is also necessary that the state should exercise its jurisdiction continuously. There must be no possibility of outsiders being able, in law, to require and enforce a temporary suspension of the state's authority so as to check some major wrongdoing and set it back on an approved course. To this as to all other jurisdictional intrusions the front door must remain firmly shut.

The analogy of the closed front door is also relevant to the third way in which the concept of jurisdictional independence finds expression. But here the door is pictured as closed against not outsiders but insiders. The suggestion is that a sovereign state is one where all internal disputes are settled internally. In law, citizens and groups have no right to complain or appeal to an external body about any of the laws which have been made by the country's legislature, any of the actions of its executive, or any of the decisions of its judiciary. The state's doors remain firmly shut in the face of those within. Dirty washing has to be cleansed at home, even if some think that the local laundering facilities are quite inadequate. In a non-sovereign territorial entity legal redress can sometimes be sought outside the territory (but within the constitutional structure of the sovereign unit which encompasses the entity in question). But the mark of sovereignty, so it is argued, is that those within a state's jurisdiction have always to make the best of such governmental arrangements as are domestically available.

The last approach to the concept of jurisdictional independence maintains that its essence lies in functional exclusivity. In other words, all sectors of national life must, from the point of view of the state's legal system, be subject to the ultimate control of its own governmental organs. There must be no aspects of domestic activity which are under the direct authority of outside bodies – as if the state's boundaries did not exist. The word 'direct' calls for emphasis. For what is being pinpointed here is not the possibility of insiders having the right to appeal to external bodies nor of outsiders having a right to be heard about internal matters, or even the right to take decisions about them which are binding on the state concerned. These possibilities may indeed form part of a functional inroad on a state's jurisdiction. But the core of such an inroad lies in an outside body having *direct* access to the sector concerned, as if it was itself part of the structure of government. In the view of this fourth concept of jurisdictional independence, inroads of this kind are impermissible. A sovereign state is one which does not let any of its functions fall into the direct grasp of externally based hands.

The matter may be clarified if the metaphor of a house is again employed. The three previous concepts of jurisdictional independence can all be exemplified by the image of the front door. Insiders cannot seek external redress because the door is closed against them, outsiders have no right to complain about what goes on behind the door, and they are not allowed through it to set up little camps of their own within. The state jealously guards its gateway so as to preserve its jurisdictional purity. The last concept of jurisdictional independence, however, focuses on a different threat. It concentrates on the possibility of some of the exterior walling being taken down so as to permit the building into the house of a fairly sizeable wedge. The pointed end of the wedge would be well within the house, encompassing an area of internal activity. But ultimate legal control over that activity would now lie not with the internal governmental organs but outside the house, in the thick end of the wedge. The controllers based there would be able to move directly into and around the relevant sector of the house without having to secure permission or assistance from its government. The front door would have been bypassed by the breaching of the walls. The state's functional exclusivity would no longer be complete, as it would have surrendered control of one aspect of its national life. This, it is argued, would be incompatible with its sovereignty.

One other introductory point should be made about this last concept of sovereignty. The use of the phrase 'functional exclusivity' should not be taken to imply that the sort of outside bodies which undermine sovereignty are all those organizations which are often described as functional. Some may present such a threat, others not, depending on the powers which a particular organization enjoys. If an organization has no independent standing within a member state, and thus has to channel its activities in respect of the function with which it deals through governmental officials of the state concerned, then it presents no threat to jurisdictional independence as defined in this fourth manner. This is, in fact, the way in which most functional bodies operate. But a few do have direct access to institutions and individuals within their member states, and it is these functional bodies which, by driving a wedge into the functional exclusivity of the state, are relevant to the concept of sovereignty which is being considered in this chapter. Such bodies have attracted the description 'supranational', which is a convenient way of distinguishing them from organizations which promote international co-operation along more traditional lines.

Domestic Privacy

This approach to sovereignty suggests that its core lies in the right of a state to go about its internal business exactly as it likes. A sovereign state is one which, so far as domestic matters are concerned, is unbeholden to outsiders. It will have no obligation to foreign states or to international organizations regarding its internal conduct. This approach may owe something to certain well-known statements about sovereignty. The French thinker, Bodin, for example, said in 1577 that it consists of 'absolute and perpetual power within a state'.[1] A rather similar instance is the pronouncement of the eighteenth-century English jurist, Blackstone, that in all forms of government 'there is and must be ... a supreme, irresistable, absolute, uncontrolled authority, in which the ... rights of sovereignty reside'.[2] To move on to the earlier part of the twentieth century, one can refer to the oft-quoted statement of the arbitrator in the case concerning the Island of Palmas. Referring to sovereignty over territory, he said that it means 'the right to exercise therein, to the exclusion of any other state, the functions of a state'.[3] The influence of these ideas could still be seen half a century later in a document from the Commonwealth Secretariat which declared that whereas a government is not sovereign in the conduct of its external policy it 'is sovereign within the purview of domestic affairs'.[4] And later still a professor of international relations observed that states have accorded each other 'liberty ... to do as they pleased within their respective territories', this liberty being 'generally dignified as the principle of state sovereignty'.[5]

However, anyone with even the most cursory acquaintance with international law knows that sovereign states are *not* unrestricted internally by the law which governs their relations with other states. Accordingly, states do have obligations to outsiders regarding their internal conduct. The most familiar example of these restrictions concerns resident diplomats, who are accorded a broad range of immunities before domestic courts. But it is also widely accepted that any alien must be treated in accordance with a minimum standard of behaviour by all the institutions of government, and that alien property, too, has certain preferential rights. There is, it is true, incomplete agreement about the exact nature of those rights, as there is about the content of the minimum international standard (the standard of civilization as it used to be called). But that does not detract from the point of principle, which is that states do not, in international law, have a free internal hand. It is even coming to be thought in some quarters that general international law places certain restrictions on how a state treats its own nationals, but acceptance of this controversial argument is by no means necessary to deny that sovereignty consists of the absence of external claims. There is plenty of other evidence to rebut such an assertion.

Sometimes, for example, a state may, by international treaty, have promised to deal with a particular group of its own nationals – a minority – in certain specified ways, with a view to the preservation of their cultural identity. Or it may have agreed that the people of a neighbouring state may have a qualified right to pass across its territory, so as to have access to the sea or a convenient port. The aircraft of foreign states may have been accorded rights of transit and landing, and foreign ships may have been promised certain privileges in specified harbours. A state may have bought arms or secured loans subject to very explicit conditions regarding their use. It may have agreed internationally that certain parts of its territory will not be used for military purposes, or that the extent to which it is so used will be subject to certain detailed limitations. It may have an obligation not to let its neighbours be adversely affected by noxious substances emanating from its side of the border. And it may even have accepted international undertakings not to cede certain portions of its territory.

The list could be continued at some length, but need not. A point which should be made, however, is that legal obligations to foreign states regarding one's internal conduct are not a recent development. There is no question, therefore, of such restrictions being seen as part of a contemporary assault on a traditionally inviolate sphere. Indeed, if anything, states have got more rather than less touchy about such restrictions over the past hundred years. But in any event there are many examples in the history books of international limitations on a state's internal legal freedom. One of the best known are those clauses of the Treaty of Paris (of 1856) which neutralized the Black Sea and obliged Russia to dismantle her bases on its coast. Towards the end of the century, the 1890 cession of Heligoland from Britain to Germany was accompanied by an undertaking that the existing rights of British fishermen of anchorage, provisioning and the sale of fish would be completely preserved. When, in 1905, Norway seceded from Sweden a demilitarized zone between the two countries was agreed upon, and, with two ancient and historic exceptions, Norway agreed to raze all fortresses on her eastern border. And, staying in the same part of the world, note can be taken of the 1920 Treaty of Svalbard by which the area concerned (also known as the Spitzbergen Archipelago) was declared to be one where military activity was forbidden.

In none of these cases was there any suggestion that the states accepting international obligations regarding their internal conduct were thereby disqualifying themselves from participation in the international society of sovereign states. Nor, subsequently, was there even the remotest hint that they were no longer among the sovereign elite on account of the legal restrictions under which they now operated. Indeed, in the case of Norway, the whole point of the 1905 arrangement was to usher her into the international society. It is therefore clear that sovereignty, in the sense of that which makes a territorial entity eligible to join in the international game, does not rest on foreign states having no legal interest in one's internal behaviour.

This is not to say that international legal restrictions on that behaviour may not sometimes be referred to as restrictions on sovereignty. The term 'sovereignty' is too malleable to prevent that, and also too attractive to those with a grievance. Thus when, in 1870, Russia took advantage both of her renewed strength and of war in western Europe to denounce the Black Sea clauses of the Treaty of Paris, it was easy to characterize this as a restoration of her sovereignty. As Bismarck later wrote, 'a nation of a hundred millions cannot be permanently denied the exercise of its natural rights of sovereignty on its own coasts'.[6] Similarly, a distinguished historian referred to the minorities treaties which were pressed on a number of central and east European states after the First World War as an obligation which 'undoubtedly was an interference with the sovereignty of the state'.[7] A representative of the Arab League, immediately after Israel's crushing victory in the Six Day War of 1967, said that the creation of demilitarized zones on the territory of Arab states would 'infringe upon [their] sovereignty'.[8] And more recently a Canadian diplomat, writing about the emergence of human rights on the international agenda, found it easy to refer in this context to the 'factors tending to erode such notions as sovereignty'.[9]

All such uses of the term, however, must be distinguished from that usage which refers to what is required if a territorial unit is to participate in international relations on a full and regular basis. Complete domestic privacy is entirely separate from constitutional independence, notwithstanding the fact that the same word is often used to designate both conditions. And, as has been seen, constitutionally independent units do not, under international law, have full internal freedom. They have it in considerable measure, it is true, which could perhaps lead to the thought that a suitable jurisdictional criterion for international statehood might be the possession of a large amount of domestic privacy. But this would not do. For, quite apart from its vagueness, this criterion is manifestly unrelated to what goes on in the world. There are many territorial units, such as the constituent states of federations, which have a good deal of internal legal freedom but which are never regarded as enjoying the same status as internationally active states. Accordingly, the idea that sovereignty, in the sense of that which makes a territorial entity eligible for an international role, is connected with the absence of obligations to external authorities regarding one's internal behaviour must be abandoned. Internationally active states do not enjoy it completely, and they are by no means alone in enjoying it partially. If, therefore, sovereignty has something to do with the extent of a state's jurisdiction, the search must be pursued elsewhere.

Executive Exclusiveness

A second possibility is to be found in the idea that a sovereign state is one within which no other state exercises, on the ground, jurisdiction of any kind. The local government's authority must run throughout its domain unimpeded by the agents of any other state. This concept is to be distinguished from the situation where one state leases some of its territory to another, so that it has nothing to do with that territory for the number of years which constitute the lease. Such arrangements may come to be a source of dissatisfaction to the sovereign freeholders, and any resultant complaints will very probably be expressed as an affront to their sovereignty. But there will be no serious suggestion that they are thereby less than sovereign so far as their eligibility for membership in international society is concerned. What they will really be saying is that they now regret the making of the lease and would like to bring it to an early end. But for as long as the lease runs the territory in question will have been transferred *de facto* from one sovereign state to another. The New Territories of Hong Kong, which administratively form a part of the British colony of Hong Kong, offer a case in point, as does the 1903 treaty (now superseded) between Panama and the United States establishing the latter's exclusive control of the Panama Canal Zone. Foreign military bases which have been arranged on the same type of legal basis, such as the American base at Guantanamo in Cuba, are another example. A further instance of this is the 99-year lease which the United States secured in 1940 with respect to certain bases in Newfoundland and the Caribbean. It might be noted, however, that technically speaking the British sovereign base areas in Cyprus do not fall into this category as they have never been part of the territory of the sovereign state of Cyprus, having been retained by Britain when its colonial rule of Cyprus came to an end in 1960.

What the second concept of jurisdictional freedom refers to, however, is something other than this, connoting a state's exclusive jurisdictional authority within territory actually under its overall control. In this view, sovereignty consists of the absence of other states ever exercising governmental prerogatives within the territory of the state concerned. As one writer has put it, sovereignty amounts to 'exclusive domination over a certain territory and its population'.[10] It is the approach which finds reflection in the vigorous complaints which are usually made when one state is discovered to be engaged in underhand or uninvited operations on the soil of another. Mexico's resentment at the murder, on its territory, of Trotsky by Soviet agents in 1940 is a case in point, as is Argentina's complaint in 1960 about Israel's abduction of Adolf Eichmann. More generally, one might refer to the fuss which is often made when espionage activities are uncovered, or the objections which are lodged when one state tries, unasked, to release hostages held on the territory of another. A rather comparable situation is the increasingly encountered American efforts to exercise jurisdiction over economic acts performed abroad which affect the interests of the United States, such as the 1982 attempt to stop certain British companies selling oil and gas equipment to the Soviet Union. The thought which states are expressing, often explicitly, in all such cases as these is that a sovereign state must at all times have jurisdiction over every part of its soil.

It follows from this that such a state would lose its sovereign status, and hence its international role, if it agreed to any other state's exercising governmental powers on its territory. For, as has been pointed out, consent has nothing to do with this approach to sovereignty. Its essence lies in the maintenance, in law, of executive exclusiveness. Manifestly, however, executive exclusiveness is legally impinged upon from time to time without loss of status by the state concerned. For states do grant executive powers to foreign states and do not cease to be members of international society on account of so doing. One such type of case is that which was known as capitulations, or extraterritorial jurisdiction. This refers to the treaty arrangements which were entered into in the nineteenth and early twentieth centuries between what were then called advanced and backward states, whereby the subjects of the former, when in the latter, were to be subject to the jurisdiction of their own states. It was to be exercised by their consuls. Such arrangements were made, for example, in respect of Japan, Turkey, Persia, China and Egypt. Britain's extraterritorial jurisdiction in Muscat ended only in 1958, and in the Trucial States of the (Persian) Gulf only when they united to form the United Arab Emirates in 1971. It might be thought that these arrangements could be accounted for, compatibly with this second jurisdictional concept of sovereignty, on the basis of the argument that the exception proves the rule, and that these were indeed, on account of local conditions, exceptional cases. However, it is not only on 'backward' territory that foreign jurisdiction is ever exercised. During the Second World War a number of dispossessed sovereigns and their governments established themselves in Britain and, by the Allied Powers (Maritime Courts) Act of 1941 were empowered to establish and maintain courts in Britain with jurisdiction to try their own nations for certain specified offences.[11] It might also be noted that, according to one writer, for a long time 'neither Turkey nor China ... regarded the immunity of foreigners from local jurisdiction as a serious impairment of its status'.[12]

A further instance of governmental activity on the soil of another state concerns not the exercise of juridical powers but the extraction of minerals. By the 1920 treaty which gave Norway possession of the Svalbard Archipelago, certain mineral and other rights were granted on an equal basis to all the signatories (numbering, in 1976, no less than forty, apart from Norway).[13] At that time the only other signatory besides Norway taking advantage of its rights was the Soviet Union (a circumstance which gives rise to some concern in official quarters in Oslo). But it could be that the possible presence of oil in the area might cause other signatories to reconsider their opportunities, the inhospitable local conditions notwithstanding. In any event, the treaty has never been regarded as undermining either Norway's status as a member of the international society or the inclusion of Svalbard within its sovereign domain.

Much more common than this type of arrangement is one where a foreign state, in connection with the presence of its armed forces in a friendly country, is granted certain jurisdictional rights over the base area and also, maybe, over the activities of its servicemen when outside the base. What is referred to here is something less than the situation which arises when complete jurisdictional authority over a leased area is signed away for a period of years. Instead, one has the position of a state exercising a measure of jurisdiction over territory and people within another state. The exact jurisdictional arrangement will vary from case to case, and will depend on the outcome of negotiations regarding the base area and the local status of the foreign servicemen. But, whatever the details of the resultant agreements, arrangements of this type have become quite common during the past forty or so years, first in consequence of the stationing of servicemen abroad during the Second World War, and then on account of the alliance structures which grew up during the cold war and the numerous bilateral defence pacts and understandings which accompanied them. In one study published in 1963, for example, it was said that about 1¼ million members of the United States armed forces were stationed abroad in at least one hundred and fifty air and naval bases and hundreds of ground installations.[14] They were probably located in at least thirty foreign states. A recent list of military bases and facilities operated in Britain by the United States included eight main bases, two standby bases maintained in a condition of constant readiness, and about fifty 'other sites'.[15] Similarly, the Soviet Union has servicemen stationed in some of its East European associates, and enjoys certain jurisdictional rights over them and the areas where they are based.[16]

A similar type of situation occurs in respect of the half-dozen or so peace-keeping forces which the United Nations has established since the mid-1950s, and the roughly similar number of military observer missions which the organization has mounted since it was set up in 1945. Here, too, states play host to foreign troops, but do not have full jurisdiction over them or their bases. Arrangements have to be worked out – informally if not, for one reason or another, in the shape of a full status of forces agreement – regarding the boundary lines between the internal (and often complex) jurisdiction of the force or observer group and the jurisdiction of the host state. Exactly the same issues arise when a multinational force is organized outside the auspices of the United Nations, such as the multinational force and observers which was established in eastern Sinai in 1982, and the multinational forces which were despatched in the same year to the capital of Lebanon.

In all these cases the host state accepts certain restrictions on its internal jurisdictional authority. But there is never any serious suggestion that by so doing it loses its sovereign status, in the sense of being eligible to participate on an equal basis in international relations. States do not, as it were, relegate those who accommodate foreign forces to an inferior class. Instead, what has happened is that the internal legal freedom of the host state has been curtailed in a rather special way – in return, presumably, for the advantage which accrues in the particular circumstances of each case from having foreign but friendly or neutral forces on one's soil. And it might be added that nowadays there are too many instances of this phenomenon for them to be explained away as exceptions to a supposed rule about the essence of sovereignty.

Reverting for a moment to international organizations, note should also be taken of how their non-military activities often impinge on a state's traditional executive role. The International Labour Organization watches over, by inquiry and fact-finding missions, the execution by member states of their international obligations on labour matters. The International Atomic Energy Authority inspects many nuclear installations to check that promises regarding the civilian use of nuclear fuel are being observed, such promises having been a prerequisite for the supply of the fuel and hence for the establishment of the installations. Schemes for economic assistance organised by the League of Nations continued well established international practices regarding on-the-spot supervision of the use of loans and the collection of revenue. And since 1945 the International Monetary Fund has had a lot of practice in the art of international surveillance. Aid consortia and credit clubs may also be organised on an *ad hoc* basis by groups of states which have a particularly keen interest in the economic health of particular countries. But in instances of these kinds it is never suggested that the operation of multilateral or international arrangements for inspection or supervision results in the loss of their international status by the states concerned. It is just that they have accepted an external presence so as to obtain the benefits that go with it. The agencies of government no longer operate exclusively in these areas, but the state itself remains an equal member of the international society.

But what about giving a foreign state the right to intervene on the soil or in the affairs of another at a moment which, in the light of its rights and obligations in the matter, the foreign state in question deems appropriate? This, it might be thought, is the sort of restriction on a state's jurisdictional authority which must surely alter its international status as a sovereign state. And certainly such situations are now both unpopular and uncommon. But such evidence as there is does not suggest that this kind of arrangement demotes the state in question from the full international league.

West Germany supplies one example. It is generally regarded as having re-entered the international society (following its total defeat in the Second World War and its subsequent occupation) in 1955, with its accession to the North Atlantic Treaty. This brought a treaty of the previous year into effect which ended the rights of the Western occupying powers over the country's foreign policy. However, Britain, France and the United States retained certain rights to intervene in West Germany in the event of serious disturbances to public order and security. These rights were only relinquished in 1968 with the enactment by the West German Parliament of what were regarded as satisfactory emergency laws.

An analogous case is that of Cyprus. Here Britain, Greece and Turkey are given the right, under a Treaty of Guarantee which is included in Cyprus's 1960 constitution, to take individual or joint action to maintain the country's independence and constitutional integrity. However, neither in the case of West Germany between 1955 and 1968 nor in that of Cyprus since independence in 1960 do these arrangements appear to have adversely affected their sovereign status and hence their ability to live a full international life. Both countries, it is true, gave certain foreign states unusual powers. But this did not stand in the way of their pushing and jostling with other sovereign states on a basis of complete formal equality. Indeed, it should be noted that both these sets of restrictions on their jurisdictional autonomy were entered into to facilitate their entry on to the international stage. Evidently, such a role is not impeded even by the granting of rights of intervention to foreign states. No more in this, therefore, than in the other ways which have been discussed is governmental autonomy the criterion for full international status.

But that is not to say that the various possible incursions on a state's executive exclusiveness may not be condemned as an infringement of its sovereignty. Quite the contrary, as all these circumstances have given rise to numerous statements denouncing the situations concerned in terms which rely heavily on the idea of an impaired sovereignty. Not all these denunciations, however, are made by the states immediately concerned. Very often an interested outsider takes on the mantle of defender of another's sovereignty, even where the other state shows no qualms about the matter in question. Indeed, the record suggests that states may sometimes have most to fear from those who affect anxiety about the preservation of their sovereignty.

Thus, for example, it was Italy that, in September 1935, opposed a League of Nations plan for something like the international government of Ethiopia on the ground that it would undermine that country's sovereignty. It was also Italy that, a few weeks later, invaded Ethiopia and before long had overrun and annexed it. Likewise, in 1947 it was Bulgaria that opposed a United Nations plan to send a commission to assist in the settlement of problems between Greece and her neighbours, arguing that this would violate Greek sovereignty. At the same time, however, Bulgaria, together with the other Communist neighbours of Greece, was doing all it could to encourage civil war in Greece and to overthrow its government.

In the matter of foreign bases, it is noticeable that those who do not want them or want to get rid of them almost always cite their sovereignty as the linchpin of their case. Mexico, for example, which has always refused to provide the United States with bases, once declared that 'our sovereignty is not for sale'.[17] Rumania, concomitantly with its independent line with the Eastern bloc, has often voiced the view that the presence of military bases and troops on foreign soil is incompatible with the principle of sovereignty. And the Prime Minister of Greece, on the United States' agreeing to close her bases on Greek territory in 1989 and 1990, said: 'For the first time, the equality of our country has been recognized. The agreement is an indication that our country has regained its national sovereignty to a great extent.'[18] Other states, presumably not having worried about this aspect of things when they first accommodated foreign troops, often discover at a later date that their sovereignty is grievously impaired and demand its immediate restoration. In 1950, for example, the continued presence of a British base in Egypt was declared to represent the slur of 'incomplete sovereignty'.[19] And when, to refer to a comparable issue, certain oriental states grew restive about the exercise on their soil of extraterritorial jurisdiction, it was because, it has been said, they had become receptive to the Western idea of sovereignty.[20]

The presence of international forces or officials, too, can arouse concern on account of their alleged undermining of sovereignty. The head of the provisional government which assumed office in the Dominican Republic in 1965 said that he intended to recover his country's sovereignty, by which he meant that he would try to ensure the departure of the Inter-American Peace Force. The implementation of a 1964 proposal to send a Nato force to Cyprus would be, declared Mr Khrushchev, the Soviet leader, a 'crude encroachment on the sovereignty'[21] of Cyprus. But he did not stand in the way, a couple of months later, of the dispatch of a United Nations force to the country. In 1973 Saudi Arabia worried lest the sending of a United Nations force to Egypt might jeopardize her sovereignty, although Egypt herself took the view that the proposed force would have the effect of safeguarding her sovereignty. Five years later, however, the suggestion that Israel should maintain certain settlements in Sinai brought a strong riposte from Egypt's President Sadat, who said that 'peace means that no one will tread on the land or the sovereignty of the other'.[22] And certainly the idea of international inspectors treading on Soviet land in connection with an arms control agreement, or even (in pre-satellite days) that military installations should be inspected from the air, has always been rejected by the Soviet Union as a violation of sovereignty. Nor, of course, is the Soviet Union alone in being touchy about the matter.

Rights of intervention are also a subject which can easily attract critical attention on account of their supposedly adverse effect on sovereignty. It happened that West Germany kept very quiet about the interventionary powers possessed by the leading Western states: this course was certainly politic, given the circumstances in which the rights had arisen, but it also reflected the fact that the external states concerned were her close allies, and, unlike the position in some other allied relationships, ones from whom she had nothing to fear. When, however, the end of these powers was in sight, comment in the West was often to the effect that West Germany would now be 'fully sovereign for the first time'.[23]

Cyprus, however, could afford to be more assertive, and at the end of 1963, barely three years into independence, President Makarios purported to scrap the Treaties of Guarantee. A few hours later he announced that what he meant was that their abrogation was greatly to be desired. Very shortly, Cyprus was saying that on account of the treaties 'the sovereignty of Cyprus is not complete'[24] and went on, most unusually, to make the very fair logical point that Cyprus should therefore not have been admitted to the United Nations. However, she gave no sign of getting out of her own volition, and before too long had persuaded the United Nations General Assembly to pass a resolution (on 18 December 1965) calling on members to refrain from any intervention directed against the sovereignty of Cyprus. This formulation was not without ambiguity, but the thought of the resolution's sponsors was clear: that it was not the right but the actuality of intervention which was now seen as a threat to Cyprus's sovereignty.

What all this amounts to is that the term 'sovereignty' has splendid potential for rhetoric. Anything which another state is doing or proposing which might have an effect on one's freedom of action can – assuming always of course that one is opposed to what is involved – be attacked in terms of its impact on one's sovereignty. The tendentious opportunities which the term offers are vast. But by the same token the numerous and varied attempts to assert (one hesitates to use the word argue) that sovereignty amounts to a governmental system which is proof against incursions by outsiders are singularly unconvincing. It all savours far too much of clutching at the handiest declamatory straw. And when it is set alongside the evident fact that states do allow other states to exercise certain governmental rights within their territory, without suffering any loss of status in the international society, it becomes very clear that sovereignty in this sense of international status has nothing to do with being governmentally autonomous.

Reasoned attempts to refute this conclusion fall down because they fail to distinguish between the varying extents to which sovereign states accept external restrictions on their internal legal competence, and what it is that gives a territorial entity international status (or sovereignty) in the first place. One lawyer, for example, has argued that sovereignty is 'like a spectrum or continuum, with different states lying at different points on it. Today many countries are subjected to substantive limitations on their sovereignty without being relegated to the category of "non-sovereign states" '.[25] The first sentence of this quotation is an accurate statement of how sovereignty might be described if it is taken to mean the extent of a state's jurisdictional freedom. But the second sentence moves on to refer to sovereignty in the sense of international status, without giving any indication of how, in terms of jurisdictional rights, the dividing line might be drawn between sovereign and non-sovereign states. The clear answer is that it is not possible to draw a satisfactory dividing line on this basis, and that as a matter of fact this is not the way in which sovereign states go about distinguishing between themselves and their non-sovereign fellows. They work on the basis of constitutional independence and not of governmental autonomy. It is perfectly legitimate to refer to the varying degrees in which states are governmentally autonomous as varying degree of sovereignty. But this is quite distinct from the use of 'sovereignty' to mean that which makes a territorial entity eligible for international life. The fact that the same term is used for both conditions must not allow the separateness of the two conditions to be obscured. Governmental autonomy is one thing (and rarely found in an absolute form); constitutional independence is another, and is enjoyed absolutely by all those states that make up the international scene.

Juridical Finality

The third way in which sovereignty may be defined in jurisdictional terms is to say that it demands the settlement of all legal issues in the courts of the land. There must be no possibility of appealing to an external court against the actions of the government or the decisions of the national courts. As Grotius put it early in the seventeenth century, that power is sovereign 'whose acts are not subject to the legal control of another, so that they cannot be rendered void by the act of another human will'.[26]

This definition echoed a famous dispute one hundred years before between Henry VIII of England and the pope, from whom Henry sought an annulment of his marriage to Catherine of Aragon. She had failed to provide him with a son – and Henry was also infatuated with Anne Boleyn. He therefore turned to the pope for assistance, as at this time the papacy exercised a wide jurisdiction in England as in other countries – a jurisdiction which Henry had vigorously defended some years before and for which he had received the title of Defender of the Faith, which is still borne by British monarchs. However, the pope found himself in a difficulty, as he was in the power of the King of Spain, who also happened to be Catherine's nephew and zealous protector. He therefore prevaricated, and in time Henry lost patience. Accordingly, in 1533 Parliament passed an Act in Restraint of Appeals, by which the whole of the pope's jurisdiction over English laymen was abolished. It was, says the historian of the affair, 'perhaps the most important statute of the sixteenth century',[27] because, in its preamble, it enunciated 'as accepted fact, a new doctrine that the king was supreme head of a realm which was a sovereign state free from all foreign authority'.[28] Now all appeals were to be determined within the realm, and only sentences pronounced within the king's courts were to take effect. The episode represented, says another historian, the 'full-grown spirit of English nationalism' which would 'no longer submit to be governed by a religious authority that was seated a thousand miles beyond the sea'.[29]

It is not hard to see this state of affairs as the mark of sovereignty. It sounds odd to speak of a sovereign state's nationals pleading their cause before a foreign court, or having the right to appeal to such a court against a decision of the state's own courts. And the reason for this is that customarily it has not happened. In the normal way a citizen has not been and is not able to go beyond the courts of his own country. The only available form of justice for him is that which is dispensed at home.

However, before concluding that here is a successful jurisdictional quarrel with the idea of sovereignty as amounting to constitutional independence, account has to be taken of two phenomena which do not accord with the 'juridically final' approach. One is now in serious decline, but the other is thriving.

The one in decline is the jurisdiction in respect of certain foreign states of the Judicial Committee of Britain's Privy Council. The Judicial Committee used to be a kind of supreme court for Britain's numerous and extensive colonies (as well as having certain domestic functions, such as acting as the final court of appeal from English ecclesiastical courts). It is principally composed of the judicial members of the House of Lords (Britain's highest court) – the Lords of Appeal in Ordinary – together with certain other office holders. And in relevant cases colonial or Commonwealth judges may sit as assessors. In theory it does not deliver judgements but opinions, which are then acted on by the Crown by way of Orders in Council.

As the British Empire turned into a Commonwealth of sovereign states, a kind of old boys' club, the newly independent members acquired the right to modify or eliminate the right of appeal to the Privy Council, and many of them did so. The Irish were quick to see the link with the Privy Council as a sign of alien government, and an Australian Attorney-General claimed not long ago, in connection with this matter, that his country was still labouring under 'relics of colonialism'.[30] A British queen's counsel has declared that appeal to the Privy Council from abroad is 'incompatible with the sovereignty'[31] of the countries concerned, and Mr Ian Smith's Rhodesia purported to choke over proposals for ending its illegal independence on the ground that appeals to the Privy Council were to be retained, which was seen as 'an unwarranted interference with the sovereignty' of a lawfully constituted Rhodesia.[32] Thus it is perhaps not surprising that the 1985 edition of *Whitaker's Almanac*[33] lists only eighteen of the forty-nine members of the Commonwealth as retaining the right of appeal to the Judicial Committee of the Privy Council, and of these eighteen only five have a population of more than 1 million: Jamaica, Malaysia, New Zealand, Singapore, and Trinidad and Tobago. And far the most populous of these five states – Malaysia – severed its link with the Privy Council in January 1985.

However, even the least of these eighteen – tiny Tuvalu with its population of 8,000 – is regarded on all sides as a sovereign member of the international society. And the same is true of the other Commonwealth members in the interval between their independence and their ending of appeals to the Privy Council. It would seem, therefore, that if a state wishes to allow its nationals to appeal to an external court this raises no questions about the state's international status as a sovereign state. All that has happened is that the state concerned has furnished its people with an appellate court beyond its borders, and to all intents and purposes that court becomes part of the judicial machinery of the state in question.[34] But technically speaking the state has undoubtedly placed a limitation on its juridical autonomy. That, as a careful student of the matter said a while ago, is, 'for what it is worth, unanswerable'.[35] And if one cares to define sovereignty as juridical finality then the logical conclusion is that a number of well-known states have been, or are, lacking in sovereignty. But that is not how states define the term when they speak of what it is that gives them eligibility to appear on the international stage.

This argument finds support in the other procedure which must be considered in this connection, which is very far from being in decline. It is the role of the European Court of Human Rights, which was set up under the European Convention on Human Rights of 1950. The twenty parties to this Convention (all of them non-Communist states) guarantee to uphold certain rights and the European Commission of Human Rights receives complaints from one member state about another's conduct. Predictably, these are few and far between. But individuals from those member states who have accepted the rights of individual petition may complain to the Commission about the way they have been treated and, if their state has also accepted the court's compulsory jurisdiction, the Commission may refer the matter to the court. The court's decision is binding. Technically speaking it is the Commission which takes the member state to court, but in effect what is happening is that an individual is appealing against some administrative practice or legal decision which is believed to be contrary to the 1950 Convention. To that extent, therefore, the juridical finality of the member state's courts has been impaired.

Most parties to the Convention have accepted the right of individual petition and the compulsory jurisdiction of the court,

Britain being among the last to do so. And when it did so, for an initial cautious term of three years (which has since been regularly extended), *The Times* observed that 'the sovereignty of the British Parliament is fractionally reduced'.[36] Now the word 'fractional' might be amended to one implying a slightly larger scope, for as a result of adverse rulings by the European Court British law and practice has been changed in respect of half a dozen or so matters. One of these is a British schoolmaster's traditional right to use a cane or a strap on those of his pupils who misbehave, irrespective of the views of the child's parents on the issue of corporal punishment. As so often happens, the consequences of a single, earlier decision were far from fully perceived.

The sovereignty of Britain, however, like that of the other signatories to the Convention who have accepted the right of individual petition and the compulsory jurisdiction of the court, has been diminished only if sovereignty is taken to mean juridical finality. Manifestly, Britain and these other states (such as West Germany and Sweden) have not lost their status as full and active members of the international society. In this sense of the term 'sovereignty', they are no less sovereign than before. Once again, therefore, the evidence points to the conclusion that sovereignty in the sense of international status is fully compatible with the right of appeal to an external court. If a different, or additional, view of sovereignty is taken, so that it connotes juridical finality, then it must be concluded both that sovereignty is something which varies in degree and that the West European arrangements here discussed do diminish the sovereignty of the states concerned. But that is not how states use the term when they refer to the basic condition which must be satisfied for a territorial entity to operate freely at the international level.

Before concluding this section, mention should be made of a few procedures which, while they do not usually involve a technical breach of a state's juridical finality, none the less are roughly analogous to the European arrangement which has just been discussed. They all relate to fairly recent attempts to provide some international protection for individual human rights.

Following the adoption in 1948 of the American Declaration on the Rights and Duties of Man an Inter-American Commission on Human Rights was set up in 1959 with the right to consider individual complaints in respect of a limited number of rights. The most the Commission could do, however, was to make recommendations. Then, in 1969, a convention was signed which made the right of individual petition to the Commission automatic for the nationals of ratifying states. The Inter-American Commission was to carry out investigations and announce its recommendations. But again it has no power to bind the parties, although in certain circumstances it does now have the right to submit cases to the Inter-American Court of Human Rights, which was also established in the 1969 convention and whose decisions are binding on the parties. The convention came into force in 1978 and has been ratified by most of the Latin American states. However, the automatic right of individual petition has not so far had much impact in practice on the protection of human rights in the region, as is seen by the fact that the states who are now bound by the convention include El Salvador, Guatemala, Haiti, Honduras and Nicaragua. And in any event, even if sovereignty is thought to be inextricably bound up with the idea of juridical finality, it has hardly been so much as dented by these provisions, as the circumstances in which the Inter-American Court may overturn an internal judicial decision or administrative action are unlikely to occur with much frequency.

Even this last qualification is unnecessary so far as the United Nations system for the protection of human rights is concerned. In 1976 the UN-sponsored International Covenant on Civil and Political Rights came into force, its principal organ of implementation being the Human Rights Committee. This committee may receive complaints from individuals only if their states have ratified an optional protocol to that effect, and even then the most the committee can do is to give its opinion on certain complaints. As of 1 July 1982 only twenty-seven states had ratified the optional protocol. Side by side with this arrangement is another whereby, under Resolution 1503 of the United Nations' Economic and Social Council, the Commission on Human Rights (to be distinguished from the Human Rights Committee) may examine individual petitions 'which appear to reveal a consistent pattern of gross violations of human rights'.[37] But this too can at most lead to an investigation – and the procedure regarding it is not only cumbersome but also shot through with political considerations.

More generally, however, the point should be made that what might be called normal international litigation can have the effect of overruling decisions which have been taken internally by judges or administrators. Such litigation is, as was noted in the last chapter, infrequent, and therefore the cases which relate just to internal matters are rare, and unlikely to show a great increase. But, as was seen in the first subsection of this chapter, international obligations can bear on a state's internal conduct, and in the sphere of human rights there have been a couple of developments specifically relating to this matter. Under the 1950 European Convention on Human Rights the Committee of Ministers of the Council of Europe may find itself acting in a quasi-judicial capacity in inter-state disputes regarding human rights, and where the states concerned have accepted its jurisdiction, either *ad hoc* or compulsorily, the European Court of Human Rights may adjudicate. Its decision will be binding on the parties. Similarly, the Inter-American Court of Human Rights may issue a judgement in any relevant dispute between states which have accepted its competence. At a wider level, it is always open to states to take disputes which relate to the application of international law to internal matters to the International Court of Justice at The Hague, and occasionally they have done so. All of which should make it quite clear that while juridical finality may customarily be associated with sovereign states it is not an essential element in their sovereign status.

Of course, observers may speak of states' reluctance to submit to international adjudication in terms of their attachment to sovereignty, and often do. On human rights, for example, it has been said that the 'resistances of national sovereignty have proved too strong to allow much effective work'[38] to be done regarding their international protection. But this is using the term 'sovereignty' to refer to states' internal jurisdictional freedom. This is not, however, how states use the term when they refer to what it is that gives them their international status.

Avoidance of Supranationalism

The three jurisdictional issues which have so far been considered in this chapter do not always arise in isolation from each other. A state may have accepted an obligation to an outsider regarding its internal conduct, and on the same matter be subject to some international supervisory mechanism which operates on its territory. Or the obligation may relate to a matter which could find its way to an external court. Or a particular topic may embrace all three jurisdictional issues. However, whether they arise singly, doubly, or three together, the argument of the chapter is not affected. State sovereignty is impaired only if it is defined to mean one, other, or all three aspects of jurisdictional freedom. And that is certainly not how states define it when they refer to that which makes them eligible for international life. Accordingly, sovereignty in the sense of that constitutional independence which offers international status is not lost by any of the possible ways in which jurisdictional freedom might be and in practice often is limited.

What have already been discussed, however, are limitations which operate within or very close to the usual framework of international relations, where states have direct contacts with each other and any limitations on a state's jurisdictional freedom are the result of specific arrangements with the state or international institution to which jurisdictional rights are granted. But when such rights are exercised by what has come to be called a supranational institution a rather different relationship emerges, at least in theory, and the question arises as to whether that relationship is compatible with state sovereignty.

The institutions which have attracted the term 'supranational' are those which have been established in Western Europe since the Second World War with the avowed purpose of removing inter-state barriers and encouraging integration in the areas of their competence. The aim was to go beyond the merely co-operative arrangements which are typical of institutional activity at the international level, and to do so by giving strong and effective power to the central organs of the new institutions. Thus it was hoped that in one sphere and another the traditional significance of state boundaries would be lost, and the territory of all the member states would come to operate in these several respects as a single unit.

The first move in this direction was the 1951 treaty providing for the European Coal and Steel Community, which was to last for fifty years. Its signatories were Belgium, France, Italy, Luxembourg, the Netherlands and West Germany – the Six as they were for a long time called. It was followed in the next year (when the Coal and Steel Community came into operation) by agreement among the Six on the establishment of a European defence community. And in 1953, in anticipation of the setting up of the defence community, a draft treaty was proposed to bring the two communities together in a European political community. However, France refused to ratify the defence community treaty, and so that scheme fell to the ground, and with it the proposed political community. It was time for a rethink. Out of this process came the signature by the Six, in 1957, of treaties of unlimited duration providing for the European Economic Community and the European Atomic Energy Community (concerned only with atomic energy for peaceful purposes). Both of them came into effect in the following year. In the mid-1960s the separate institutional arrangements of the three communities were merged into a single set of institutions. Henceforth, reference would be made simply to the European Communities or even just to the European Community, although it should be noted that the founding treaties were not substantively altered, so that the Community's common institutions operate under three separate and different sets of powers. In 1973 the Six became the Nine, with the accession of Britain, Denmark and Ireland. Norway had also planned to join, but the proposal was rejected in a national referendum. In Britain, by contrast, and following a change of government, membership was confirmed by the constitutionally most unusual step of a referendum, held in 1975. Greece joined in 1981, and in 1986 the Ten are due to become Twelve with the addition of Portugal and Spain.

The term supranational was used in the Coal and Steel Community treaty, the defence community treaty, and in the draft treaty regarding the proposed political community. However, it was deliberately omitted from the Economic and Atomic Energy Community treaties as by now the term was thought to have, in some ears, a possibly ominous ring. But these treaties were recognized on all sides as being in the same vein as that which had set up the Coal and Steel Community, and thus the term 'supranational' may appropriately be applied to all three arrangements. It is not, however, a term of art, as states have not given it an exact and agreed meaning. Rather, it is a helpful means of classification in that it draws attention to features in these organizations which are both distinctive and significant. In elucidating this point, illustrations and terminology will be taken only from the Economic Community (or Common Market, as it is often called) as this is far and away the broadest and most important of the European Communities. But the general observations which will be made are equally applicable to all three, all of them being clearly and similarly distinguishable, at the theoretical level, from the way in which international co-operation has hitherto been institutionally conducted.

The attempt by academics to highlight the distinctive character of supranationalism, and thus to provide an overall view of this international development, has led to a number of suggestions. One student[39] has drawn attention to six possible criteria, but is not fully satisfied with any single one of them. However, the one which he admits as having the best claim does provide, on its own, a very solid base for the supranational concept. It is that the essence of supranationalism lies in an organization having the legal power to bind natural and legal persons within the member states.[40] In the more usual manner of international co-operation, an organization, even if it has the power to bind its members, only binds the state as such. Thus the member state in question would have an international obligation to do what the organization required it to do. If it failed to honour its obligation, then the organization would have a legitimate ground for legal complaint. But the organization could not, as it were, go behind the state's back, enter the state, and demand of particular individuals, institutions, or enterprises that they do what was necessary for the state's international obligation to be carried out. In the case of a supranational organization, however, the relevant individuals, institutions, or enterprises may be directly bound by a supranational act. It is not so much a case of the supranational body going behind the state's back as of there being no back to go behind. For the supranational body has direct access to the territory of its members. In respect of matters within its jurisdiction, it is as if state boundaries do not exist. The supranational body is like the central authority in what has been called a functional federation.[41]

In the case of the European Communities the organs which have the power to act with this kind of supranational effect are three in number: the Commission, the Court and the Council. The Commission is the executive body of the Community. It is made up of individuals who must act independently in the interest of the whole organization. It takes decisions by simple majority. The Court, too, is not subject to instructions from the member states, but acts in the normal judicial manner. At the centre of the Community is the Council, composed of the representatives of the member states. It is responsible for the general direction in which the Community moves, although in the normal way it only acts on the basis of proposals received from the Commission. It may take decisions by majority vote or by a qualified majority, with the votes of the members being weighted on an agreed formula. But in practice the Council works on the unanimity principle if any member declares that the matter under discussion affects its vital national interests – this being the effect of the Luxembourg Agreements of January 1966.

Besides giving opinions and recommendations, the Council and Commission take three other kinds of decisions, all of them having binding effect. Their regulations are like statutes in national law, and all individuals and organs within member states are bound directly and immediately. Directives are policy orders to member states to bring about, in their own way, certain results. And decisions tell a member state to take some particular action or order an individual or business enterprise to do something specific. The Court interprets the law of the Community, which takes precedence over internal law where any conflict arises between the two. For, as the Court has made very clear, the Community treaties do not merely impose obligations on the signatory states but have brought a new legal order into being which, within the area it covers, stands above the domestic law of the various members.

Manifestly, arrangements of this sort have a considerable impact on the jurisdictional freedom of their member states. The state becomes subject to additional international rules regarding its internal conduct. An external executive receives the right to operate on the soil of the state, and to have direct dealings with its nationals. Moreover, that external executive may, if thwarted, call on the local courts for support. And an external court may hear appeals regarding internal matters, being empowered to invalidate legislative and executive acts done by the member's legislature and government. If, therefore, sovereignty consists of 'supreme decision-making authority'[42] within a territory, the state concerned no longer has it, or at the very least is no longer fully possessed of it. And yet, the members of the European Community are still members of international society. The Community's substantial inroads on their jurisdictional freedom have not resulted in their expulsion from the international league. Nor, it is worth emphasizing, are they now less than full members of that league. A special, lesser, category of membership has not been created to accommodate those who have fallen somewhat from grace by accepting supranationalism.

The only possible conclusion to draw is that while 'sovereignty' may certainly be used to mean jurisdictional freedom (whether in absolute or relative terms) this is not how states use it when they refer to what it is which equips them for participation in international society. Accordingly, sovereignty in this hugely important sense is not lost by joining a supranational organization. And the reason is that such an organization does not, on its own, amount to a constitutionally superior system of government. Its legal system is superior to that of the member states with respect to the area of its competence. But that area of competence is strictly limited. The supranational body does not have general 'legislative power'.[43] Accordingly, even though at least one lawyer has referred to the European Community having equipped itself with 'a constitution',[44] the Community is not in possession of a basic legal arrangement of equivalent breadth to those which are operative in all sovereign states. Certainly the member states have entered into a new 'constitutional situation'.[45] But that situation is not one of subordination to a higher constitution in the sense in which the term 'constitution' is used when it denotes the distribution and limitation of general governmental power within a particular territory. A supranational organization is not the same thing as a federal state. Thus the members remain constitutionally independent, and hence in full possession of their prized international status. In this sense of the term they are no less sovereign than they were before entering the supranational body.

The issue of supranationalism and sovereignty cannot, however, be left at this point. For there is no doubt that a supranational arrangement is, in principle, different in kind from the usual run of organizations which are set up to facilitate co-operation between states, being governmental rather than international in nature. And in consequence there is certainly a question as to whether this difference in kind might encourage the undermining of sovereignty in the sense of that which makes a territorial entity eligible for membership in international society. The debate on Britain's entry to (and continued membership of) the European Community provides a useful peg on which to hang an examination of these questions.

In this debate the longer-term impact of membership on Britain's international status was not much ventilated. Instead the tone was set by the governments of the day, who were, of course, advocating entry. In official pronouncements it was first claimed that Community law would not involve Britain in any 'constitutional innovation', this remarkable statement being followed by the bland, and disingenuous, suggestion that the legal restraints which membership would involve were similar to '[m]any of our treaty obligations . . . for example, the Charter of the United Nations, the European Convention on Human Rights and GATT'.[46] This was Mr Wilson's Labour government speaking. Four years later the Conservative government led by Mr Heath declared, in a passage chiefly notable for its vagueness, that there 'is no question of any erosion of essential national sovereignty; what is proposed is a sharing and an enlargement of individual national sovereignties in the general interest'.[47] Four years on, with Mr Wilson back in power, it was now admitted that the 'Community has certain distinctive features which make it unique among international groupings'.[48] But it was argued, if that is the word, that British membership was desirable because it made us 'better able to advance and protect our national interests – this is the essence of sovereignty'.[49]

These points, especially the last two, were repeated time and again on one side of the debate. Nor were politicians the only ones to participate along these lines. One academic, for example, spoke of the 'choice between theoretical sovereignty and practical effectiveness'.[50] And from the Community's headquarters came a contribution from the leading Briton on its staff (Britain now having joined), who contrasted what he called operational and non-operational sovereignty. The former consisted of being able to influence important decisions, whereas the latter, for Britain, amounted to 'sulking in a corner and saying: "Look, I am free to suck my own thumb" '.[51] Thus sovereignty was being presented, by the proponents of entry, as jurisdictional in character, and the amount lost by entry to the Community was said to be well worth the benefit of being able to participate in important decisions.

The other side of the debate, too, approached the issue of sovereignty chiefly in jurisdictional terms. The prospect of bureaucrats from Brussels poking their noses into British affairs was dwelt upon. The fact that an external court would have overriding authority in Britain was underlined, and it was sometimes darkly added, as in *The Times* on one occasion, that the court was likely to be 'supervisory and activist in the continental tradition'.[52] But above all it was pointed out that entry would involve a loss of parliamentary sovereignty – of the very long tradition whereby Parliament is the supreme law-making body in Britain, unfettered even by any internally entrenched rules, let alone by an external authority. Of the longer-term threat which the Community might present to Britain's international status less was heard. The issue was certainly not ignored. Early in the debate a professor of international relations suggested that sovereignty, in the sense of international status, was blurred by supranational arrangements, and that substantial abatements by Britain of her international legal freedom would make the eventual loss of her international status 'inescapably, merely a matter of time'.[53] Later, a leading Conservative campaigner against British entry suggested that a member state 'would in practice have no option except to proceed, along with its fellow members, to participation in a federal Western Europe, if those others so desired'.[54] But this approach suffered under the dual handicap of being both academic (in that it turned on a concept of sovereignty, and a fairly unfamiliar one at that) and speculative. Not surprisingly, it did not cut much ice.

However, it is clear that a federal state was the goal of the founders of the supranational movement. The person who played a very large part in getting the idea of the Coal and Steel Community off the ground has said that the aim was to 'breach the ramparts of national sovereignty'[55] with a view to the eventual establishment of a European federation. Similarly, the preamble to the Economic Community Treaty spoke of the determination of the signatories 'to lay the foundations of an ever closer union'.[56] The hope was that the Communities set up in the 1950s would result in the economies and social systems of the members becoming very deeply intertwined, with two consequences. First, that it would become impractical for any member to withdraw, even if it thought that it was legally entitled to do so. (In Britain, much had been made of the point that it would always be open to Parliament to repeal the Act of Accession whatever the European Court might say about it.) And, second, that the progress of the Communities in the economic field would lead, ineluctably, to the harmonization of policy and institutions in other areas, so that one interlocking pattern of supranational arrangements would emerge. Effectively, the members would have become one territorial unit, and before too long would recognize this by bringing the formal situation into line with that which had emerged *de facto*. As a former American Secretary of State put it, the essence of the supranational method is 'not to attack the question of sovereignty head-on. Architecturally, the plans are defective and bewildering. But as living organisms rooted in the soil of European life, their very growth changes and modifies that life until they may become so entwined with the inseparable from it they may crack even the masonry, as the roots of a tree will do.'[57]

These arguments have a certain force. If the economies and social systems of ten or so countries become fully integrated, up to and including the operation of a single currency, it would be very hard indeed for any one of them to abandon the enterprise, or for the states to go their separate international ways in non-economic fields. Thus other integrative activities would probably have been set in hand, and the member states, and outsiders, might one day scratch their heads over the question of whether, from the international point of view, they were many or one – whether their central arrangements did not reflect the existence of a single, superior constitution rather than the co-operation of a number of constitutionally independent entities. This process would then be an instance of one of the two ways in which sovereignty, in the sense of constitutional independence, can be voluntarily lost – the other being its formal renunciation at a grand international ceremony. It would be similar to cohabitation leading to what used to be called common law marriage, as distinct from the establishment of matrimony by way of a particular event held on a particular day.

However, for institutional momentum to work in this way at the supranational level it is necessary for the states concerned to get beyond the point of no return in their integrating activities, so that instead of each of them having their own hand on the brake they merely have a say as to when it should be operated. Where that point of no return lies is very far from clear. In Western Europe a number of observers, not too long ago, perceived it as coming into view. The 'obsolescence of national sovereignty' was said by one to be 'the key'[58] to what was going on. In 1969 a high-level committee, referring to the unification of Europe, said that within ten to fifteen years 'the importance of relations between the individual governments of Europe will begin to decline'.[59] And a close student of the West European scene opined that the 'survival of nation states as they are today . . . is in my view unlikely. The strengthening of functional systems of interdependence . . . makes some changes in the present nation state system inevitable'.[60]

But politics is not a matter of moving steadily forward to one's initial goals, not even if, as is perhaps unlikely in the European case, they are unambiguously stated and genuinely shared. International integration, until it gets beyond recall, remains under the ultimate control of the states concerned. It has no necessary organizational momentum, no inescapable inner logic, and the point of no return is perhaps further down the road than many tended to think. Certainly, during the last decade or so it has been increasingly apparent that the members of the European Community are not minded to merge their separate international identities into a single West European unit. A member of the European Commission described the term 'European Union' as 'happily fuzzy'[61] and a former high-level member of the Commission secretariat said that 'what is emerging is a loose functional confederation'.[62] Another commentator, noting the re-emergence of 'the dogma of national sovereignty',[63] has concluded that the national state's exit has been at least temporarily halted and that 'intergovernmentalism [is] the most appropriate term to describe the broad character of relations within the Nine in the 1970s'.[64] Altogether, the view of Britain's 1973 Reith lecturer that the Community was on its way to an 'unknown destination'[65] seemed increasingly apposite, as did his description of the Community as like a bag of sticky marbles.

Thus the European Community does not yet threaten sovereignty, in the sense of the members' constitutional independence, and hence their international status. It consists of a group of states which are working closely together on a wide range of economic and social issues, and this approach has been extended into the field of foreign policy through the mechanism known as 'political co-operation'. It is not unreasonable to anticipate that co-ordination in these fields will remain at least at its present level and perhaps get more intense, without, however, necessarily moving in the direction of federalism. The apprehensions which were once entertained about the possibility of sovereignty being submerged by the Community were not ill founded. For undoubtedly a new kind of arrangement has been established, one involving a very high measure of co-operation and possessed of a framework which gives scope for developments of a clearly federalist type – which may yet occur. As of the mid-1980s, however, the Community is moving very much along the familiar route of international co-operation (albeit on a special kind of road) with the member states securely in the driving seat. The national interest, nationally perceived, is still their clear criterion, and each of them has a reasonably firm hand on a separate system of control.

If the Community did begin to pick up speed towards closer integration and, ultimately, a federal goal, this would, of course, have adverse implications for the sovereignty (meaning international status) of the member states. But it would have no effect on the role of sovereignty in the world at large. Other states would not be so impressed by the West European example as to tumble over themselves to give up their constitutional independence, with a view to the early establishment of a world state. Of that, at least, one can be sure. All that would happen internationally would be the replacement, in Western Europe, of ten or a dozen states by one. Whether or not, at the level of values, that would be a good thing would depend on one's assessment not only of the West European scene but also of the general role of sovereignty in international relations. Opinion on this matter will be examined in the next chapter. But so far as the analysis of supranationalism and sovereignty is concerned one just needs to note that, while such arrangements certainly diminish the jurisdictional freedom of the member states (and hence their sovereignty if one cares to use the term in that way), they have not yet had an adverse effect on the international status of the members. Sovereignty, in the sense of constitutional independence, has not been impaired by supranational organizations, nor is there any necessary reason why it should be.

Notes: Chapter 9

1   Quoted in F. H. Hinsley, *Sovereignty* (London: Watts, 1966), p. 22.
2   Quoted in Paul Johnson, *The Offshore Islanders* (London: Weidenfeld & Nicolson, 1972), p. 227.
3   Quoted in Michael Akehurst, *A Modern Introduction to International Law*, 3rd edn (London: Allen & Unwin, 1977), p. 140.
4   Commonwealth Secretariat, *Diplomatic Service: Formation and Operation* (London: Longman, 1971), p. 14.
5   Susan Strange, 'Looking back – but mostly forward', *Millennium*, vol. 11, no. 1 (Spring 1982), p. 43.
6   Quoted in M. Wight, *Power Politics*, ed. Hedley Bull and Carsten Holbraad (Leicester: Leicester University Press, 1978), p. 259.
7   René Albrecht Carrié, *The Meaning of the First World War* (Englewood Cliffs, NJ: Prentice-Hall, 1965), p. 104.
8   *The Times*, 13 October 1967.
9   Geoffrey Pearson, 'Emergence of human rights in international relations', *International Perspectives*, July/August 1978, p. 10.
10   H. Lubasz (ed.), *The Development of the Modern State* (London: Collier-Macmillan, 1964), p. 2.
11   See Lord Gore-Booth (ed.), *Satow's Guide to Diplomatic Practice*, 5th edn (London: Longman, 1979), p. 11.
12   George W. Keeton, *National Sovereignty and International Order* (London: Peace Books, 1939), p. 38.
13   See letter in *The Times*, 18 February 1976, from Norway's Minister of Foreign Affairs.
14   See G. Stambuk, *American Military Forces Abroad* (Columbus, Ohio: Ohio State University Press, 1963), pp. 4–5.
15   *The Times*, 4 November 1983.
16   See, for example, A. Korbonski, 'The Warsaw Pact', *International Conciliation*, no. 573 (May 1969), p. 34.
17   *The Times*, 23 July 1969.

18 *The Times*, 16 July 1983.
19 Quoted in Elizabeth Monroe, 'Mr. Bevin's "Arab policy" ', in Albert Hourani (ed.), *Middle Eastern Affairs Number Two* (London: Chatto & Windus, 1961), p. 47.
20 See Keeton, *National Sovereignty*, p. 38.
21 Quoted in James A. Stegenga, *The United Nations Force in Cyprus* (Columbus, Ohio: Ohio State University Press, 1968), p. 45.
22 *The Times*, 21 January 1978.
23 *The Times*, 30 June 1967; cf. *New York Times*, 28 May 1968.
24 Cyprus Government, *The Roots of Evil* (21 February 1964), quoted in T. Ehrlich, *Cyprus 1958–1967* (London: Oxford University Press, 1974), p. 74.
25 M. H. Mendelson, in *The Times*, 15 November 1972.
26 Quoted in P. Taylor, 'The concept of community and the European integration process', *Journal of Common Market Studies*, vol. 7, no. 2 (December 1968), p. 84.
27 Geoffrey de C. Parmiter, *The King's Great Matter. A Study of Anglo-Papal Relations, 1527–1534* (London: Longman, 1967), p. 221.
28 ibid., p. 223.
29 G. M. Trevelyan, *A History of England*, 3rd edn (London: Longman, 1945), pp. 301–2.
30 *The Times*, 15 January 1973. Subsequently in 1975, Australia's Labour government abolished appeals to the Privy Council from courts under federal jurisdiction. However, the right of appeal to the Privy Council from state supreme courts on state matters remained. Early in the 1980s, again under a Labour regime, the federal government and the state governments agreed to sever these legal links. But in February 1984 the Australian High Court ruled that as the constitution had not yet been changed, the right of appeal remained. See *The Times*, 11 February 1984. Subsequently it was announced that Britain and Australia had agreed on constitutional changes which would end the remaining appellate jurisdiction of the Judicial Committee of the Privy Council in respect of Australian Courts. See *The Times*, 17 August 1985.
31 *The Listener*, 24 September 1964.
32 Quoted in John Day, 'A failure of foreign policy: the case of Rhodesia', in M. Leifer (ed.), *Constraints and Adjustments in British Foreign Policy* (London: Allen & Unwin, 1972), p. 159.
33 *Whitaker's Almanac 1985* (London, 1984), p. 693.
34 cf. J. E. S. Fawcett, 'Note', in J. B. D. Miller, *Survey of Commonwealth Affairs. Problems of Expansion and Attrition 1953–1969* (London: Oxford University Press, 1974), pp. 426–9.
35 R. T. E. Latham, 'The law and the Commonwealth', in W. K. Hancock (ed.), *Survey of British Commonwealth Affairs, Vol. 1, Problems of Nationality 1918–1936* (London: Oxford University Press, 1937), p. 559. (This chapter was reprinted in R. T. E. Latham, *The Law and the Commonwealth*, London: Royal Institute of International Affairs, 1949, same pagination.)
36 *The Times*, 8 December 1965.
37 Quoted in A. H. Robertson, *Human Rights in the World*, 2nd edn (Manchester: Manchester University Press, 1982), p. 55. See also, generally, I. Weightman, 'The establishment, operation, and development of the 1970 procedure by which the United Nations examines complaints concerning human rights violations', unpublished MA thesis presented to the University of Keele, 1981.
38 Evan Luard, *International Agencies* (London: Macmillan for the Royal Institute of International Affairs, 1977), p. 184.
39 P. Hay, *Federalism and Supranational Organizations* (Urbana, Ill.: Illinois University Press, 1966), pp. 29–38.

40   cf. G. Schwarzenberger, 'Federalism and supranationalism in the European Communities', in G. W. Keeton and G. Schwarzenberger (eds), *English Law and the Common Market* (London: Stevens, 1963), pp. 17–33.

41   ibid., p. 19

42   B. Buzan, *People, States and Fear* (Brighton: Wheatsheaf, 1983), p. 41.

43   R. Aron, *Peace and War* (New York: Praeger, 1967), p. 745.

44   J. D. B. Mitchell, 'The sovereignty of Parliament and Community law: the stumbling block that isn't there', *International Affairs*, vol. 55, no. 1 (January 1979), pp. 34 and 40.

45   ibid., p. 40.

46   Cmnd 3301, May 1967, para. 23.

47   Cmnd 4715, July 1971, para. 29.

48   Cmnd 6003, March 1975, para. 118.

49   ibid., para. 151.

50   M. Niblock, *The EEC: National Parliaments and Community Decision-Making* (London: Royal Institute of International Affairs and Political and Economic Planning, 1971), p. 107.

51   Sir Christopher Soames, quoted in *The Times*, 31 December 1974.

52   *The Times*, 27 February 1975.

53   C. A. W. Manning, in *The Times*, 18 July 1961.

54   Sir Derek Walker-Smith, *The Times*, 31 July 1969.

55   Jean Monnet, *Memoirs* (London: Collins, 1978), p. 296.

56   Quoted in R. Vaughan, *Post-War Integration in Europe* (London: Edward Arnold, 1976), p. 73.

57   Dean Acheson, *Sketches from Life* (London: Hamish Hamilton, 1961), p. 49.

58   Max Beloff, *The United States and the Unity of Europe* (London: Faber, 1963), p. 119.

59   Cmnd 4107, *Report of the Review Committee on Overseas Representation 1968–1969* (Duncan Report), misc. no. 24 (1969), s. IV 15.

60   Paul Taylor, 'Britain, the Common Market, and the forces of history', *Orbis*, vol. 16, no. 3 (Fall 1972), p. 757.

61   Ralf Dahrendorf, 'The foreign policy of the EEC', *The World Today*, vol. 29, no. 2 (February 1973), p. 57.

62   Michael Shanks, *The Times*, 30 December 1977; cf. his 'The EEC – a community in search of an identity', *Three Banks Review*, no. 115 (September 1977), pp. 52–66; cf. also his article in *The Times*, 9 December 1980.

63   Paul Taylor, 'Intergovernmentalism in the European Communities in the 1970s: patterns and perspectives', *International Organization*, vol. 36, no. 4 (Autumn 1982), p. 766.

64   ibid., p. 741.

65   Andrew Schonfield, *Europe: Journey to an Unknown Destination* (Harmondsworth: Penguin, 1973).

10

Moral

Those who quarrel with sovereignty on moral grounds are not arguing about the exact meaning of the term. They are not addressing themselves to the question of whether constitutional independence is a correct statement of what a territorial entity needs if it is to acquire international status. What they are doing is to express their view about the desirability of the world being organized on the principle of sovereignty. They are suggesting that, for one reason or another, it is a poor basis for politics at the global level, and that it ought to be abandoned for something better as soon as possible.

It might be thought that the analysis of such views meets an immediate difficulty arising from the variety of ways in which the term 'sovereignty' is used. For given this varied usage it could follow that the moral critics perceive the problem in dissimilar lights. The sovereignty on which one of them focuses could be very different from that of another, and so on. In which case an overall treatment of their approach would not be possible. As it happens, however, there is no real difficulty here. For, although the essence of sovereignty at the international level is seen in different ways, there is little dispute over the fact that it has to do with the separate political entities – the sovereign states – which make up the international society. And it is this general arrangement and its attendant practices that arouse the ire, or the grief, of the moral critics of sovereignty. Accordingly, there is no need for them to agree on precisely what it is that lies at the core of the phenomenon which is being criticized. All they need to do is to hit the target, and in this particular exercise the target is large enough not to require pinpoint accuracy on the part of the marksmen.

Two main lines of criticism are advanced. First, there are those who imply that sovereignty is a bad thing because of its psychological power. The suggestion is that the very word itself, or the idea to which it refers, has a baleful influence on men's minds, causing them to arrange their affairs and behave in ways which would profitably be abandoned if they shook themselves free of this semantic or conceptual encumbrance. It is, as it were, a secular case of the word being made flesh, and it is therefore the word and its associated thought processes that must be erased if the world is to be improved. The second moral quarrel with sovereignty looks at things the other way around, in an inductive rather than a deductive spirit. It sees sovereignty as just the term which expresses the form in which the globe is organized. By extension, the term is also used to refer to some of the behavioural characteristics which are thought to be inherent in such a system. These characteristics are disliked, and the nature of this disapprobation is conveyed by the pejorative use of the term 'sovereignty'. But, unlike the first line of criticism, it is understood that the immediate remedy lies in structural rather than conceptual change. The prime task is to alter the world's political arrangements; once that is done, the term 'sovereignty' will simply wither away on account of its lack of contemporary relevance.

In practice, of course, the dividing line between these two critical approaches is not as clear-cut as the previous paragraph suggests. Those who concentrate on the need for structural change are usually aware of the independent psychological strength which the term 'sovereignty' possesses, and that some attention must therefore be paid to this aspect of the matter. Likewise, those who focus on the importance of words and thought processes almost always understand that these phenomena do not have a completely autonomous existence, but may be modified or eroded by alterations in the political realities to which they refer. None the less, each of these approaches is sufficiently distinct to warrant separate examination.

Conceptual Criticism

This type of argument is well exemplified by the allegation of a close student of European affairs that the problem of sovereignty is 'an issue not of substance but of form . . . we have, all of us, got hung up on a word'. He went on to say that in consequence we have been using 'a system of categories that has simply ceased to fit', and the consequence of that has been that 'we have got ourselves into the sort of international jungle that reached its apogee and reduction to the absurd and horrible in two world wars'.[1] Strong stuff. A comparable observation is that of a distinguished philosopher of religion, who expressed the view that the 'failure of the European system has been primarily due to the unlimited and unrestricted development of the principle of sovereignty', which he saw as having 'dominated' the political development of Europe ever since the Renaissance.[2] And, putting the point more generally is the Chairman of the Institute for World Order, himself a town planner, who declared that 'We are stuck in a mindset that accepts the sovereignty of nations, the inevitability of war, the absolute necessity of building this huge and increasing armaments program'.[3]

In a similar vein, a lawyer writing on the eve of the Second World War said that the 'fetish of national sovereignty assumes the shape of the evil genius in the modern European forest of international intercourse';[4] and a generation later another lawyer doubted whether 'any single word has ever caused . . . so much international lawlessness'.[5] A much-travelled political scientist and philosopher, however, took the view that the lawyers themselves bore some responsibility for the problem, condemning sovereignty as 'a poisonous lawyer's myth'.[6] But the Director of Britain's Royal Institute of International Affairs (a former politician) refused to ascribe specific blame in making his judgement that states would cultivate their military strength 'so long as the concept of national sovereignty retains its present hold upon most governments and nations'.[7] In an analogous way, the fourth Secretary-General of the UN has observed that the 'war syndrome is an inevitable outgrowth of the doctrine of state sovereignty'.[8]

It is hard to avoid the conclusion that remarks of this nature greatly exaggerate the importance of sovereignty, as a concept, on national decision-making and international relations. It is, of course, impossible to arrive at an accurate conclusion on the matter: it is all a question of judgement and intuition. And there is no doubt that status-related concepts can acquire a certain resonance of their own. Thus they may come to affect a person's feelings or self-image, and in turn his behaviour. But even at the individual level, where there is greatest scope for such influences, it is doubtful whether more than a small proportion of rulings and relationships are much altered or inflated by the term which declares a person's status. There may, quite possibly, be some change in a person's outlook and demeanour after elevation to the episcopate, the judicial bench, the peerage, or even to a university chair. But it is improbable that a man would behave very differently if the terminology used for his new position was less (or more) imposing than professor, lord, Mr justice, or bishop.

Internationally, the impact of a concept referring to status – that is to say, sovereignty – is likely to be even less, for three reasons. First, the decision-making process will usually be more complex than is the case with individuals, in that more than one person will be involved. This should decrease the influence of emotional considerations. Second, the fact that the decision-makers are acting not on their own behalf but in the name of the state may work in the same direction, inducing a greater sense of caution and responsibility. This may not always be so: a slight to a state may have more serious consequences than one to an individual, partly, perhaps, because the idea of sovereignty may lend a greater air of enormity to the action in question. But, third, account should be taken of the fact that to the extent to which the term 'sovereignty' has emotive associations they are generally defensive rather than offensive in character. The idea of sovereignty comes chiefly into play when an action has been taken by another state which calls for a response, rather than as a ground for a forward policy of one's own. Thus sovereignty will commonly be invoked to justify a reaction which has already been planned or executed, as in the case of the Soviet Union's account of the shooting down of a South Korean civilian aircraft in 1983. On the other hand, the term alone lends itself less easily to an out-of-the-blue attack – whether verbal or physical – on another state.

Despite, therefore, the variety and weight of opinion which was cited at the start of this section, there seems good ground for denying that the concept of sovereignty, on its own, has the consequences which have been attributed to it. It may sometimes increase a state's sensitivity, but it is taking the matter too far to see tension and war as generally the result of the fact that states call themselves sovereign. However, it is manifestly undeniable that tension and war occur not infrequently in the international society of sovereign states. Whether that is enough to condemn the structure of the existing system is the issue which will next be considered.

Structural Criticisms

It is very easy to relate the undesirable aspects of international relations to the fact that the state system is based on the principle of sovereignty. As one political scientist has put it, the 'essence of traditional sovereignty lies in the control of the state over its own means of going to war'.[9] From which premiss the conclusion has often been drawn that international disputes can ultimately be settled only by war. There is, says a well-known political philosopher, 'no other last resort'.[10] And from this position it is hardly any step at all to the conclusion, voiced here by a political economist of considerable eminence, that 'wars will remain not merely possible but inevitable'.[11] Or, as it was put rather more generally two hundred years ago, 'To look for a continuation of harmony between a number of independent, unconnected sovereignties in the same neighbourhood, would be to disregard the uniform course of human events, and to set at defiance the accumulated experience of ages'.[12] A more up-to-date version of the same argument is that of a very distinguished writer, who declared, 'Sovereignty is the respectable word for the chauvinist nationalism that has already launched our planet on a thousand wars.'[13] For, as another well-known figure, this time a lawyer and international civil servant, has put it, governments invoking sovereignty 'mean red-blooded, and all too often red-clawed, sovereignty, sanctified lawlessness, a juristic monstrosity and a moral enormity'.[14] No wonder that two students of international relations have concluded that the sovereign state is a kind of 'parochial tribalism' sustaining 'a fragmented international order more relevant to the seventeenth than to the twentieth century'.[15]

Pausing for breadth after this spirited assault, one might note that the structural critics of sovereignty pay little attention to the positive aspects of the existing system. There is, after all, a vast amount of co-operation between states as well as conflict, conducted in the expectation of mutual benefit. This will not satisfy the most radical critics of present arrangements, who see the idea of national interest as meaning in effect 'the interests of the ruling groups', and thus leading to 'insoluble conflicts over issues that in no way reflect the needs and aspirations of the people of these societies'.[16] But less extreme observers might have been expected to take account of the fact that there is benefit as well as pain to be had from an international society organized on the principle of sovereignty, and that states usually go a long way towards making the most of it, with consequential advantages for their peoples.

A much less familiar point, but one which the structural critics might none the less have looked at, concerns the basic premiss of their argument – that tension and war are inextricably bound up with a society organized on the basis of sovereignty. Both history and *a priori* considerations certainly point very clearly in this direction. But it is worth noting that there is nothing in the international system which makes the use of armed force a logical necessity, for offence or even for defence. As one observer has put it, it is mistaken to 'think of the military dimension as being integral to the very concept of sovereignty'.[17]

However, it is not surprising that this matter is not much explored, especially as those who take moral exception to the structure of the present system are often hot in pursuit of their own nostrums for its improvement. These are sometimes of very little practical or intellectual value. The matter is not, for example, advanced by the recommendation of a psychiatrist that 'the concept of unlimited national sovereignty' be 'replaced by an orderly rather than anarchic international system';[18] nor by the urging of an international civil servant that 'a broader loyalty' needs to be substituted for 'age-long prejudices';[19] nor even by a Judge of the International Court of Justice lending his authority to the view that one of the 'essential issues of international law' is 'the curbing of the pretensions and aberrations of the doctrine of sovereignty'.[20] While long on exhortation, such calls for the taming or supersession of sovereignty are notably short on ways and means. They are also hugely imprecise about the arrangements which would give expression to the improved world for which they call. But perhaps their biggest deficiency lies in the fact that, while assuming the problem to arise from the coexistence of separate states, they none the less usually speak in terms – such as 'the international system' or 'international law' – which imply the continuation of coexisting states. Thus they often sound little better than vague efforts at both having a cake and eating it.

There is, of course, no theoretical reason why there should not be an improvement in the moral condition of the existing international system, assisted, perhaps, by an increase in the number and extent of the present arrangements for international co-operation. But no matter how many co-operative arrangements are made, or international functional agencies established, if states continue to coexist in the absence of government the essence of the present system will remain unaltered. In that event, all the empirical and *a priori* evidence suggests that tension will often develop between states and that from time to time war will break out. In this sense the structural critics of sovereignty are right in claiming that war is both a theoretical and a practical hazard of the present system. It is not something which can be ruled out and is very likely to rule itself in.

It was with this thought in mind that West Europeans were advised in 1951 by a leading American general (shortly to become his country's president) that they should get rid of their 'patchwork territorial fences'.[21] And at this time there were many local calls to the same effect. As one of its advocates put it in 1948, only a 'federation of the West, including Britain, will enable us to solve our problems quickly enough, and finally prevent war'.[22] But the creation of a larger state in Western Europe, even if it had occurred or may yet occur, will by no means solve the problem of sovereignty. It would just mean that the number of sovereign states in one part of the world had diminished through a voluntary merger. One large state would have replaced ten or however many lesser ones, somewhat reducing the total number of states making up the international society. But the organizing principle of that society – sovereignty – would remain in place. And if the world's political ills are perceived to flow from its basis in sovereignty those ills would not be much, if at all, diminished. Some, indeed, might fear their increase, on the ground that one large state is more dangerous than a number of smaller ones.

The logic of the argument therefore points unmistakably to a single world government. As a very distinguished historian has put it, 'The institution of war between states is a parasite on the institution of local sovereignty; a parasite cannot survive without its host; and we can abolish local sovereignty pacifically by voluntarily entering into a world-wide federal union ... This is the positive solution of the problem of war.'[23] Moreover, some years ago a much-respected student of the international scene bore the news that the world was already at the 'halfway house between state sovereignty and world government'.[24] And not long afterwards an international lawyer declared that there was 'no longer a question [as to] whether we will have world government by the year 2000'.[25]

If the world does indeed develop in this direction some huge political changes are in the offing. And sovereignty would lose all significance as a term applied to states in their international capacity, for the very simple reason that if there were only one state in the world it could have no international capacity in the sense in which the term 'international' is now used. There would be no international society for it to be admitted to, and therefore no point in ascertaining whether it met the requirement for entrance. And while the world state would certainly have a constitution there would be equally little point in speaking of the state as constitutionally independent, as there would be no equivalent constitutions for it to be independent of. Sovereignty as the core feature of international society would have entered the history books.

There is no logical reason why such a development as this should not take place. There is nothing sanctified about the idea of sovereignty. The world has got along without it in times past, and in theory it could do so again in the future – even tomorrow.

In practice, however, there is no chance of such a development in the foreseeable future, however generously viewed. It is all very well for the moral critics of the present system to call for a world state, implicitly if not explicitly. But they are remarkably coy about supplying the necessary particulars regarding the way from here to there. And not surprisingly, for there is no clear likelihood of any of the three possible routes being followed. One is by way of ever-increasing co-operation between all the world's numerous states and the concomitant emergence of something in the nature of a central authority. This would not mean that world government would creep in unawares, but it would do so slowly and painlessly. But the likelihood of this happening is nil. If the states of Western Europe, with all their close ties, find this enterprise difficult, the world as a whole, with all its distrustful divisions, is not going to effect a fundamental transformation. For the same reason the second route – a constitutional convention of the whole globe, with all states signing away their sovereignty on the same dotted line, and honouring their pledges – can also be ruled out. This just leaves the third possibility of a world empire, of one superstate imposing its formal hegemony on all the rest of the globe. Just conceivably it might happen in the wake of a nuclear war, but hardly in any other circumstances.

Whatever, therefore, the indignation that some feel about the structural implications of a world which takes sovereignty as its organizing principle, it is far from obvious that anything can be done about it. Moreover, there is a final question to be asked about the prescription which has been proposed, and that is whether, even if a world state was attainable, it would serve the purpose which is desired of it – the eradication of war. In a formal sense, the answer is necessarily positive. War as it is usually thought of, between states, could not occur if there were only one state. But in the more fundamental sense of organized physical violence between social groups it is not at all clear that war would be unknown in a world state. Not a few sovereign states have experienced civil war, reflecting their insufficient social solidarity. If the bounds of one state encompassed the whole globe, there would be very little likelihood of much overall loyalty towards it and its institutions, with ominous implications for its internal peace. Any subsequent outbreak of fighting between some of its various provinces, or a substantial revolt in a distant part against the rule of the centre, could come to look not very dissimilar from war as it occurred in the defunct international society. It might even be worse, given the propensity of civil war to take a particularly brutal form, and the likely outrage of the central government at the threat to its authority.

Viewed in this light, the present international system does not look so bad as some of its structural critics have made out. It may not be ideal, and certainly there is plenty of scope for improvements within the existing international scheme. But evidently states, and their peoples, are attached to their sovereignty. Moreover, the clear tendency over the last generation or two has been in the direction of a strengthening and not a weakening of the idea of sovereignty, in the sense of that which makes a territorial entity eligible for international life. The implications of this liking for constitutional independence will be considered in the final chapter.

Notes: Chapter 10

1   Uwe Kitzinger, 'The realities of sovereignty', in A. Moncrieff (ed.), *Britain and the Common Market* (London: BBC, 1967), pp. 67–8.
2   Christopher Dawson, *Understanding Europe* (London: Sheed & Ward, 1952; Garden City, NY: Image Books, 1960), p. 63.

3 James W. Rouse, 'We need a model of the world that works', *Transition*, vol. 2, no. 6 (December 1975), p. 3.

4 George W. Keeton, *National Sovereignty and International Order* (London: Peace Book Co., 1939), p. 35.

5 Michael Akehurst, *A Modern Introduction to International Law* (London: Allen & Unwin, 1970), p. 26.

6 George Catlin, quoted by C. A. W. Manning in his unpublished work 'Sovereignty for the common man', p. 30.

7 Kenneth Younger, 'The spectre of nuclear proliferation', *International Affairs*, vol. 42, no. 1 (January 1966), p. 23.

8 Kurt Waldheim, 'The United Nations: the tarnished image', *Foreign Affairs*, vol. 63, no. 1 (Fall 1984), p. 93.

9 Roy E. Jones, *The Changing Structure of British Foreign Policy* (London: Longman, 1974), p. 91.

10 Hannah Arendt, *Crises of the Republic* (Harmondsworth: Penguin, 1973), p. 188.

11 J. A. Hobson, quoted in K. Robbins, *The Abolition of War. The 'Peace Movement' in Britain 1914–1919* (Cardiff: University of Wales Press, 1976), p. 205.

12 Alexander Hamilton, quoted in Martin Wight, *Power Politics*, 2nd edn, ed. Hedley Bull and Carsten Holbraad (Leicester: Leicester University Press, 1978), p. 104.

13 Barbara Wood Jackson in a letter to *The Times*, 4 January 1975.

14 C. W. Jenks, *A New World of Law?* (London: Longman, 1969), p. 133.

15 H. and M. Sprout, quoted in R. J. Vincent, *Nonintervention and International Order* (Princeton, NJ: Princeton University Press, 1974), p. 374.

16 Noam Chomsky, *Peace in the Middle East?* (London: Fontana, 1974), p. 52.

17 N. Sims, *Approaches to Disarmament* (London: Friends Peace and International Relations Committee, 1974), p. 68.

18 Jerome D. Frank, *Sanity and Survival* (London: Barrie & Rockliff, 1967), p. 290.

19 C. W. Jenks, *The World Beyond the Charter* (London: Allen & Unwin, 1969), p. 182.

20 H. Lauterpacht, quoted in a review by G. I. A. D. Draper, *International Affairs*, vol. 54, no. 3 (July 1978), pp. 477–8.

21 Dwight D. Eisenhower, quoted in Jean Monnet, *Memoirs* (London: Collins, 1978), p. 359.

22 Jean Monnet, quoted in ibid., p. 272.

23 Arnold Toynbee, *Experiences* (London: Oxford University Press, 1969), p. 84.

24 Stanley Hoffman, *The State of War* (New York: Praeger, 1965), p. 70.

25 Saul H. Mendlovitz, 'Remarks', in *American Journal of International Law*, vol. 57, no. 5 (November 1973), p. 118.

11

Q.E.D.

The purpose of this inquiry was to examine the significance, in international relations, of the concept of sovereignty, with particular reference to that usage which refers to what makes a territorial entity eligible for membership in international society. It was suggested that there must be some criterion for membership, and that states have adopted one which is both neat and operable without fuss. They say, in effect, that an entity must, like them, be sovereign if it is to be admitted to their circle. And by sovereign, in this context, they mean constitutionally independent. The result is an arrangement which works very well, and is clearly understood by all the territorial participants, and would-be participants, in the international game.

However, many observers get very confused about the use of the word 'sovereignty' at this level. Partly this is because states themselves are rather free with its use, and rarely trouble to point out that now they are meaning this rather than that or the other. But confusion chiefly arises because the observers themselves do not draw distinctions between the various usages of the word. In turn, the reason for that is usually due to an observer having a fixed and single idea about the proper meaning of the term 'sovereignty', which is most unlikely to accord with the way in which states use the term when they refer to their international status. The observer's idea will probably have been derived from one of the various ways in which the term is used in the context of domestic politics, or, perhaps connectedly, from an acquaintance with the work of a political theorist. In any event, it will be noticed that there is a considerable gap between the 'proper' meaning and the condition of states in international society. Perplexity follows, and very possibly impatience or even annoyance, for states are seen to be making misrepresentations about themselves. The thought that the term 'sovereignty' might legitimately refer to several distinct concepts appears not to enter many observers' heads. And the possibility that one of these concepts might relate to what is necessary for a territorial entity to be eligible for admission to the international society is generally even more remote from their thought processes.

It has been shown, however, that this is in fact one of the ways in which the word 'sovereignty' is used in international relations. The relevant concept was elucidated, and its application examined. Consideration was then given to a number of doubtful or embarrassing cases, but none of these was seen to invalidate the general rule. Attention was next paid to a number of other usages of the word 'sovereignty' at the international level. It was argued in each case that there was no incompatibility between it and the use of the term 'sovereignty' to mean constitutional independence. All that was needed was an awareness of the need to make a distinction between different uses of the same term. Finally, for the sake of completeness, a brief survey was made of certain moral objections to that concept of sovereignty which has been at the centre of the present work.

Organizing Principle

Of all the internationally related concepts which the word 'sovereignty' connotes, the one around which this inquiry has been built is the most fundamental. This is because of its intimate connection with both the practice of inter-state relations and the way in which, for the purposes of understanding such relations, they may be characterized by the scholar. So far as the first of these matters is concerned, sovereignty, in the sense of constitutional independence, acts as a fundamental organizing principle. If political communities are to have regular and orderly dealings with each other it is necessary that the extent of their competence is clear and accepted by all concerned. There is no theoretical reason why such communities should not have varying degrees of international competence so that a constitutionally independent state might need to negotiate on one matter with another such state, but on a second matter with a body with limited autonomy within that other state, on a third with yet another, even less autonomous body within the other state, and on a fourth with a non-territorial group which has wide-ranging ideological or theological claims and allegiances. Such a mixed system could not claim to be based on the equality of all its participants, but it would encompass entities of varying status and authority, each of them handling all the external matters which came within its purview. The system's organizing principle would therefore be that of accepted international competence.

It might be imagined that such a system, while theoretically possible, would come under considerable practical strain. In part this is due to the complexity of the modern world, where the connectedness of things makes it difficult to separate out, in a sensible way, the matters which may be dealt with, internationally, by constitutionally subordinate bodies and those which should be left to the constitutional superior. In part, too, the difficulty of operating such a system lies in human nature, in that the officers of a constitutionally superior body would be most reluctant to allow a subordinate body to engage in extra-national negotiations. And nowadays the bureaucrats of central government usually have the ability to make their authority felt in all parts of the country which they serve. Of course, one further possibility would be to do away altogether with arrangements which involve claims to constitutional superiority and subordination, and just to have a system of entirely free-standing but greatly overlapping jurisdictions – a kind of multi-functionalism. Again, in theory, this would be possible. But its contemporary practicality is even more in doubt than a system which relies at least in part on the idea of constitutional superordination.

All these remarks, however, are in the purely theoretical realm, in that they do not relate to what goes on in practice. At the practical level, developments moved decisively, a long while ago, in the direction of an international system in which the regular territorial participants were all of the same kind. This meant, at one period, that they were all sovereigns, each of them speaking for states which, in a very real sense, were their own. They were also all independent of each other, formally speaking. Over time internal political developments resulted in changes in the distribution of power, which was evidenced by the development of written constitutions setting out the new arrangements. Now it was the state, as such, that was deemed to be the sovereign entity, rather than the sovereign himself. Thus inter-state relations became relations between not sovereigns but sovereign entities, the mark of their sovereignty residing in their constitutional independence of each other. But it remained a system in which the participating units were all of the same kind. Its organizing principle was still simple, straightforward, and single. Any territorial entity which satisfied it was eligible to join in the international game.

An organizing principle of some kind is necessary if chaos is to be avoided in the relations of those who have more than a minimal amount to do with each other. In theory it does not matter what it is, so long as it is clear and generally accepted. Then everyone knows how they stand, in the sense of knowing who is entitled to act at the external level, and in respect of what issues. It happens that the particular direction in which extra-national or trans-societal relations have developed has been to establish sovereignty, in the sense of constitutional independence, as the one and only qualification that must be obtained by a territorial entity which aspires to full participation in inter-state relations. In other words, sovereignty is the organizing principle of inter-state relations. All those states which are seen playing the international game are doing so not just because they wish to play (and others have agreed to play with them) but also, and fundamentally, because they have what participation in the game requires: sovereignty.

International Society

Sovereignty is thus a concept of some practical import. Additionally, however, its role greatly facilitates the use of the term 'society' to describe the collectivity of states. States may then speak of themselves, if they wish (as they sometimes do), as forming a society. And scholars may also use this terminology in their efforts to characterize the collectivity of states in a way which fellow scholars and students and even states themselves will find illuminating. There are several grounds on which it does make sense to talk of sovereign states making up a society. One relates to the extent of their dealings with each other. They are, at any one moment, transacting a great deal of international business, of various kinds. Another ground for using the term 'society' is the continuity which is found in the relations of states. They are not here today and gone tomorrow. This may be true of their governments, but the vast majority of states live on, and, by and large, each government assumes unquestioningly the obligations undertaken by its predecessor, and that government's predecessor, and so on. Thus there is not only a lot of contact but also, over time, some stability in the collectivity of states, or the society, as it might be called. Yet another argument for this terminology lies in the fact that accepted forms of behaviour and patterns of action (and reaction) have grown up among states. This enables them to make some fairly reasonable assumptions about the sorts of things which are done and expected in their grouping – or society, as one might naturally say – and, on the other hand, the sorts of things which are not done and which will therefore occasion surprise, and unusually strong objection. By the same token, students of international relations can make some sense of what is going on, out there, between states, finding it possible to identify elements of order amidst the clash of competing policies.

The most basic argument for speaking of the collectivity of states as a society, however, rests on the exclusivity of the grouping. A society, in the sense of a social organization, is by definition a body which includes some and excludes others. It is, putting it differently, based on the concept of membership. How the membership principle is operated will vary from one group to another, depending very largely on the nature and purpose of the group in question. But the existence of such a principle is indicative of the fact that the group may helpfully be called a society. And, as this work has made clear, such a principle operates at the international level. Not every territorial entity is fitted, by virtue of its territoriality, to play the international game, or join the international club. It has to possess territoriality of a certain kind – the sort indicated by the phrase 'constitutional independence'. Such entities may confidently knock on the international door. Those lacking the requisite condition know there is no point in their doing so.

It is, of course, this common possession of sovereignty which enables the territorially based members of international society to speak of their sovereign equality. There is no suggestion here at all, and never has been, that they are equal in territory, power, population, influence, rights, or anything – other than status. It is thus mistaken to imply that something is wrong when it is possible to draw 'a contrast between the fact that all states are supposed to be sovereign, and the fact that the rights which are at the disposal of some states are inferior to those at the disposal of others'.[1] And it completely misrepresents the position of states to say that 'though lip service continues to be paid to the concept of "sovereign equality", it now bears less relation than ever to the realities of the world'.[2] For, to use the familiar formulation of Vattel, 'A dwarf is as much a man as a giant; a small republic is no less a sovereign state than the most powerful kingdom'.[3] Or, to quote the Prime Minister of Nigeria at the first Pan-African summit in 1963: 'There must be acceptance of equality by all states. No matter whether they are big or small, they are all sovereign, and sovereignty is sovereignty.'[4]

But, as has been made clear by frequent use of the word 'eligible', the possession of sovereignty does not automatically result in a state being ushered in to the international society. Sovereignty is the necessary condition, but is not sufficient. That much is evident. Beyond that there is some uncertainty surrounding the matter, arising from the fact that the international society, as such, is wholly lacking in formal arrangements and procedures of the kind which are common in other societies. There is no lack of provisions whereby states can communicate with each other, enter into legal undertakings towards each other and establish institutions for the better conduct of their mutual business. The universality of such provisions enables the scholar to refer to them as the procedures of the international society. But they are not formally spoken of in this way by states. And there has never been an attempt to institutionalize the international society, with the accompanying requirement to equip it with a constitution dealing with all the matters which customarily fall under that head, including the basic ones of admission and expulsion. Some have been tempted to regard the League of Nations and the United Nations as a move in that direction. But such a view is imperfect in respect of both the theory and the practice of the two organizations in question.

What must be turned to, therefore, is the always reliable test of state practice. At one time it might well have been possible to have sought an answer to the question of whether a sovereign state was a member of international society via the test of recognition. This is a legal doctrine which enables one state to give formal notice to another that, in the view of the recognizing state, the other state has 'arrived' on the international scene, thus clearing the way for ordinary international relations to occur between the two. It is an attractive device, and continues to appeal to a number of scholars in the discipline of international relations. Indeed, some of them are to be heard saying not only that the members of international society may be identified through the test of recognition but also that recognition confers sovereignty – a sovereign state being one which has been recognized as such by other sovereign states. As one of them puts it, 'After recognition a state possesses sovereignty', and in this way 'bare struggle become[s] transmuted into a regular interchange'.[5]

However, it was never clear that states were 'constituted' (as the saying went) through recognition, for there was always the problem of the extent of recognition that was necessary – in terms of both the number and weight of the recognizing states – for it to be deemed that a legitimate state had appeared. And nowadays recognition (of governments as well as states) is much more a political act than ever before, often expressing not a judgement about whether an entity exists but a political view about the desirability of having dealings with it. Thus recognition is now an even less satisfactory test than hitherto for establishing whether or not a state is a member of international society. And, by the same token, it is of little value in determining whether an entity is sovereign, in the sense of eligible to participate in international society.

Thus the way is now rather clearer than it was for the acceptance of the view that, in the words of the then (and subsequent) Lord High Chancellor of Great Britain, sovereignty, like 'domicile or sex ... is a question of fact'.[6] However, this does not solve the matter of how it is to be known whether a sovereign state is a member of international society. An attendant problem here, of course, is that as membership procedures are not formalized the very concept of membership itself has not been explicitly elucidated. However, both common sense and the practice of states suggest that a state may reasonably be regarded as a member if it is not faced with any formal obstacles to the conduct of international relations of the usual kind. Or, putting it a little differently, a sovereign state is a member of international society if other states raise no objection in principle to having relations with it in the normal international way. This negative criterion, rather than the positive one of explicit recognition, reflects what actually happens when a new state appears. For in the overwhelming majority of cases the assumption of sovereignty by a territorial entity thereby brings about, without further question or action, a new relationship with existing sovereign states. The process may fairly be characterized as the according of membership in international society to the new state. Such a state may not, especially if it is small, involve itself to any great extent in the international hurly-burly. It may not even apply to join the United Nations. But there are no formal hindrances to it doing either of these things, or anything else which states customarily do. It is simply choosing to abstain from some areas of activity – but is not being excluded.

This practice, however, does not quite amount to a rule of automatic admission, for the pre-existing members of international society retain the right to shun a new state, or, for that matter, an existing member. This could give rise to the problem of having to decide whether or not a state was pointedly ignored by enough members to throw doubt on its own membership, or continued membership. Such a problem could, for example, occur in respect of a contentious secession, as it might have done, but did not, in respect of the emergence, in 1971, of Bangladesh. It could also arise over the pursuit by a state of internal policies which were viewed with increasing abhorrence by virtually all other states, as could yet happen in respect of South Africa, or, perhaps, Israel. Thus it must be allowed that at the margin of the concept of membership in international society there is a grey area where uncertainty could exist. But this does not undermine the clarity with which the concept can be applied elsewhere, and so does not throw any theoretical doubt on its viability. At the level of practice it may be noted that such cases have not given rise to any problems as yet, and that it seems unlikely that they will occur in significant numbers in the foreseeable future.

Where, by contrast, a state is shunned universally, or as universally as makes no difference (being supported, perhaps, only by its creator or its immediate backer), the answer to the question regarding membership in international society is almost entirely clear: that it is not a member. This was so, for example, with regard to Rhodesia during the period of its unilateral declaration of independence, and is so regarding the black homeland states set up by South Africa, the Turkish Republic of Northern Cyprus (declared in 1983), and of Taiwan since the admission of the Beijing government to the UN in

1971. Indeed, the lawyers would deny the term 'state' to such entities[7] (and presumably also the term 'sovereignty') and doubtless this approach would be endorsed by all those who are politically opposed to the entities in question. This is going rather far, for the word 'state' has a clear meaning which would appear to be entirely applicable to Taiwan and the rest. It could easily be qualified by 'illegal' or some such word by those who wish to make that kind of point. Be that as it may, there is very little difficulty in speaking of such states, or entities, as non-members of international society.

But, as the terminology of the last paragraph implies, the approach it suggests is not wholly free from problems. They relate to the position of non-members of international society to international law. In the usual way the members of a society are bound by its rules, as are visitors, but those who are external to or excluded from a society are not so bound. They cannot claim the rights of members and, correspondingly, they cannot be called upon to perform the duties which are expected of those within. At the international level, however, this would lead to non-members being in a very curious position, somewhat analogous to that of the outlaw in medieval Europe. They would, in law, be free from all restraints in respect of other states, and all other states would be free to do what they liked to the outlaw state. There would be no legal protection in this situation, for example, for its territorial integrity and political independence. This is an unappealing position, and in fact it is not the one which is deemed to exist. Indeed, international law is regarded as applicable to illegal states or entities.[8] In practice, of course, such a state might get the worst end of any legal argument, simply on account of its minority and unpopular situation. Majorities are no more averse internationally than they are elsewhere to interpreting the law to suit themselves, if that is at all possible – as it usually is among states. But the asserted applicability of international law to allegedly illegal states will not necessarily displease the latter. It may give them the opportunity to show how law-abiding they are. And they may value the opportunity to call up the law in their support – always, of course, also keeping their powder dry. It is, on the face of it, a somewhat anomalous situation. But it can be justified on the grounds that the international society is itself somewhat unusual, and that in any event life is never so neat and tidy as to dispense with all anomalies.

One way around the problem of deciding whether or not a state is a member of international society would be to drop the concept of membership altogether and instead speak of participation. For whereas membership is an absolute concept, requiring a yes or no answer, the idea of participation is one which calls for an assessment in terms of degree. Some participate a lot, others a little, some not at all, and so on. The possession of sovereignty, in the sense of constitutional independence, would make a territorial entity eligible to participate in international society in a full and regular manner, but the actual extent to which it became a participant would depend on the ebb and flow of actual relationships. International law would continue to apply to all such relationships, being, as now, a law for sovereign states. However, the concept of participation is less compelling and meaningful than that of membership, and accords less well with the concept of a society. Accordingly, as there are no major problems in the way of applying the concept of membership to what actually goes on between states, and some distinct advantages, there is no reason to urge a change in ideas and terms. Moreover, this leaves the concept of participation available for sole use with regard to the international activities of non-state actors. Such bodies certainly get involved in the affairs of states but cannot be described as members of international society, on account of the fact that the concept of sovereignty, meaning constitutional independence, is necessarily inapplicable to them. They may, however, very properly and tellingly be referred to as participants in the state-run society.

States and Statehood

The question does arise, however, as to whether states are as important as they used to be, whether they have been or are in the process of being toppled from their pre-eminent position at the international level. The answer will partly depend on how 'international' and 'important' are defined. Clearly, if 'international' is used in its popular sense of 'inter-state', then by definition international relations can be no less inter-state in character than they have ever been. If, on the other hand, by 'international' is meant everything that goes on across state boundaries, then there is a great deal more to consider than inter-state relations. And the importance of one as against the other will be determined by the view of the observer as to what is important. To some an international evangelical crusade will doubtless be of far greater significance than talks about arms control, or whatever else states are doing. To others, international encounters in the field of sport may dominate the transnational or trans-societal horizon. On such issues there is no possibility of progress in comparative analysis: it is all a matter of one's point of view. However, the question with which this paragraph opened usually refers to one of two possibilities which are, in principle, open to disciplined examination. One is that states are, or are becoming, the mouthpieces for non-state international actors, so that really it is not this or that state which is making a claim but a body which is both distinct from the state and lies, at least in part, outside its territorial domain. The other is that, as states go about their international business, they find that the defence of their positions or the advancement of their interests requires that they chiefly have dealings not with other states but with non-state actors. In other words, the environment within which states compete is dominated, or becoming dominated, by bodies not of their own kind.

These are large possibilities, but for the purpose of this inquiry they can be given short shrift. Without doubt, non-state actors now have some impact on the international activities of states. Terrorist groups and multinational corporations are commonly cited in this connection, and the latter may also sometimes have an influence on the internal policies of individual states. Nor must the part played by non-governmental international organizations be forgotten, as they often act as internationally based pressure groups. Governmental international organizations are also frequently mentioned in discussions of non-state actors, but such references are usually ill founded.[9] For, in as much as such organizations are made up of states, they cannot be regarded as separate from their members. Only if considerable freedom is given to its secretariat may a governmental international organization be properly spoken of as falling into the non-state actor category. And usually international bureaucrats, like national ones, are kept on a tight rein – or one which can quickly be tightened if they step too far out of line.

But although states sometimes talk to and jostle with non-state actors, this is by no means the case for most of the time, or anything like it. Nor can states be realistically pictured as puppets at the end of strings controlled by international bodies of a non-state kind. Thus the claim that 'the territorial state is declining'[10] lacks conviction. On the contrary, the 'modern national state is . . . the most inclusive, deep-seated popular institution of our time'.[11] Accordingly, 'it would be premature to suggest (much less to declare, as many contemporary writers do) that the nation-state is dead or dying'.[12] Indeed, what is found in the contemporary world is 'not the state in atrophy but, if anything, the state triumphant'.[13]

One popular response to this line of argument is to point out that many sovereign states (often the phrase is prefaced by 'so-called') are hardly very successful or effective instances of their kind. It may be that they find themselves in a disadvantageous geographical position. For example, speaking during the First World War of the possible emergence of a number of small states in eastern Europe, one commentator said that few advocates of such a development 'even paused to consider whether a little land-locked Bohemia or a diminished but independent Hungary could maintain their sovereignty under the pressure of the great military Empires which would surround them'.[14] The substitution of the phrase 'political independence' for sovereignty would give this remark virtually continuous relevance throughout the succeeding two-thirds of a century. Or it may be that a sovereign state is without much by way of natural resources – the plight of many Third World countries today. Or, even if well endowed by nature, it may be that incompetence and/or corruption results in a state finding itself in very poor shape – of which, again there are many contemporary examples. Sovereignty, in other words, is by no means the recipe for a safe or prosperous life, nor for internal stability. A territorial entity needs much more than sovereignty if it is to do well in the world, or to keep on an even domestic keel.

But none the less sovereignty is the condition that a political community must achieve if it is to have the chance, on its own, of doing anything at all. And it happens that in the twentieth century the idea that political communities should govern themselves has become orthodox. Even a fairly manifest lack of preparedness for the task is deemed to be an inadequate reason for the postponement of the grant of sovereignty. Thus it has been widely bestowed, and numerous new states have appeared. Moreover, the point deserves emphasis that the acquisition of sovereign status does, in itself, constitute a material, and not just a nominal, change in a territory's position. For this alteration in its status is not simply a matter of words but has some practical implications, which can be of considerable significance.

When, for example, in 1965 the Soviet Union wished to criticize the United States for its involvement in the internal affairs of the Dominican Republic (a sovereign state), the Soviet representative in the UN Security Council charged the United States with trying 'again and again to conduct itself in Latin America – and not only in that area – as if it were in its own private domain . . . [it uses] as cover the dirty and thoroughly dishonest pretext of the "need to restore law and order" in other countries, as if it were a question of Alabama or Mississippi'.[15] The point is that if it had been a question of Alabama or Mississippi the Soviet Union would have been most unlikely to have raised its voice, just as all states are very loath to bring internal matters on to the international agenda, no matter how repulsive a state's behaviour. This is because a different set of rules and understandings applies to what a state does inside its own borders from what it does outside. On account of this a political community may feel itself much safer as a weak sovereign state, even close to a big and avaricious or insecure neighbour, than as a constituent unit of a federal state. Of course, states do not always obey all of the rules, and thus things may go ill with a weak state in a poor position. But short of physical occupation and total control – annexation in fact if not in law – a community is likely to do much better for itself if it possesses sovereignty than if it does not.

The position of the states of Eastern Europe offers an illustration of this point. Following the collapse of the Russian Empire and the defeat of the Austro-Hungarian Empire in the First World War, a number of new, and often relatively small, sovereign states were established (or in some cases re-established) in that area. They included the states which continue to appear on the political map, and also the three Baltic states of Estonia, Latvia and Lithuania. During the Second World War the Soviet Union, by now having succumbed to the traditional impulses of Tsarist Russia, took advantage of the conflict to annex the three Baltic states and incorporate them in the union as constituent republics. Subsequently many efforts were made, and continue to be made, by the Soviet government to stamp out separatist national feeling in its recent acquisitions. Meanwhile, the Soviet Union established its hegemony over the remaining sovereign states of Eastern Europe. But they remain sovereign, and thus the Soviets do not behave there, generally speaking, as they do in the Baltic areas of their country. And when they do behave badly, as in Hungary in 1956 and Czechoslovakia in 1968, much is made of it by the rest of the world. It is also very significant that the Soviet Union did not intervene physically in Poland in the early years of the 1980s, despite her worries about the train of events in that country.

It is therefore a great mistake to bracket the former Baltic states and the other East European states so far as their experiences at the hands of the Soviet Union are concerned. It will not do to write, as one well known political scientist has done: 'Czechs and Poles, Estonians and Latvians, are less fortunate than the inhabitants of the sovereign republics of Senegal or Bangla Desh [*sic*]; in those Eastern European places neither the individual nor the nation has hardly anything worth the name of liberty.'[16] At the individual level, maybe; but at the national level there is certainly a difference between Czechoslovakia and Latvia. As another political scientist has put it (one with much more than a passing interest in the international dimensions of his subject): 'it takes a strange blindness to claim that "sovereignty" or "independence" no longer means anything. Even within the Soviet bloc the persistence of a Polish state means a great deal to the Polish people, both in idea and in fact, both in the immediate present and in the long run. Between the condition of the Baltic ex-states and that of the satellite states . . . the difference is at least substantial.'[17]

This points to the reasons why sovereignty has been so much sought after, and continues to be sought. If offers a remedy to those political groups who feel themselves to be oppressed, or with wholly insufficient opportunity for the expression of their national culture, whether Basques or Kurds, Quebeckers or Sikhs, Tamils or East Timoreans. And if they win sovereignty they can then do things which they would have had no chance of doing had they remained in a position of constitutional subordination. They can, in short, play at the international game, and take advantage of what sovereign status affords even to the smaller states. Thus Tunisia, sovereign in 1956, was henceforth able to assist the rebels in neighbouring Algeria in their fight against the French. When tiny Seychelles, with a population of only about 60,000, became sovereign in 1976, worries were expressed about the possibility of Soviet ships being given naval facilities there. In the following year Somalia, an impoverished state with a population of only a few million, ordered a large number of Soviet advisers out of the country at seven days notice. They went. Early in 1985 South Africa felt very frustrated by what it saw as the harbouring of guerrillas by the neighbouring, and immeasurably weaker, state of Botswana. Almost two decades earlier Nigeria, far and away the most populous African state, was greatly irked by the offer from its very small neighbour, Dahomey (now Benin), of a staging base for humanitarian flights by the International Committee of the Red Cross to the Biafrans. Biafra, of course, was fighting for sovereignty, believing this to be the only way of providing security for its people, who were, at that time, fearful of remaining within the Nigerian state.

As it happens, the Biafrans were unsuccessful (but, remarkably, were treated with great leniency and humanity by the victorious government of Nigeria). This has not, however, caused other entities to have second thoughts about the desirability of their sovereignty, or their aspiration for it. Sovereignty thus remains a notion with huge appeal, reflecting, as it does, the liking which political communities have for governing themselves. Accordingly, while there is nothing innately sacrosanct about the concept, the world will in all probability remain organized, politically, on this basis for a very long time. Instances of the actual working of the sovereignty principle, in the sense of a territory being translated from non-sovereign status to that of membership in international society, are likely to become increasingly rare, as there are hardly any colonies left which are suitable for the change and the dismemberment of existing sovereign states is very hard to achieve, in part because it is so strongly frowned upon on all sides. But in another sense the concept of sovereignty is at work all the time, in that it is the constitutive principle of inter-state relations and, theoretically speaking, the foundation stone of the international society. Some such principle is essential in the international scheme of things and sovereignty, meaning constitutional independence, has shown itself to be a neat and economical way of supplying this need.

Notes: Chapter 11

1 Stanley Hoffman, *Duties Beyond Borders: On the Limits and Possibilities of Ethical International Politics* (Syracuse, NY: Syracuse University Press, 1981), p. 144.
2 Evan Luard, *Types of International Society* (New York: The Free Press, and London: Collier-Macmillan, 1976), p. 224.
3 Quoted in P. Butler, 'Legitimacy in a states-system: Vattel's *Law of Nations*', in M. Donelan (ed.), *The Reason of States* (London: Allen & Unwin, 1978), p. 52.
4 Sir Abubakar Balewa, quoted in John J. Stremlau, *The International Politics of the Nigerian Civil War 1967–1970* (Princeton, NJ: Princeton University Press, 1977), p. 16.
5 Murray Forsyth, *Unions of States. The Theory and Practice of Confederation* (Leicester: Leicester University Press, 1981), pp. 10 and 11.
6 Lord Hailsham, *The Times*, 14 July 1971.
7 See James Crawford, 'The criteria for statehood in international law', *British Yearbook of International Law, Vol. 48, 1976–1977* (Oxford: Oxford University Press, 1978), pp. 144–5.
8 See ibid.
9 See Alan James, 'International institutions: independent actors?', in Avi Shlaim (ed.), *International Organizations in World Politics. Yearbook 1975* (London: Croom Helm, 1976), pp. 76–84.
10 Oran R. Young, 'The United Nations and the international system', *International Organization*, vol. 22, no. 4 (Autumn 1968), p. 919.
11 R. E. Osgood and R. W. Tucker, *Force, Order, and Justice* (Baltimore, Md: Johns Hopkins University Press, 1967), p. 7.
12 Robert Gilpin, *War and Change in World Politics* (Cambridge: Cambridge University Press, 1981), p. 18.
13 Osgood and Tucker, *Force, Order, and Justice*, p. 324.
14 H. N. Brailsford (1917), quoted in Michael Howard, *War and the Liberal Conscience* (London: Temple Smith, 1978), p. 79.
15 Ambassador Fedorenko, quoted in T. M. Franck and E. Weisband, *Word Politics* (New York: Oxford University Press, 1971), p. 4.
16 M. Cranston, *The Mask of Politics* (London: Allen Lane, 1973), p. 46.
17 R. Aron, *Peace and War* (New York: Praeger, 1967), pp. 748–9.

Select Bibliography

Benn, S. I., 'The uses of sovereignty', *Political Studies*, vol. 3, no. 2 (June 1955), pp. 109–22.

Blair, P. W., *The Ministate Dilemma* (New York: Carnegie Endowment for International Peace, 1968).

Brewin, C., 'Sovereignty', in J. Mayall (ed.), *The Community of States* (London: Allen & Unwin, 1982), pp. 34–48.

Bull, H., *The Anarchical Society. A Study of Order in World Politics* (London: Macmillan, 1977).

Crawford, J., *The Creation of States in International Law* (Oxford: Clarendon Press, 1979).

Crawford, J., 'The criteria for statehood in international law', *British Yearbook of International Law, Vol. 48, 1976–1977* (Oxford: Oxford University Press, 1978), pp. 93–182.

d'Entrèves, A. P., *The Notion of the State. An Introduction to Political Theory* (Oxford: Clarendon Press, 1967).

de Jouvenal, B., *Sovereignty* (Cambridge: Cambridge University Press, 1957).

de Smith, S. A., *Microstates and Micronesia* (New York: New York University Press, 1970).

Forsyth, M., *Unions of States. The Theory and Practice of Confederation* (Leicester: Leicester University Press, 1981).

Franklin, J. H., *Jean Bodin and the Sixteenth-century Revolution in the Methodology of Law and History* (New York: Columbia University Press, 1963).

Franklin, J. H., *Jean Bodin and the Rise of Absolutist Theory* (Cambridge: Cambridge University Press, 1973).

Gilmour, W. C., 'Requiem for associated statehood?', *Review of International Studies*, vol. 8, no. 1 (January 1982), pp. 9–25.

Gilpin, R., *War and Change in World Politics* (Cambridge: Cambridge University Press, 1981).

Goodwin, G. L., 'The erosion of external sovereignty?', *Government and Opposition*, vol. 9, no. 1 (Winter 1974), pp. 61–78.

Gunter, M. M., 'What happened to the United Nations ministate problem?', *American Journal of International Law*, vol. 71, no. 1 (January 1977), pp. 110–24.

Harden, S. (ed.), *Small Is Dangerous. Micro States in a Macro World* (London: Frances Pinter, 1985).

Hay, P., *Federation and Supranational Organization* (Urbana, Ill.: Illinois University Press, 1966).

Herz, J. H., *International Politics in the Atomic Age* (New York: Columbia University Press, 1959).

Hinsley, F. H., *Power and the Pursuit of Peace* (Cambridge: Cambridge University Press, 1963).

Hinsley, F. H., *Sovereignty* (London: Watts and New York: Basic Books, 1966).

Ionescu, G. (ed.), *Between Sovereignty and Integration* (London: Croom Helm, 1974).

Jackson, R. H., and Rosberg, C. G., 'Why Africa's weak states persist: the empirical and the juridicial in statehood', *World Politics*, Vol. XXXV, no. 1 (October 1982), pp. 1–24.

James, A. M., 'The contemporary relevance of national sovereignty', in M. Leifer (ed.), *Constraints and Adjustments in British Foreign Policy* (London: Allen & Unwin, 1972), pp. 13–34.

James, A. M., 'International institutions: independent actors?', in A. Shlaim (ed.), *Yearbook of International Organization 1975* (London: Croom Helm, 1976), pp. 72–92.

James, A. M., 'International society', *British Journal of International Studies*, vol. 4, no. 2 (July 1978), pp. 91–106.

James, A. M., 'Comment on J. D. B. Miller', *Review of International Studies*, vol. 12, no. 2 (April 1986), pp. 91–3.

Keeton, G. W., *National Sovereignty and International Order* (London: Peace Books, 1939).

Klein, R., *The Idea of Equality in International Politics* (Geneva: University of Geneva, 1966).

Lubasz, H. (ed.), *The Development of the Modern State* (London: Collier-Macmillan, 1964).

MacIver, R. M., *The Modern State* (Oxford: Clarendon, 1926).

Manning, C. A. W., 'The legal framework in a world of change', in B. Porter (ed.), *The Aberystwyth Papers* (London: Oxford University Press, 1969), pp. 305–9.

Manning, C. A. W., *The Nature of International Society* (London: Bell, 1962; repr. London: Macmillan, 1975).

Marshall, C. B., *The Exercise of Sovereignty* (Baltimore, Md: Johns Hopkins University Press, 1965).

Mattingley, G., *Renaissance Diplomacy* (Boston, Mass.: Houghton Mifflin. 1964).

McIlwain, C. H., *The Growth of Political Thought in the West* (New York: Macmillan, 1932).

Miller, J. D. B., *The World of States* (London: Croom Helm, 1981).

Miller, J. D. B., 'The sovereign state and its future', *International Journal*. vol. 39, no. 2 (Spring 1984), pp. 284–301.

Miller, J. D. B., 'Sovereignty as a source of vitality for the state', *Review of International Studies*, vol. 12, no. 2 (April 1986), pp. 79–89.

Monnet, Jean, *Memoirs* (London: Collins, 1978).

Northedge, F. S., *The International Political System* (London: Faber. 1976).

Northedge, F. S., and Grieve, M. J., *A Hundred Years of International Relations* (London: Duckworth, 1971).

Osgood, R. E., and Tucker, R. W., *Force, Order, and Justice* (Baltimore. Md: Johns Hopkins University Press, 1967).

Parmiter, G. de C., *The King's Great Matter. A Study of Anglo-Papal Relations, 1527–1534* (London: Longman, 1967).

Schonfield, A., *Europe: Journey to an Unknown Destination* (Harmondsworth: Penguin, 1973).

Schwarzenberger, G., 'Federalism and supranationalism in the European communities', in G. W. Keeton and G. Schwarzenberger (eds.), *English Law and the Common Market* (London: Stevens, 1963), pp. 17–33.

Stambuk, G., *American Military Forces Abroad* (Columbus, Ohio: Ohio State University Press, 1963).

Stankiewicz, W. J. (ed.), *In Defense of Sovereignty* (New York: Oxford University Press, 1969).

Strayer, J. R., *On the Medieval Origins of the Modern State* (Princeton, NJ: Princeton University Press, 1970).

Taylor, P., 'Intergovernmentalism in the European communities in the 1970s: patterns and perspectives', *International Organization*, vol. 36, no. 4 (Autumn 1982), pp. 741–66.

United Nations Institute for Training and Research, *Status and Problems of Very Small States and Territories* (New York: UNITAR, 1969).

Wight, M., *Systems of States*, ed. H. Bull (Leicester: Leicester University Press, 1977).

Index